BOOM TIMES FOR THE END OF THE WORLD

BOOM TIMES FOR THE END OF THE WORLD

SCOTT TIMBERG

Heyday, Berkeley, California

"Down We Go Together" originally appeared in *Culture Crash: The Killing of the Creative Class*, © 2015 by Scott Timberg, published by Yale University Press. The other essays and articles in this book originally appeared in the following publications, sometimes under slightly different titles: *New Times LA*, the *Los Angeles Times*, the *New York Times*, *Salon, Al Jazeera America, Los Angeles Magazine*, and *Vox*.

Library of Congress Cataloging-in-Publication Data
Names: Timberg, Scott, author.
Title: Boom times for the end of the world / Scott Timberg.
Description: Berkeley, California : Heyday, [2023]
Identifiers: LCCN 2022033100 (print) | LCCN 2022033101 (ebook)
ISBN 9781597145985 (paperback) | ISBN 9781597145992 (epub)
Subjects: LCSH: Creative ability--United States--History--21st century.
Social classes--United States--History--21st century.
Social change--United States--History--21st century.
Popular culture--United States--History--21st century.
Classification: LCC BF408 .T545 2023 (print) | LCC BF408 (ebook)
DDC 305.5/50973--dc23/eng/20220922
LC record available at https://lccn.loc.gov/2022033100
LC ebook record available at https://lccn.loc.gov/2022033101

Cover Design: Anna Jordan
Back Cover Illustration of Scott Timberg: Eric Almendral
Interior Design/Typesetting: Roland Pilcz

Published by Heyday
P.O. Box 9145, Berkeley, California 94709
(510) 549-3564
heydaybooks.com

Printed in Saline, Michigan, by McNaughton and Gunn

10 9 8 7 6 5 4 3 2 1

CONTENTS

Introduction by Ted Gioia 1

Eye on Cool 9

Being Spike Jonze 29

Unwanted Thoughts 43

The Romantic Egotist 55

Indie Angst 79

High-Tone Talk 93

Hitting a Nerve 107

Mars in Apogee 115

The Cult of Glenn Gould 123

His Back Pages 133

Music on the Edge 145

Retooling Form and Function 157

Boom Times for the End of the World 165

Drawn to a Dark Side 173

Highbrow. Lowbrow. No Brow. Now What?   179

The Novel That Predicted Portland   185

Will Any Band Ever Break Up?   191

Can Unions Save the Creative Class?   201

Chasing Musical Legends in Joshua Tree National Park   217

How the *Village Voice* and Other Alt-Weeklies Lost Their Voice   223

Down We Go Together   233

Leaving Los Angeles   253

Searching for a Great American Rock Show   263

The Revenge of Monoculture   269

How Music Has Responded to a Decade of Economic Inequality   277

After a Decade, Will Gustavo Dudamel Stay at the LA Phil
or Leave on a High Note?   289

Acknowledgments   303

About the Author   305

INTRODUCTION

Ted Gioia

I.

WHEN SOMEONE CLOSE to you takes their own life, your first reaction is not just pain, but also denial and disbelief. Especially when it's someone younger than you—vibrant, healthy, blessed with so much talent and smarts. This can't be real, you tell yourself. You want an explanation, but the tragedy defies any attempt to find meaning in it.

That was the case with Scott Timberg. Years have passed, and I'm still reeling in the aftermath of his suicide on December 10, 2019. But in the midst of the grieving, a kind of larger significance to his death emerged in the days following the event. I felt it, and others who knew him—either personally or through his writing—felt it too.

For many of us, Scott's death revealed uncanny and disturbing connections with his professional life over the last decade, when he emerged as our leading chronicler and champion of creative professionals who had been squeezed and displaced in the "culture business." This large and growing demographic included, as he saw it, everyone from journalists like himself all the way to the film lover who once worked at the local video rental store (before it closed) or the minimum-wage clerk at the defunct indie bookstore.

They had all been part of a healthy cultural ecosystem, and he had watched it collapse over the course of just a few years.

And then it happened to him too.

Scott lost his job at the *Los Angeles Times* shortly before he turned forty. In a final ironic twist, he had just received a glowing performance review a few days before the round of layoffs that left him unemployed. He never really recovered from this. It may sound glib, but I absolutely believe Scott would still be alive today if the *Times* hadn't let him go.

I know how tough the newspaper business can be. Even so, I was mystified by this turn of events, because Scott was one of the finest arts and culture writers in the country, engaged and passionate and capable of delivering insightful articles at short notice on almost any subject. In a fair world, Scott Timberg would be competing for a Pulitzer Prize in criticism, but instead he was shut out in the cold.

He never recovered his bearings after leaving the *Times*. Thrust into the turbulent freelance economy, he continued to do outstanding work, but with fewer opportunities and smaller rewards.

But there was one consolation: Scott found a new vocation as champion for other creative professionals who, like himself, had been marginalized in the shrinking arts economy. He drew on his own experiences in writing a book on the subject, the harrowing (even more so after his death) *Culture Crash*, published by Yale University Press in 2015.

In his death, Timberg got turned into a kind of martyr, a patron saint for all the forgotten writers, artists, musicians, and other victims of the gig economy—and his personal tragedy became a commentary on both his life and theirs. It's easy to criticize this way of packaging a death that (for me and others) will never lose its sting. But there's a large dose of truth in it too. All the pieces fit together, almost too well.

II.

I never met anyone who loved journalism more than Scott Timberg.

For him, the newspaper business was more than a vocation, it was almost his destiny—at least that's how he saw it. You might even say it was in his blood.

His father, Robert Timberg, was a celebrated journalist who had started out as a soldier in the US Marine Corps during the Vietnam era. An exploding landmine had left him with serious injuries, requiring thirty-five reconstructive surgeries. Yet the elder Timberg somehow managed to reinvent himself as a writer—although he had never previously published anywhere, not even a school newspaper—after earning a master's degree in journalism from Stanford University.

That was where Scott was born, in Palo Alto on February 15, 1969. Like his father—and brother Craig, a writer for the *Washington Post*—Scott wanted to work for a newspaper. So after graduating from Wesleyan, he got a master's degree in journalism from the University of North Carolina, then plunged headfirst into the newspaper business, still in boom times during those pre-Internet days.

In our conversations I would often make some cynical remarks about the state of US newspapers, but Scott vehemently defended the journalist's life. He believed it was a noble profession. And the way he practiced it, it was just that.

I often felt chastened by his idealism. He was almost like a news reporter in one of those movies or TV shows you've seen. Somehow he combined a deep earnestness and total dedication to his craft with a childlike innocence. Perhaps I'm still too cynical, because I can now see how inevitably he would be punished for that pure faith in the goodness of his chosen vocation.

But at first there were successes. After working for *The Day* in Connecticut and the alt-weekly *New Times* in SoCal, Scott got hired by the *Los Angeles Times*. This was the ideal job for him, and again and again he delivered remarkable articles on tight deadline, never losing his enthusiasm for the next concert, the latest art exhibition, the forthcoming book, the hot new film, and anything else that came his way.

What made the *LA Times* gig so perfect was that Scott loved Los Angeles almost as much as he loved the newspaper business. If you had any doubts how much Scott Timberg cared about Los Angeles and its messy, complex cultural riches, you merely needed to look at the name of his blog (*The Misread City*) or his Twitter handle (@TheMisreadCity). If you didn't love LA as much as Scott loved it, you were just misreading it, and he would soon set you straight.

Here, too, Scott was a wide-eyed innocent. After all, the rest of us know how shallow the cultural waters are in SoCal. Hollywood is almost an emblem of phoniness. In LA, commerce squeezes out artistry—it always has and always will. If you're a creative person with integrity and love LA, you need to do it like Randy Newman in his song of that same name: with a heavy dose of skepticism and dark humor.

But Scott didn't see it that way. He had met his future wife, Sara Scribner, at the Troubadour, the quintessential LA club, and that was almost a symbol for the romance he had with the entire city. It might be sprawling, congested, cruel, and uncaring. But he saw only its beauty and endless promise.

As a result, Scott had a knack for finding the best in the cultural scene on the dream coast. We would have long, rambling conversations about California—which for him was a rich tapestry in which the threads, on any given day, might include West Coast jazz, Ross Macdonald's Lew Archer mysteries, Spike Jonze's movies, Ed Ruscha's pop art, Robinson Jeffers's Hawk Tower, sci-fi from Ray Bradbury or Philip K. Dick, *La La Land, L.A. Confidential*, the California history books of Kevin Starr, the photos of William Claxton, or Gustavo Dudamel's latest performance. Some of those turned up as subjects in his published writings, but the surviving articles and essays only begin to sketch out his endless curiosity and passion for his adopted home state.

Over the course of many years, Scott sometimes seemed like an adopted member of my own extended family as well, and even in this connection he revealed the breadth and depth of his intellect. Long before I met Scott, he had struck up a friendship with my older brother Dana, a well-known poet, and they would discuss literary matters by the hour. But when he spoke with my nephew Mike, an aspiring filmmaker, he would shift gears and converse about movies like a die-hard cinephile. When I chatted with Scott, we would focus on jazz and musical matters, which he knew well. He would even ask me to send him lead sheets for jazz songs, and get my advice on substitute chord changes and improvising modes.

I mention this because readers got only a small taste of how deeply he was immersed in creative pursuits. I'm sure I'm not alone in feeling that Scott's greatest gift might have been for smart conversation. I wish everyone reading these words could have had the experience of talking to this devoted and caring polymath, even for just a few minutes.

III.

Scott tried to leave LA, and for a time settled in Athens, Georgia. He writes about that painful decision in "Leaving Los Angeles," one of his finest essays. I encouraged him in that move, and assumed that, like many of us, Scott would find it was best to love the City of Angels from afar.

But he couldn't do it. Like a jilted lover, Scott dreamed of rebuilding an intimate relationship with the city of his broken dreams. He returned to Los Angeles, and made one final attempt to get his life back on track as an arts and culture writer.

With the benefit of hindsight, it's easy to view Scott Timberg as a victim, but that doesn't do full justice to how hard he fought to reestablish himself in the shrinking journalism business. We spoke every few days, and he was always pursuing leads and opportunities. Even in our last conversation, a few days before his death, he was still brainstorming on ways to reinvent himself and relaunch his career. On a few occasions it felt like Scott was on the brink of a big break, but the luck never ran his way.

In those final years, he continued to work the freelance circuit, and managed to write *Culture Crash*, a book that gets more sadly relevant with each passing year. He was scrambling and probably struggling financially, but you never saw it in the published work. He wrote brilliantly and with just as much insight as ever, maybe even more so. Only the paychecks were getting smaller and smaller.

I assumed it was just a matter of time before Scott found his place in the SoCal culture ecosystem. He was too talented, too good at his craft, to fall through the cracks. Maybe even the *Times* would bring him back one day—that seemed like such an obvious move. Who could they find better than Scott Timberg?

The one thing I never guessed is that he would give up hope.

But he did. I lost a dear friend, and Los Angeles lost its most devoted lover. And all we are left with is Scott Timberg, patron saint of the displaced creative spirit.

That after-the-fact canonization gives some tiny circumference of meaning to a death otherwise so meaningless. And, frankly, I suspect Scott would have no disagreement with such a framing of his life and times. He saw the challenges he faced echoed in the lives of so many others, and he cared deeply about all those who suffered in the same way he did. The notion that his abbreviated life might serve as a rallying point for the compassion owed to those squeezed by our culture shift would have given Scott a small bit of gratification. I know it provides me with some consolation.

But Scott would also want people to remember the joy and exhilaration he felt in pursuing his chosen vocation. His selected writings do just that. Here he still survives in the role he played best: the passionate and earnest culture writer who loved his misread city. I only wish it had loved him half as much in return.

EYE ON COOL

ONE OF THE MOST POWERFUL PHOTOGRAPHS in the annals of jazz depicts the charismatic alto saxophonist Art Pepper trudging up a long, lonely hill near his house in Echo Park, cradling his saxophone under his arm and holding a lit cigarette. Pepper's saxophone playing was a thing of beauty, but it was a delicate and precarious beauty, scarred with the pain that would at times send the man himself into tailspins of drugs and thievery. Looking back, four decades later, the picture almost has the quality of prophecy: Pepper, for all his early success and his many heartbreaking solos, never really reached the top of that hill, never stopped laboring, Sisyphus-like, to outrun his own inner demons.

William Claxton, the tall, mild-mannered man who shot the image, remembers his meeting with Pepper on that day in 1956; the saxophonist had gotten out of jail the day before and was waiting for his connection. "He looked very healthy, but he was kind of shaky," the photographer recalls. "He cut his hand opening a can of soup or something." The shot, Claxton says, was simply common sense.

"I saw this steep hill, and he'd been telling me how hard his life was. He was a very sweet, ingenuous guy. He seemed very naive, like his life had been all uphill."

The photograph has become the definitive shot of the sensitive and lyrical Pepper and a key image for the glamorous and tragic world of West Coast jazz. But Claxton, unimpressed with his own artistry, never used it as an album jacket or publicity photo. Only years later, in fact, did anyone but Claxton see it. "The one of him walking up the hill I never showed to anybody—that was for me."

Claxton tells the story sitting in his home on a foggy afternoon. From the high windows of his Spanish bungalow, the cantilevered houses and rough, patchy flora of Benedict Canyon dissolves into a mist below, as if he were musing above the clouds. Staring from the walls, bathed in the room's natural light, are many of his photographs—depicting such jazz artists as Duke Ellington, Ben Webster, Gerry Mulligan, and Chet Baker.

But Claxton did more than shoot striking photographs of great musicians. He created the visual reality of West Coast jazz, a whole new way to picture the art. Even people who have little musical knowledge of "cool jazz"—the mostly white, often mellow-toned scene that flourished in California in the 1950s—know what it looked like: Blond, high cheek-boned singer/trumpeter Chet Baker in undershirts and Hawaiian prints. Baritone saxophonist Gerry Mulligan's sharp suits and redheaded crew-cut. Dave Brubeck's round horn-rimmed glasses and nerdy smile. And Claxton placed these players and their peers in previously unthinkable settings. Instead of laboring in a studio, shrouded in shadow and hidden beneath coiling cigarette smoke, the musicians relaxed outside, blowing saxophones by the beach, riffing on ships, joking in garden groves.

"Claxton's image of Chet Baker was very important in creating the mystique of West Coast jazz," says Ted Gioia, the school's leading chronicler. "There's no parallel in East Coast jazz." James Gavin, who's nearing completion of a book on Baker, calls these photos "as important a chronicle of the music as the music itself."

As the fifties waned, the luster of West Coast jazz began to fade and, in an unfortunate consonance, Claxton went on to other things—television directing, Hollywood, fashion, even ads for The Gap that replicated the simple, white-background style he made famous.

But he never gave up music photography completely, and now he's nearing the end of five full decades with a camera. He was an exceedingly young man of twenty-four when he helped found the seminal Pacific Jazz label in 1952; because he's lived clean and avoided hard drugs, he's remained in good health while the boys in the band have dropped off. As a result, he's one of the last survivors of the great West Coast scene. And the last year or so has seen a revival of interest in Claxton's work and in the era he chronicled.

In 1998, Blue Note—which owns the Pacific Jazz catalog—reissued sixteen titles by artists like Baker, Mulligan, Jack Sheldon, and Bud Shank, most with suitably cool covers by Claxton. The University of California has reissued Ted Gioia's crucial history of the era, *West Coast Jazz*, with a section of Claxton photos. In a sign of the photographer's ability to reach beyond the insular and often backward-looking world of jazz enthusiasts, he's been increasingly enlisted by rock artists— among them Elvis Costello, who recently asked Claxton to shoot the cover for his celebrated Burt Bacharach collaboration, *Painted From Memory*. And the Fahey/Klein Gallery on La Brea will host a show of Claxton's work next month, timed to precede the publication of *Jazz Seen*—Claxton's collected jazz shots—by the German publisher Taschen.

The result is that Claxton's profile is suddenly as high as it's been since the height of Pacific Jazz. Or at least his public profile—despite his fame, little is known about Claxton the man, even by jazz die-hards.

Gregarious, warm, slightly absentminded, and sometimes politely mischievous, Claxton projects both rumpled ease and a slightly formal Old World politeness. He calls himself "a hippie, relaxed type," though he's using the term hippie in its short-haired 1950s and not its 1960s psychedelic sense.

While Claxton has made a living shooting some of the most beautiful and meticulously dressed people on the planet, he carries himself casually and unselfconsciously; he favors heavy work shirts with square pockets, as if he were a village electrician. He projects little ego; some describe him as the kind of artist who "disappears into his work." And so, as wide as he's ranged—from photojournalism to fashion to movie sets—Claxton knows exactly how he'll be remembered: "I think I'm so deeply rooted in jazz," he says in his slightly hoarse voice that recalls worn leather, "that it'll say on my tombstone that I was a jazz photographer."

Pacific Jazz trumpeter Jack Sheldon, who Claxton captured in the glare of a car's headlight in the 1950s, is more succinct: "To me, he's just like one of the cats."

As a kid, Claxton loved listening to swing—Benny Goodman, Artie Shaw. He dreamed of opening an art deco club—all checkerboard and palm fronds in black and white, with the people providing the only color. And he loved photography; not only the gritty journalistic dispatches of Robert Capa and W. Eugene Smith but the clean, airy fashion photography of Irving Penn and Richard Avedon that he found in his sister's copies of *Harper's Bazaar*.

Claxton's first in-person experience with jazz was as a teenager, driving from La Canada to clubs on Glendale's Brand Avenue. By the time he began college, still living at home, he would borrow his father's Packard and drive with a girlfriend from his leafy, white neighborhood in the hills above Pasadena to the jazz clubs that lined LA's Central Avenue. Claxton was so tall that bouncers assumed he was of age, and he would slip into Jack's Basket, Brother's, the California Club and the other clubs on Central—many of them "homes, behind the stores on Central Avenue"—that offered camaraderie, jazz dancing, and, of course, music. They opened after midnight and served booze in coffee cups. Despite the mostly male performers, he remembers the scene as a matriarchy, with church-bred women, many of them transplanted Southerners, running the show. Claxton, in fact, was struck by Central's formality. "I was treated very well, even when I was the only white in the place," he recalls. "Everybody wore ties and jackets, no matter what they did, and everyone was taught to be courteous. No one was revolutionary; there weren't any Farrakhans around. But I also noticed that the big hotels would not let the black musicians in. The racism was quiet."

Claxton went there to hear what he calls "my heroes"; one night, when his parents were gone for the weekend, he invited the great Charlie Parker to his house in La Canada after a show. ("Did you give him something to eat?" his mother asked when told of the visit.) This was not the behavior of your typical San Gabriel Valley teenager; it was hard even to get word of the jazz scene out there. The *Los Angeles Times* and other mainstream papers chronicled Central sporadically or not at all, and the black papers were little better. When the *Times* turned its attention to Central, it often described the district's happenings with both enthusiasm and condescension.

"It was a kind of daring thing to do that nobody else was doing," Claxton recalls. "We were really out of place." The only other whites he saw were musicians and movie stars, and his friends knew little about his nocturnal excursions. "We didn't really brag about it," he says. "It was our own private, little world."

Thanks to a neighborhood friend who had introduced him to photography, Claxton's visits to hear Dexter Gordon, Billy Strayhorn, Slim Gaillard, and Benny Carter on Central often became impromptu photo sessions. "I liked the way the musicians looked, their body language; the instruments were beautiful, the way they caught the light . . . I thought it was a great combination of sound and visuals."

Not long after Claxton began attending, though, Central started to fade. According to *Central Avenue Sounds*, last year's informative oral history, the loss of defense jobs after World War II put much of the audience out of work; police harassed and arrested interracial couples and white women; and R&B supplanted jazz as the music of choice for black Angelenos. As with Harlem, one reason for Central's demise was a relaxing of the strict segregation and redlining that had made Central a high concentration black neighborhood; many blacks started settling along Western or Crenshaw.

But as Central's audience dispersed with the dawn of the 1950s, a new chapter of LA jazz began, one that resembled Central only vaguely. Made up mostly of white musicians too excited by the flashes of bebop and modernism to remain in big bands, this gang collected around clubs like the Haig, a bungalow near Wilshire's Ambassador Hotel, and the Lighthouse Café, a boisterous, Polynesian-decorated place not far from the Hermosa Beach surf. Though these clubs were mostly white, Claxton often saw the black celebrities of the day—Lena Horne, Harry Belafonte, Sidney Poitier, Cab Calloway—checking out the new sound.

While Central's musicians were dedicated to modernity—which by the late forties meant manic, harmonically knotty, small-group bebop—many of these white players were more melodic, emulating the pleading tones and smooth lines of tenor saxophonist Lester Young. Some players came out of the New Orleans revival that had thrived among white Angelenos during Central's heyday. Others had been involved in a strange experiment led by an East Coaster: Baritone saxophonist Gerry Mulligan and alto saxist Lee Konitz had taken part in Miles Davis' *Birth of the Cool* chamber jazz sessions in 1949, in which French horns, tubas, and saxophones strove for a kind of smooth, introspective pan-European harmony. Still others, like trumpeter Chet Baker, an Okie who had recently gone AWOL from the army and settled in the South Bay, had played with Charlie Parker, the greatest of all modernists, during Bird's rare West Coast appearance.

And it was this world that Bill Claxton walked into one night in 1952, now a kid striving to close out a degree at UCLA. Claxton had tried all kinds of things that hadn't worked out. He'd spent a summer working in a Kodak lab, an experience he compares to Charlie Chaplin struggling with the conveyor belt in *Modern Times*. His academic work in psychology was supposed to lead him to the source of creativity and the artistic temperament, but never did he think he'd ever make a living as a photographer.

Claxton went to hear Mulligan's controversial "piano-less quartet" and got the musician's permission to photograph. Claxton was drawn to this group for the same reasons as many Southland music fans: By dropping the piano out of the band, Mulligan had created a new kind of harmonic freedom, and his soulful, almost drowsy baritone playing made him the instrument's undisputed leader. While he was shooting, a young man named Richard Bock approached him and said he'd just started a new record company called Pacific Jazz. Bock wanted to know if he could use

Claxton's photos for an album cover. The label had at this point released exactly zero records.

As Claxton developed his prints a day or two later, it was Mulligan's trumpeter, Chet Baker, that kept drawing his eye. Face to face, Baker had seemed distinctive looking but comical, too: "A fifties pompadour, pale white skin, a tooth missing—he looked like an angelic prizefighter. A sweet, pretty, rough guy." In pictures, though, he had a power over the camera that Claxton couldn't have predicted on first meeting. Baker, he says, taught him what the word "photogenic" really meant.

"As a photographer I meet a lot of good looking guys, and great-looking girls, and take pictures of them. And the pictures are not very good. It has nothing to do with how beautiful you are. A lot of it has to do with how you project emotionally. I know it sounds mysterious, but it's true."

The recording of that show was soon put together as a Pacific Jazz record called *The Gerry Mulligan Quartet*. Baker and Mulligan's melodic, open, airy, delicately arranged sound—miles away from the bluesy, often thunderous bebop that was thriving in New York—helped define an emerging West Coast sound, and Pacific Jazz soon became synonymous with it. And since this batch of musicians toured less frequently than their New York peers—some of the best West Coast players never even graced New York's clubs during cool's heyday—and since jazz rarely got much exposure on television, it was Claxton's photos that spread the word to the rest of the country. As Ted Gioia puts it, "He did as much as the musicians to create the image of West Coast jazz."

When Claxton began shooting, there was already an established school of jazz photography, dominated by photos of New York musicians in darkened studios or clubs, brooding behind cigarette smoke. Claxton was familiar with the work of such Gotham shooters as William Gottlieb and

Herman Leonard, who had memorialized the great New York musicians, aloof in the shadows or hard at work.

"The musicians were always perspiring," Claxton says with a gentle laugh. "I said to myself, 'It's not like that out here.'" It was a jazz subculture, after all, as different from the East Coast jazz scene as LA's sprawl was from New York's skyline. "They played at the beach. They wore Hawaiian shirts, there was sunlight everywhere."

Among other things, it was a jazz world that drew far less critical attention and praise than the East Coast's and, perhaps because of this, was less self-serious. It was a world in which, as Claxton delights in pointing out, "even the junkies were into health food." So instead of entombing them in the studio, Claxton put players in boats, on beaches, on streets, on cable cars. He wondered, "Wouldn't it be great to see musicians in totally different, incongruous settings? And the musicians loved it . . . I shot them up in trees, in the backs of convertibles."

"His pictures are just like the sounds of cool," says author Gavin. "The music is about order, but also about beauty; soft sounds and round corners, and Bill's aesthetic is all about people looking cool and beautiful."

The clubs in those days were filled with great, innovative players, among them horn player Jimmy Giuffre, pianist Hampton Hawes, drummer Shelly Manne. To the general public, the best known was Baker, who was as popular for his winsome singing voice as his crisp, detached trumpet playing. Though Claxton has created the image by which the world knows the trumpeter, he feels little warmth for the man himself, judging him "a tough person to get along with." Though his most distinguishing characteristic was his sullen, passive withdrawal, Baker was also, according to Claxton, "absolutely spoiled rotten. He was the only child of poor dust-bowl parents, but they gave him everything he wanted." The two would sometimes, in Claxton's phrase, "smoke grass" and talk records. Both loved fast cars; Claxton fancied sports cars, Baker went for Lincolns and Cadillacs.

"I think our closest bond was that we both liked pretty songs, and I introduced him to a lot of standards by Rogers and Hart or Gershwin that he didn't know." Baker, of course, was hungry for this kind of cultural education; his Okie parents had offered him little exposure to the genteel, necktie-wearing world of Tin Pan Alley pop. ("Oklahoma is a cultural waste-land," Baker recounted in a 1988 interview. "I mean those people listen to the most terrible kind of music in the world—hillbilly, rockabilly, and all that crap.") Among the tunes to which Claxton introduced the trumpeter was "Deep in a Dream," which a wrinkled Baker recites to the camera in the aptly titled documentary *Let's Get Lost*.

"With guys," Claxton says, "his relationships were pretty passive—except when he turned around to do exactly what he wanted."

Whatever his personality flaws, Baker's playing skills—when he wasn't strung out and had all his teeth—are rarely disputed. Yet despite such talented players, the new West Coast cool was greeted with condescension from critics, most of them headquartered then, as now, in New York or Chicago. New York jazz writers often characterized the scene as driven by gimmicks, not bluesy enough, not black enough (ironic, since nearly all these critics were white), a conspiracy of Hollywood marketing, and generally too soft or "cool." The historian Joe Goldberg, for instance, in his otherwise exemplary *Jazz Masters of the Fifties* refers to "the West Coast jazz fiasco" and assumes the reader shares his assessment of the music's "sterility." But it may have been the success of Claxton's covers in creating the music's image that caused West Coast jazz to be taken less seriously.

"On the basis of record covers, one might wonder whether these musicians ever saw the inside of a studio," Gioia writes in *West Coast Jazz*. "If the

New York critics wanted to prove that West Coast jazz was all image and no substance, certainly these flighty jackets played right into their hands."

But while Claxton's shots documented a life of ease and were often marked by a sense of humor, he rarely delved into the truly cheesy side of cool jazz. He maintained a sophisticated and playful relationship to his subject matter—which was really the mystique of West Coast jazz itself.

"He knew when to parody it, when to play it up, when to play it down," Gioia says, speaking specifically about a shot in which The Lighthouse All-Stars riff improbably on the Hermosa Beach strand. "When [his shooting] does become hokey, it does so consciously, and there's an element of self-parody."

Claxton has shot a few silly or cleverly sexy covers—the Art Pepper/Chet Baker collaboration *Playboys*, for instance, on which a busty, topless blonde wears puppets on her fists and holds her arms crossed at chest level, or the *Jazz West Coast Vol. 3* jacket, which shows a deep-sea diver emerging from the ocean with a trident in one hand a trumpet in the other. But he's not responsible for the most egregious examples of the form, like the Art Pepper and Friends *Surf Ride* LP, which shows a shapely, bikini-clad babe balancing atop a surfboard. Even when Claxton did shoot cheesecake, he had the integrity to credit it to his imaginary alter ego Lou McGilla.

And corny iconography aside, California jazz didn't deserve the smugness it was greeted with from East Coast critics, who were so unrelenting on their assaults on cool or West Coast jazz that even the musicians who'd helped forge the style were afraid of the label. Sometime Californian Stan Getz, for instance, made a record called *East of the Sun*, which made his alliances clear. In researching West Coast Jazz, Gioia found that the stigma still cut, even forty years later. "In interviews for this book," he writes in the preface, "any inquiry about 'West Coast jazz' inevitably resulted in a perceptible rise in tension in the interviewee, followed by vehement denials of any connection with that music, almost to the point of pulling out birth certificates to show out-of-state origins."

Consider the dissing an earlier and more genteel version of later rivalries in hiphop. But those who looked down their noses at this music missed some of the most fluent and probing sounds of the decade. And some musicians are even willing to admit as much.

"When I moved from New York to Los Angeles in 1957, I quickly realized the East Coast was extremely conservative," woodwind player Paul Horn wrote in his autobiography. "California was wide open—an experimental, innovative, and exceptionally creative environment. People felt free to try new ideas, anything at all. If it was new and interesting, they went for it."

Good, bad, or ugly, the heyday of cool jazz didn't outlast the decade. "It seemed like the scene was folding up," Claxton says. "What they seemed to be doing, from my point of view, was refining the bop era," and making "a really cerebral kind of music . . . Nothing really new was happening."

What was happening—free jazz, ushered in by saxophonist Ornette Coleman's recordings with Don Cherry—was occurring elsewhere. Coleman had spent most of the fifties in LA as an obscure and at times controversial presence, and made his first recordings in the city. But by the time he asked Claxton to shoot the cover for the epochal *The Shape of Jazz to Come*, he was on his way to New York, where his reputation took off with the dawning of the 1960s. Indeed, many of the important and innovative black players of the era—Coleman, Dexter Gordon, Charles Mingus—had left California for New York to build national reputations. The best players of the cool scene, instead of leaving the coast, went into internal exile, losing themselves in drugs and crime. Perhaps even worse, some were lost in the no man's land of faceless film and TV studio work. As for Claxton, he toured New Orleans and the Deep South, then left for New York himself.

Once in New York, Claxton slowly moved away from jazz, and then photography itself. He made a second career as a fashion photographer for German designer Rudi Gernreich. (Claxton's best-known photo, oddly enough, is not of a jazz player but of Modera model Peggy Moffitt—now the photographer's wife—in Gernreich's once scandalous "Topless Swimsuit," from 1964.) He would eventually return to Los Angeles, and—though he has to be coaxed into such curmudgeonly moments—has since been frustrated with the slow, downhill slide of the city he helped mythologize in the 1950s.

"The taste—the restaurants, the art, the way people dress. I think it's really ugly," he says, apologizing for his bitterness. "And the personalities seem to be really aggressive."

Claxton got a front row seat to LA's decline, in fact, when he and his wife returned to LA in 1969 to check on the hillside bungalow they'd bought a few years before. Claxton and Moffitt arrived at the airport just as the corpses at Sharon Tate's mansion were being discovered.

"And it was like one of those corny scenes in a movie where you turn on the radio and it says, 'and more about the murders in Benedict Canyon.'" Unfazed, they moved back permanently in 1971, and a son arrived in 1973. "After living in New York and Paris and London, we couldn't stand living here. Things moved so slowly, you could only make one appointment a day, and you spent all your time in your car."

By the early 1970s, Claxton had little to do with jazz, less to do with jazz photography. The photographer found work documenting the making of Hollywood films. He would direct commercials, "lots of terrible sitcoms," and episodes of the seventies show *Love American Style*. As far as jazz was concerned, there was little left to chronicle, especially in LA; as Gioia jokes, nearly all of the West Coast players went to the studios, to prison, or to New York. The players who'd once seemed the most promising as musicians and the most beautiful as photography subjects seemed the hardest hit: In 1968, Chet Baker's teeth had been knocked out by a vengeful drug dealer; by the seventies, the wrinkled, often strung-out trumpeter was pumping gas.

Alto saxophonist Art Pepper—whose dashing looks, romantic temperament, and bouts of meanness were similar to Baker's—went through a similar downward spiral. In the fifties, Pepper had managed to move in and out of prison and heroin convictions with his playing unblemished, cutting historic recording sessions during breaks from San Quentin. Nothing seemed to break his stride. Back then, Claxton was amazed when he was discussing prison with Pepper, and the saxophonist described his life there with nostalgia and fondness. "He said, 'It was a small, confined world, and everything was provided for me. Anything I wanted I got.'" And Pepper, the leading white interpreter of what was considered a black man's art, was a hero to many of the black prisoners.

Years later, though, with race relations in the country far different, and an acrid racism coloring Pepper's worldview, Claxton bumped into Pepper again, and asked him if he still enjoyed Quentin. Now seeming worn with the years and weary from maintaining his tightrope dance, Pepper "looked at me like I was crazy . . . He said, 'The whole world has changed. They don't know my records. They don't know who I am.' He had no reputation in prison." It didn't help that Pepper had recorded only sporadically since his great run in the fifties. "What had happened," says Claxton, "was that the whole world had passed him by." A few years later, Pepper was considering a career in bookkeeping. (He eventually cleaned up and regained his virtuosity.)

It was during the seventies, a time so hard on many of his old peers, that Claxton—tired of working on crummy TV shows—decided to get back to what made him. "I just cooled it, stayed at home and played with my son, and thought about photography for a while, which is really where my roots were." He eventually returned to photography, but not to jazz. Like much of the music's former audience, he was turned off by where jazz was going—or not going. "Charlie Parker had changed the sound of jazz so much that you couldn't find a saxophone player who didn't play like him," Claxton says with a bitterness that's uncharacteristic. "That was boring to me the seventies."

By the eighties, when Claxton got back into shooting musicians after two decades in movies, fashion, and photojournalism, much had changed. First, there was a blow to Claxton's creativity. It's not just Indie rockers and old-school audiophiles who lament the shift from vinyl to compact disc. CDs literally shrunk the space Claxton had to work with. He describes the shift with a characteristic easygoing demeanor—the words "my canvas has been diminished" and a self-deprecating smile—but one look at the typical new jazz, rock, or pop cover and it's clear how the record cover has declined as a forum for good shooting.

Even worse, shooting a musician had grown to include countless faxes and meetings and a glut of lawyers, art directors, accountants, agents, and various record company weasels.

"I think it was due to the rock guys that made such a huge amount of money," he says. "There were so many people you had to go through before shooting the picture. They became enormous productions. I say it's so many people just justifying their jobs. It became hard for me to recreate the spontaneity I used to have—now the person is rolled out onto the stage looking too perfect. And these people standing in the background saying, 'Can I fix your hair, can I change your shirt?'"

Lost, too, was Claxton's ability to spend time with a musician before shooting, to establish his essential rapport. The only time he can work at the same creative level as the old days, he says, is with an unknown or up-and-coming artist. He saw just how deadening the once pleasing process had become while shooting an album for Bruce Springsteen in the early nineties. After dealing with "every legal hanger-oner, every record company hanger-oner—it just drove you nuts," he showed up for the shoot in Hollywood.

"I had to go through two security clearances and a lawyer," he recalls. "I had to sign an agreement saying I wouldn't shoot him in the red jacket, only in the blue jacket, something like that." After a hard day of shooting, Claxton felt good about several "moody, emotional, candid" shots. But the Boss' lady friend had done a few Polaroid's and Springsteen chose to use them instead.

Claxton knows the historical reason for this shift but still finds it frustrating. Much of it, he says, goes back to Sinatra, who broke famously with Capitol Records in the early sixties, forming Reprise and launching the era of musician-run labels. Musicians began to talk about "complete creative control." While the phrase sounds high-minded, what it often really means, Claxton says, is that "his three-year-old may pick the cover."

Claxton's response, he says, is to shoot what he thinks is good, keep the best of the shots for himself, and let the labels and execs take what they want. "I try to shoot for myself, to trust my own visual instincts," Claxton says. "So I got some great pictures, and I don't care if they don't use them."

Though he's associated with the cool school, Claxton's body of work goes beyond lighthearted shots of California boys in Hawaiian shirts.

His most evocative photos peek into a musician's soul: A photograph of Baker staring down into a piano—a shot that captures his reflection in the instrument's polished top—conveys the trumpeter's sullen beauty as well as his unrelieved narcissism. Other shots hint at the distinctive music of a player or singer. Claxton shows hard-bop pianist Horace Silver, muscles tensed, delighting in his own playing in a way that makes his own rhythmically adroit musicianship almost audible.

An overhead closeup of Dizzy Gillespie blowing furiously into his famously bent trumpet reminds us of the slashing angles, wild curves, and cramped musical space that characterize Dizzy's breed of bebop.

Sometimes Claxton's photos reveal more than their subjects intended, like his shot of Baker with his girlfriend Lili, in Hollywood in 1955. With Lili engaging the camera in a protective, maternal gaze and Baker averting his eyes boyishly, it deepens our understanding of the trumpeter's almost pathetic dependence on women to help him through a reckless life.

Claxton's tools were unusual. He often used a Rolleiflex, a large-format camera that captures more information than a normal 35 mm, and has both a square field the shape of a record jacket—and a very quiet shutter, which doesn't interrupt a musician's playing. And after he met Richard Avedon during a New York trip in the late forties, Claxton also relied on natural light whenever possible. But as sophisticated as Claxton's artistry, much of his success comes from such simple virtues as the power of persuasion. When trying to get Thelonious Monk to pose on a cable car for the 1959 *Alone in San Francisco* session, Claxton had to convince the notoriously individualistic pianist that the shot wouldn't look corny.

"I don't want to have some postcard record cover," he recalls Monk saying. Claxton told Monk that he knew a bar in North Beach that served "champagne cocktails." ("I didn't even know what they were," admits Claxton. "It sounded exotic.")

The two ducked into the first bar they came to in North Beach, and after a few champagne cocktails, Monk was happy to pose wherever Claxton wanted. On the way back from the bar, they passed an abandoned Elk's Lodge with antique chandeliers and a battered old piano; Claxton got a shot of Monk with both.

Many of Claxton's most legendary shots were taken in this sort of casual, spontaneous manner. His celebrated cover for Sonny Rollins' *Way Out West* LP plays on the incongruity of Rollins as the ultimate New Yorker, adrift in the sunbaked West. According to Claxton, the creative negotiations with Rollins, arguably the leading jazz saxophonist at the time, were slightly less complicated than deciding where to stop for lunch: "Sonny said, 'I've never been to the West before, so let's do something Western.' And I said, 'Do you want to wear a cowboy hat?' So I went to a place called Western Costumers on Melrose, and rented him a ten-gallon hat and a holster and gun, and a steer's skull." The ensuing cover shows Rollins in the Mohave desert, grinning sardonically and leaning back like a gunslinger.

Claxton tries to see a player perform so he can "listen with his eyes"—and to see how a player moves, gestures, catches the light.

"My technique is no secret—I try to spend as much time as possible with a person before I shoot them. I usually get to know their fears. Some people are afraid of being photographed." It's also important to allow people to get accustomed to his physical presence. "I'm such an awful tall guy that if they didn't get used to me I'd be a terrible annoyance. I kind of blend into the background. They think I'm another mike stand."

Unlike a lot of photographers, says veteran cool jazz saxophonist Bud Shank, Claxton understands musicians and their rhythms. "What we're doing takes enormous concentration, and anything that breaks that concentration is bad." Shank and Claxton's connection goes back to the 1950s, when both drove Jaguars; the former still uses Claxton as his photographer whenever possible, including the shots for a recent record on a Japanese label. "These Japanese photographers were all over the place—they made me nervous! They didn't know when to shoot and when to stay away. But I'm very relaxed around Claxton. You don't even know he's there—and the guy's six-foot-six."

"Bill has a real flair for putting people at ease," says Gavin. "You can tell that when you sit with him for five minutes."

"I got a reputation for taking really difficult people and getting along with them," Claxton says. "Nobody wanted to shoot Sinatra because he was a headache. Nobody wanted to shoot Streisand because she was a headache. People trust me, because they know I won't do them in. I think it was because of my personality. Some people said it was too sweet or too gentle." He laughs. "But for me it works."

Perhaps now more than ever. Those who lived in LA in the fifties often feel a powerful nostalgia for a less crowded, less commercial, less self-conscious city. Jazz fans who remember the music's great era often have a similar difficulty regarding the present with the same degree of fondness as the past. Perhaps because Claxton's style represents a high point from which jazz photography has fallen, and because even those not old enough to remember the time and place respond to its crisp, simple style, Claxton has more work than he can handle these days. ("I'm sort of enjoying a renaissance in the last couple years," he says.) He's begun to shoot jazz again, too. His upcoming book of jazz photographs falls off steeply at 1960, but picks up in the last few years with young players like Jacky Terrasson and Stephen Scott.

"There's a lot of young guys shooting pictures, but I can't think of anyone who really stands out like Claxton," says Ray Avery, the founder of the Jazz Photography Association's LA branch and a longtime friend and admirer. "I think a lot of us are photographers, but he's an artist."

[*New Times LA*, February 4, 1999; *Los Angeles Times*, February 10, 1999]

BEING SPIKE JONZE

IN A STRANGE NEW FILM THAT OPENS THIS WEEK, people pay for the pleasure of slipping through a small door in an anonymous office building and spending fifteen minutes inside John Malkovich's head. Turns out celebrity's not all it's cracked up to be: Those who make the trip watch Malkovich reading *The Wall Street Journal*, heating up leftover Chinese food, and ordering bathroom towels over the phone.

According to Malkovich himself and some of the film's other stars, this is pretty much what it's like to be famous. "When we go to McDonald's, we have to decide if we want to park or go through McDrive," says the edgy and inscrutable star of stage and screen.

Cameron Diaz, the former model and *There's Something About Mary* lead, who appears in this new film as a frizzy-haired pet-store owner, concurs: "I think what the movie says is that the grass is always greener—everybody else [seems to] have it better."

For most of the film's stars, and for its producer, R.E.M.'s Michael Stipe, celebrity is a known quantity, something they wrestled with long ago, but one member of the crew of this Kafka-meets-*Alice in Wonderland* satire— director Spike Jonze—has little to say about celebrity or voyeurism. He has even less to say about himself and his own background. For Jonze, who's developed a formidable underground reputation over the past decade as a video director *par excellence*, the real demands of celebrity have come calling for the first time.

Though he has made one of the year's funniest movies—*Being John Malkovich* is up there, in its own eccentric way, with *South Park* and *Rushmore*—and is MTV's most celebrated director, he has almost no public profile. Jonze—who also appears as one of the *Three Kings* in David O. Russell's Gulf War action film, playing a hick from a group home in Dallas who longs for a nice split-level in Garland—turns down interviews, decides not to show up for others, and stages bizarre pranks in lieu of others. His publicity firm has to hire paparazzi photographers to get a shot of him. Walking into a New York press conference that seems to fill him with fear, and asked by a reporter when he changed his name, the blond and sheepish twenty-nine-year-old responds: "Ah, 1933."

Despite the director's frequent impersonation of an innocent bystander, Jonze's new work is one of the most personal and unpredictable films to arrive in a long time. Incongruously, it's also controlled and polished. Much of the movie takes place on the seven-and-a-halfth floor of an obscure New York skyscraper and involves a hundred-year-old lech who survives almost entirely on carrot juice and a monkey struggling to get in touch with its inner child. But it's hard to know whether *Being John Malkovich* will go down in history as "the last great movie of the century," as *Esquire* has called it, or as an endless midnight movie.

As ubiquitous as his work is, Jonze himself is a study in the elusive. Most Americans under the age of thirty-five have probably seen one of his videos for acts such as Sonic Youth, Björk, Dallas' own MC 900 Ft Jesus, or Dinosaur Jr., but the man himself exists only as a vague mystique. His videos are consistently the best and most inventive in the business: His clip for

Weezer's "Buddy Holly" sets the alternative-rock band onstage at Al's Diner, with old, kitschy footage of Richie Cunningham, Potsie, even The Fonz. His manic video for the Beastie Boys' "Sabotage"—an imitation seventies cop show, complete with bad mustaches and reflector sunglasses—is equally beloved for its retro fashion sense and its constant onscreen movement. Björk's "It's Oh So Quiet" was a Busby Berkeley homage set in a Valley tire shop, with dancing mechanics and twirling umbrellas, and this year's video for Fatboy Slim's "Praise You," which chronicles an amateur dance troupe, swept the recent MTV Music Video Awards. The fact that those who admire his videos know little more than his name is no accident.

"He just doesn't like to talk about himself," says Megan Baltimore, who, with Jonze and two others, owns the Torrance, California-based Girl skateboard company and also was once his roommate. "I don't know if I should say anything," she replies when asked more about him. "I don't want to give away any of his secrets." Asked whether Jonze attracts misinformation and mythology, she says, "Would I be giving away his mystique if I said yes?" This kind of closed-mouth treatment is typical of the way Jonze's friends from the skateboard world discuss him.

"Spike has a wonderful persona, because the people around him help create his mythology," says Jacob Rosenberg, a fellow skater and video director who has known Jonze casually since the early nineties. Rosenberg says Jonze likes to play with his image and reputation out of the same sense of boyish fun that motivates his shooting and directing. "Life is much more interesting the way he does it."

Part of the Spike Jonze myth is that he's a reclusive, almost pre-verbal genius—the image he likes to convey when members of the media are around. When, in 1995, a *New York Times* reporter asked Jonze whether his real name was Adam Spiegel (which it is), his response was, "Yeah, that's a . . . you know, it's all . . . it's a mastermind P.R. plan I'm working on." Or when asked whether he was dating actress and director Sofia Coppola, daughter of the *Godfather* director: "You know, it's all a . . . I have no . . . I don't know what you're talking about." (Jonze married Coppola this spring at her father's Northern California vineyard in a ceremony serenaded by Tom Waits.)

For an early segment for an MTV series of interviews with video directors, Jonze sent his friend Chris Pontius, who writes for skateboard magazines, to pretend to be him. For *Mean* magazine, Jonze posed as a frazzled publicist who couldn't get Jonze to cooperate. For *Spin*, he asked some friends to act like strangers and repeatedly beat the hell out of him in front of a reporter. Even when interviewing with friends at a skateboard magazine, he invents stories and agrees to every outlandish rumor—wild honeymoons, cross-country BMX bike rides—the reporter serves him.

Jonze plays similar games with his identity on the screen. In his much hailed video for Fatboy Slim's gospel-flavored "Praise You," he appears as the leader of The Torrance Community Dancers, a clumsy and, thankfully, imaginary group that awkwardly expresses itself in front of a Los Angeles movie theater. Despite his reported bashfulness, Jonze stars in the video, venturing extroverted, breakdance-inspired moves that most people would keep to themselves. Then, in a voice even more nasal than his real one, Jonze—speaking to an offscreen interviewer—spins another imaginary identity.

"A lot of people tell us we have a very hip-hop feel," he says. "Growing up in Manhattan, I performed with several B-Boy posses." He enthusiastically hugs the other dancers and says: "That's sort of our background, sort of our inspiration!" At the annual MTV video awards in September, where "Praise You" collected three awards, Jonze accepted his prize as "Richard," the leader of the Torrance troupe, the icon of ironic cool posing as a pretentious performing-arts geek.

Jonze's real identity is less romantic. He was born Adam Spiegel, heir of the once stylish, now frumpy Spiegel catalog, and he grew up in Bethesda, Maryland, the affluent suburb of Washington, DC, where he was more interested in BMX bikes and skateboards than in TV or movies. He's been called Spike since age twelve, named—by staffers at the bike shop Rockville BMX—for the spiky haircuts he gave them. (Jonze was added on, most think, in homage to the surreal forties bandleader.) He moved to LA as a teenager in the late eighties and has remained there since, establishing and maintaining a hallowed role in the local skateboard scene and doing his best to stay invisible to the local media. These days he's into yoga, which he does every day at lunch.

Slight of build, with fine hair and an affinity for baggy but neat clothes, Jonze looks like the kind of polite kid who might still be arguing with his parents about whether law or medical school should be his next step. It's unlikely he passed his high school public-speaking class: When he discusses himself or his work, his sentences collide and interrupt each other, and he seems to have trouble sitting still for more than a few minutes, running to get more water whenever possible. He's more or less the opposite of press-crazed Harmony Korine, the other boy-wonder director with a new film (*Julien Donkey-Boy*) at the New York Film Festival.

Jonze's friends—nearly all of whom, famous or obscure, refuse to speak for attribution—use the words "sweet" and "unassuming" when speaking about him, and a few describe him as shy with people he doesn't know, crazy or wild with those he does. Shyness aside, in the last few years he has begun to come out of hiding, appearing not just in that MTV video but also in cameos in several films, among them *Mi Vida Loca* and his friend

David Fincher's *The Game*. His role as the Judas Priest-loving redneck Army private Conrad Vig in *Three Kings* marks the first time he's been given any substantial role in a feature film.

Jonze left Bethesda at age seventeen to work for *Freestylin'*, an LA bicycling magazine. He was hired to write and edit, but instead drifted into the darkroom. "He was kind of notorious in the BMX scene as a prankster," says Andy Jenkins, the editor who hired Jonze mostly on the basis of his funny, anarchic personality. Jonze also began shooting photos of skaters and a series of skateboard videos—quick-cut, mostly half-hour films made by skateboard companies to show off their stars and to sell boards and clothing—and quickly developed a reputation as a groundbreaker.

His first major effort was 1991's *Video Days*, made for the Blind skateboard team, which included not only skating legend Mark Gonzales but also the actor Jason Lee, best known from Kevin Smith's films. That video contains the seed of what's become a widely celebrated style: fast, risky camera work, smart choice of music, offbeat humor.

"For anyone from my era, it's *the* video," says Ed Templeton, a Huntington Beach skater who was internationally ranked in the early nineties. "When I want to get stoked to go skating, I watch the Blind video." This video, and other Jonze skate films such as *Rubbish Heap*, made a real impact on their medium. Says a skateboarder and photographer who asked that his name not be used: "It portrayed kids as kids—doing crazy stuff and getting into trouble." Earlier skate videos had tended to be polite and safe. "There was this etiquette to the way skateboarding was portrayed. People weren't doing crazy things. Spike did this video, and it was just the rawness of kids. He shot a lot of night spots, which allowed the subjects to stand out more. It was rad."

Skater and photographer Rosenberg praises Jonze's camera movement, his ability to describe a skater's personality through short interviews, and his innovative choice of music. "Skateboard music was almost all punk rock," Rosenberg says. "But Spike came in with things like The Jackson Five's 'I Want You Back.'" He also used a dynamic John Coltrane song from the 1950s and War's funky "Low Rider," which plays as the teenage skaters uncap beers and crash their car in the desert badlands.

These videos drew the attention of Thurston Moore and Kim Gordon of Sonic Youth, who asked Jonze to star in and shoot the skateboard passages of their rock video "100%." On the set, Jonze worked with director Tamra Davis (director of *Billy Madison* and Hanson's "MMMBop" video) and learned from her the rudiments of rock-video directing. Meanwhile, *Freestylin'* had gone out of business, and Jonze moved on to *Dirt*, a magazine for teenage boys that was, during its short-lived run, the counterpart of the more successful *Sassy* for girls. R.E.M. singer Michael Stipe met Jonze while he was working at *Dirt* and remembers him being "like a skate kid—a very smart one." In some ways he still is: Almost a decade after he broke in, skaters are still Jonze's people, and skaters feel proud of his success, as though he were a boy from the old 'hood.

In 1995, Sony/TriStar asked Jonze to direct *Harold and the Purple Crayon*, a live-action-animation feature film based on the Crockett Johnson book about a boy whose crayon drawings take on a life of their own. David O. Russell, who went on to direct *Spanking the Monkey* and to cast Jonze in *Three Kings*, was brought in as scriptwriter, but for reasons no one will discuss, the film was never made. Jonze continued to make skate videos and to shoot for magazines, and he branched into commercials—including clever, imaginative spots for Nike and Nissan and a Levi's jeans commercial in which a patient on a stretcher is saved by the Soft Cell song "Tainted Love"—and short documentaries while building the definitive portfolio of alternative-rock videos.

Stipe concedes that it's difficult to pin down Jonze's directing style, which is built from the rapid juxtapositions that mark the work of his namesake. Like most of the director's admirers, Stipe speaks about Jonze's ability to see the world from "a different angle," but can't be much more specific. "It's more of a freedom to fuck with the medium, and that for me is what sets him apart from the average director. He doesn't see the limitations, and if he sees them, they don't translate for him."

Much of the appeal of Jonze's style has to do not just with rapid onscreen movement and guerrilla camera work but with tone, the way he borrows images and iconography from other times and places and treats them with empathy and even affection instead of scorn. It's clear in his use of the fifties and seventies in his Weezer and Beastie Boys videos, in the way he pokes fun at the clumsy dancers in "Praise You"—who persevere through the indifference and hostility of passersby—but also makes this leotard- and tank-top-clad bunch the heroes of the story.

"He employs a certain contemporary irony that is inevitable for his age," says Sonic Youth singer-guitarist Thurston Moore. "But it is refreshingly lacking in the bitterness I see in other hepsters his age, like Harmony Korine."

Jonze's ability to see the humor in his subjects without trashing them is most clear in *Amarillo by Morning*. This short documentary from 1997 captures a group of Texas teens who dream of a future in the rodeo and nearly makes a star of a sixteen-year-old named Little John, a baby-faced kid in an enormous cowboy hat who speaks in the earnest, rapid-fire patter of a teenage televangelist. The documentary came about by accident, while Jonze and his director of photography, Lance Accord, were visiting

Texas to shoot rodeos. They met some kids and, as Jonze puts it during our interview, "just couldn't stop videotaping them." Part of what drew Jonze to these boys was the absurdity of their conviction, but he never mocks them. "For me, I was just so into how they were sixteen years old and they were so vocal about what they thought their lives would be like."

When he speaks about his projects, Jonze often adopts an innocent's fecklessness, as if he were an accidental genius. As he told the Los Angeles Reader in a 1995 interview: "It's probably because I'm like Chauncey Gardener, the guy from Being There. I'll say something like, 'A big table!' and then someone says, 'Oh, great. Let's give him a lot of money. Go make it.'"

Despite Jonze's image as a fun-loving boho who just lucks into his triumphs, there's a rigor and degree of difficulty to all of his work. Thurston Moore saw it immediately when he and Tamra Davis first watched Video Days.

"We were marveling at how some of the shots were being made, and we figured the cameraman was on a skateboard following the skaters, which is something we had never seen, at least not with so much inventiveness," says Moore, adding that Jonze's command of technique is such that "he can throw a camera in the air and create cool-looking stuff."

Being John Malkovich began its life not with Spike Jonze, but as an idea inside the head of rookie screenwriter Charlie Kaufman, who is nearly as shy and evasive as the director. Originally the story of a married man who fell in love with another woman, the script morphed into the tale of a harried puppeteer (John Cusack) who takes a job as a filing clerk on the seven-and-a-halfth floor of a Manhattan office building and discovers a portal into John Malkovich's head. He and a sexy, sharp-tongued co-worker (played by Catherine Keener, of Your Friends and Neighbors) set up a scheme to advertise the experience and charge $200 for the trip.

"You get to be John Malkovich for fifteen minutes," says a matter-of-fact Joe-Sixpack character waiting in line, as though explaining a gimmicky ride in a run-down amusement park. It's one of the film's many deadpan moments, in which strange developments are treated as just part of the landscape.

Kaufman says that he proceeded intuitively with the story that became *Malkovich* and that the script is still, mostly, a mystery to him. "It was always John Malkovich," Kaufman says. "It was part of the original idea. And I can't tell you why I liked it."

After Jonze had been brought in to direct but before they'd contacted Malkovich, Kaufman and Jonze threw other names back and forth, trying to come up with someone who'd work as suitably in case the actor declined to participate. "We couldn't come up with somebody else who works as well," Kaufman admits.

Kaufman and Jonze passed the script to Malkovich's agent, who passed it to the actor, who might never have read it if not for a severely delayed flight out of Los Angeles International Airport. Headed back to his home in the south of France, Malkovich expected his role to be little more than a passing reference. "I thought it would be a one-line joke or something," he recalls. Upon completing the script, he was struck by the daring humor and the unlikeliness of a film so eccentric ever getting made.

Jonze's main contribution to the film had nothing to do with the dynamic camera moves, lost-in-time quality, or sudden juxtapositions that characterize his skate or rock videos. Says Jonze, sitting in a New York hotel room: "I always thought of playing it very naturalistically and emphasizing the characters and the script and the story."

Instead of getting in its way, he says, letting the script be insane and hilarious was the best way to go. Jonze's choice was an unlikely one in a year that's seen kinetic, MTV-influenced movies such as *Run Lola Run, The Matrix,* and *Fight Club* and the emergence of more and more rock-video directors into the world of feature film.

His take on the script helped keep some of the film's big names, who found the story funny and original but were skeptical of it working as a full-length film. (The movie's rumored budget, $13 million, suggests that much of the cast's high-priced talent worked for far less than their standard fees.)

"When I first read it, I thought, 'Oh, God, I hope they don't try to make it into something wacky,'" says Diaz, who signed on only after discussing it with Jonze. Keener found the script "amazing," but felt similarly: "You take a script like that, and you wonder where it could end up."

Cusack was one of the first people to see the script, which he had heard described as long as five years ago as "this underground script that would never be made." He found it "part vaudeville and black comedy and absurdist farce and existential, completely original. I never thought he could sustain it for a whole film." He wanted to meet with Jonze, whose reputation he knew only vaguely, before committing to the movie. Though he'd seen some of his videos and liked them, Cusack wasn't yet convinced. "They showed he was inventive. None of them suggested that he could make a feature film."

Cusack says he's usually hesitant to play guinea pig for first-time directors, who most often just tell him what they think he wants to hear. Jonze, it turned out, was different.

"Spike immediately started talking about character, character, character, and tone," Cusack says. "He didn't talk about visuals. And that's when I knew that this kid was smart." Tricky, kinetic direction works for some films, he says, but not this one. "*The Matrix* and *Run Lola Run* were not really about characters; they're about creating worlds. You're being taken on a wild, science-fiction ride. If you're gonna make a movie about people, you can't overwhelm it with visuals, because you can't settle down and look at behavior."

People who have worked with Jonze talk about a contrast between his image as a daffy slacker and the driven, hard-working reality. "I think Spike has a great sensibility," says Malkovich. "For a kid who seems like a goofball, who's skateboarding or taking pictures and doing tricks on his bicycle, he's very smart. He has a really delicate touch. He really watches you—unlike a lot of directors who sit by the video monitors. He's very stubborn—he has very strong opinions. He's a little bit relentless." Adds Keener: "I found him very focused on the set. In a benign, conservative way, he kept us all on track."

Mark Pellington, who has also made the transition from rock videos (for Pearl Jam and Nine Inch Nails) to feature films (most recently *Arlington Road*), calls Jonze "a great conceptualist." Jonze is stylish, he says, but all his work is driven by fresh, left-field ideas. Pellington compares Jonze to David Fincher (the video director who graduated to *Fight Club* and *Seven*) and Tim Burton in his ability to tell a story with visual verve without overwhelming it with effects.

"God gave him a special way to see the world," Pellington says, "and he does it with tongue in cheek and a good heart."

Though a rumor has floated that Jonze was worn-out by the process of working on *Malkovich* and *Three Kings* and wants to return to shorter projects, he says he's ready for more. He's spoken recently to Rage Against the Machine about a video and always has his eye out for other documentary ideas. But he's also known for being choosy, and when it comes to features, he'll continue to hold out for scripts as good as the movies he loves, among them such recent films as *The Straight Story* and *Election*.

"He's a genius—everybody knows it," says a friend from the skateboard days. "Whenever he does something, people just wait. People put everything aside. You just don't know what's going on in his head—*ever.*"

[*New Times LA,* November 4, 1999]

UNWANTED THOUGHTS

AN ENORMOUS COFFEE CUP, welling with black java, fills the screen. A man with a thick Boston accent and enormous glasses—his face reflected blearily in the coffee's darkness—describes how he met his wife, a Dunkin' Donuts waitress: "I'm a good tipper," he says, "and she used to bring me extra coffee." Multiple images of him replicate across the coffee shop's bar, and she talks about how the two of them married, how he taught her how to shoot a .22; he tells how they spent their honeymoon at Auschwitz. Okay, so it's not a Maxwell House commercial: We're in an Errol Morris film.

Most of the director's movies concentrate on odd, obsessive men—guys who drift into reveries as they describe worm farming, lion taming, the joys of collecting opossum, a jar of atomic sand that grows slowly each year. Their eyes light up with an otherworldly glow. They seem to identify with their obscure objects of desire. One bow-tied zoologist in 1997's *Fast, Cheap & Out of Control* exclaims that his study of the African naked mole rat had become "a form of self-knowledge."

Morris's latest movie, *Mr. Death*, begins in the same vein as *Fast, Cheap*, with an unfashionable man coolly discussing electric chairs—the sizzle of flesh, the conductivity of urine, and so on. With fondness in his voice, Fred Leuchter recounts picking up the electric chair tradition from his dear old dad, a prison guard—"I learned all kinds of strange things as a youngster" he intones seriously—and we hear how excited he was when a chair was delivered and sat in the driveway. We see a snapshot of Fred smiling and strapping himself in.

The guy seems to have a heart, though, weird as he is: Leuchter drops his matter-of-fact engineer's tone when he talks earnestly about making death by electric chair and lethal injection more "dignified." With his polyester shirts and bland enthusiasm, he comes off like a nebbishy high school chemistry teacher, but Leuchter was once known as the Florence Nightingale of Death Row.

Thanks to the director's perfect timing and winking ironies—when Leuchter suggests that prisoners waiting for execution could be placated with music and art, Morris cuts to a cornball Currier & Ives painting—the first few minutes of the film are hilarious. A passerby walking beside the LA County Museum, where the film screened earlier this month, might have guessed he was overhearing the audience at a Marx Brothers retrospective.

But a half-hour into the film, *Mr. Death* takes a dark, sudden turn: Because of his fame with lethal injection and electric chairs, Leuchter was asked to serve as the expert witness for the trial of Ernst Zündel, a German national living in Canada who calls the Holocaust anti-German propaganda and published *The Hitler We Loved and Why*. Leuchter travels to Auschwitz on Zündel's dime, where he takes samples of the crematoria walls, finds no significant trace of the cyanide used to gas prisoners, and concludes that the Holocaust never happened. His *Leuchter Report* is published, translated, and spread through the Internet, and he's swept into the role of hero to the Holocaust denial crowd, speaking to neo-Nazi groups about "a responsibility to countless future generations that come after me, a responsibility to the truth!"

And, before long, thanks to the efforts of a few Jewish activists and his own carelessness, Leuchter falls and falls hard. As David Irving, a notorious revisionist historian who was converted to Holocaust denial by Leuchter's work, says: "He came from nowhere, and he went back to nowhere."

Instead of treating Leuchter like a malevolent anti-Semite, Morris, who is Jewish, portrays him as a kind of Everyman—a hapless fellow who chose his friends unwisely and gave in to vanity and self-deception. Morris, who is known for empathy toward his interview subjects, says he has all kinds of conflicting feelings about Leuchter and that the film opens up plenty of weird questions. "There's something really odd, truly odd and interesting about people," he says the day after the LACMA screening. "Do we know other people? Do we know ourselves?" Or, as he told the New Yorker: "What happens if you really need to be loved and the only people who will love you are Nazis?"

In person, Morris is less an absent-minded philosophy professor than an obscure and intellectual kind of Borscht Belt comedian. He paces, makes strange half-serious pronouncements ("What is the real defense against genocide? Consumerism!"), jokes about his TV commercials as "my very, very *finest* work," riffs on the novelist Vladimir Nabokov, and addresses a wide variety of serious issues with a David Letterman-like facetiousness. He looks at a hotel's couch and thinks of Freud. "I had a psychiatrist when I was a little boy—he asked me if I ever had *unwanted thoughts.*" Dropping his voice a little: "Another good title for a movie. I was going to perhaps use it as a title or an autobiography." Full-throated again: "And I remember saying, 'Is there any other kind?'" Pause for laughter. Cup of coffee in hand, he wonders aloud what he would be like if he drank forty cups a day, the way Leuchter does. Morris is a slightly manic fellow to begin with; it's frightening to think of him any more amped up.

"I guess what's so remarkable about Fred's story is how out of touch he is," he says of Leuchter, whom he also describes as a kindred spirit. (Morris lost his father when he was two and has conceded that he, like Leuchter, has almost always been obsessed with death.) "On one level, telling a truth or telling a falsehood is a simple kind of linguistic deal: There's a real world out there. If they say what happened happened, they're telling the truth. But if you get to the knottier question of *what they think they're doing*, it becomes this ghastly hall of mirrors. Are they somehow convincing themselves they're telling the truth even though they should know better? Are they consciously lying? And there's this crazy slippery slope where they try to convince themselves. Because people, unfortunately, can convince themselves of anything. Our capacity to believe nonsense is virtually unfettered."

Morris is no less animated the night before at the LACMA screening, where the film plays to a near-capacity audience as part of a retrospective of his films. Something about the crowd's temper and Morris' extroverted style seem a little off as he paces the stage at the museum's Bing Theater just a few minutes after screening shots of death camps: There's massive, uproarious laughter almost every time he speaks or pauses. It's the kind of jarring emotional dissonance that doesn't exist in his understated, artfully balanced film.

While Morris jauntily takes questions from the audience after the screening, a woman, visibly upset, stands up and denounces the film and its audience. Speaking with a Central European accent and wearing a shapeless red sweater that contrasts with the chic black and gray of the industry-heavy crowd, she says she's "extremely disturbed by the mockery that has been made of a very serious issue. You are extremely insensitive to what happened at Auschwitz. People died horrible deaths, and yet you are laughing."

Morris listens closely, then admits: "There's this question of course of whether people should even *make* this kind of film—a question I've had to deal with repeatedly." But he doesn't apologize for his work. "All I can say is that I find Holocaust denial fascinating."

This woman was not the only person to be thrown by *Mr. Death*. Shelly Shapiro, who directs the Holocaust Survivors and Friends Education Center in Upstate New York and has written a book assaulting Leuchter, is impressed with the film's artistry. But the movie, she says, removes Leuchter from his real context. "He comes across in the end like a fool—but he's *not* a benign fool." Shapiro, who appears in the film, says there's danger in making Holocaust denial seem funny when it helps create people like alleged racist gunman Buford Furrow. "It's not a laughable issue. It's the basis for militias, for anti-Semitic violence. Fred Leuchter is the scientific core of their argument. The real truth is that it's the Buford Furrow kind of person who subscribes to Leuchter's point of view, hard-core people who would kill small children at a Jewish community center."

Similar criticism has come from the press, though the film has drawn heavily positive reviews. Writes Blake Eskin, the arts editor of the New York-based Jewish monthly *The Forward*: "Morris wants to make *Mr. Death* another open-ended epistemological entertainment, but how open-minded can you be when dealing with the claim that gas chambers at Auschwitz couldn't have been the site of mass murder?"

At times, Morris has been deeply troubled by his Leuchter project, and he says it crossed his mind from time to time during the filming that he shouldn't make it. He understands the people who are hurt by the film. "There's usually one person who is upset for whatever reason," he says. "They have every right to be upset. But I'm *not* making light of the Holocaust. Hopefully I'm opening it to examination. I don't learn anything from hearing again and again and again that the Holocaust was bad. I *know* it was bad, I've known it all my life. Learning that the Germans were anti-Semites doesn't tell me much either.

"You know, there was someone from the Simon Wiesenthal Center who objected to the screening, they called the LACMA just before the screening that day and said they should not show the movie, because it was pernicious, the movie was soft on Fred. Quite the contrary; I think it's a very important movie to be shown, because it forces us to look very deeply into the Holocaust and what might have produced it."

The process of filming *Mr. Death* hit a strange snag partway through. Morris originally made a film that was all Leuchter's show. He let the engineer's oddball assertions—like the loopy theories of the lion tamer or topiary gardener in *Fast, Cheap* or the turkey hunter in *Vernon, Florida*—go unchallenged, figuring that Leuchter was so clearly nuts he would incriminate himself.

But when Morris, who lives in Cambridge, Massachusetts, showed a rough cut of the film to students at Harvard ("which is supposed to be a good school"), he found something very disturbing: Some of the students were convinced by Leuchter and started to wonder if the Holocaust had ever happened, while others thought that the filmmaker himself was convinced by Leuchter and thought the Holocaust had never happened.

It was here that Morris turned to several historians and Holocaust activists for balance, hoping they could advise him and go onscreen to counter Leuchter. One of the first he called was Robert Jan Van Pelt, a Dutchman who teaches at Canada's University of Waterloo and cowrote a book about Auschwitz. "The first description I got of what Errol was doing made me very uneasy," Van Pelt recalls by phone. He rented some of Morris' earlier films, and saw that they operated through dramatic irony—keeping information from its subjects or operating on the assumption that the audience knew better. "One of the problems with irony is that you have to be very smart to see it. I thought Errol was too smart for his own good." But when he met Morris, he found him smart and a good listener, and Van Pelt made one unbudging condition for his appearance: "I said, 'I really want you to go to Auschwitz.'"

Morris had already spent more money than he'd planned and taking a film crew of fifty people to Auschwitz would not be cheap. But the trip, says Van Pelt, produced a real change in Morris. "When he was in Auschwitz," he says, "whatever sort of smart-ass attitude he'd ever had completely disappeared."

Morris says the trip made an enormous impact. "There's no way you can go to that place and not be completely bent out of shape one way or another. Trying to imagine how such a thing is possible. Egyptian in size. I remember walking in Birkeanu for the first time and thinking, 'This is some kind of vast temple of death.' Immense, and I mean immense. The way it was geometrically arranged, mirror images, *Krema 1* and *Krema 2*, and that line drawn from the rail terminal. There is no question that this is one of the truly dark, evil episodes of human history. What does it really tell us about ourselves? Who were these people? What did they think they were doing?"

It's easy to imagine a world in which Leuchter becomes a creepy Holocaust-denier version of *Shine* pianist David Helfgott, touring the world in the wake of his bio film to clear his name before rapt halls. But he's unlikely to reemerge. He's rumored to be living in California, working on the world's fastest modem. Though Morris says Leuchter enjoyed the film and the two men remain on good terms, the filmmaker won't say anything more of Leuchter's whereabouts and refuses to appear in public with him.

Morris got to this point—this confluence of comedy and tragedy—from a path as twisted and unlikely as that of any working filmmaker. Born in 1948 and raised on Long Island, he spent the seventies drifting in and out of graduate school, first at Princeton, then at Berkeley, studying the history of science and philosophy and devouring all kinds of obscure movies— noir, Third World, and otherwise— at the Pacific Film Archive. Those who knew him then describe him as intense and a little paranoid. "I had to defend him to my staff," Tom Luddy, then archive director, told the *New Yorker's* Mark Singer. "What made him eccentric? Well, for one thing, he dressed strangely. Remember, this is Berkeley in the early seventies. And Errol was wearing dark suits with pants that were too short, white dress shirts, and heavy shoes. He looked like a New York person gone to seed." His remarkable achievements during this time included spending a year immersed in the world of Ed Gein (the Wisconsin murderer who served as the model for Hitchcock's psycho, Norman Bates), getting caught sneaking into a mental institution, and making the German director Werner Herzog eat his shoe in public (long story).

His film career began no less conventionally with a trip to Vernon, a Florida swamp town where residents were blowing their arms and legs off in order to collect insurance money. But the dwellers of "Nub City," as it's known, weren't too keen on a city slicker snooping around, and after some intimidation Morris left Vernon. He dropped the project when he read about a pet cemetery in Napa Valley, and in 1977, he shot *Gates of Heaven*, one of the slowest, strangest movies ever made. This film played in 1978 in

New York and Berkeley but had to wait two years for a theatrical release. In the meantime, Morris headed back to the swampy hamlet and shot *Vernon, Florida,* a film about everything but the insurance scam, which he'd been warned away from; he calls it his "philosopher kings in the swamp" movie.

These early films used almost no camera movement and rebelled against the conventions of the verité documentary form by using artificial lighting and fixed cameras. With his next film, 1988's *The Thin Blue Line,* Morris crafted his current style, further breaking from the documentary tradition. The film, about a man wrongfully accused of the murder of a Dallas policeman, used a haunting Philip Glass score, arty reenactments, campy cuts from old movies, and the kind of repeated close-up shots critics call "fetishistic"—soaring milk shakes; silent, whirring sirens; popping popcorn. The film has become famous for clearing the accused man's name and brought the director his current profile. *A Brief History of Time,* from 1992, about astrophysicist Stephen Hawking, 1991's largely ignored feature *Dark Wind,* and 1997's *Fast, Cheap* followed.

With *Fast, Cheap,* Morris began using an invention of his own—the Interrotron, named by his wife for its suggestion of the words "interview" and "terror." A combination of cameras, mirrors, and half-silvered lenses, the Interrotron projects the interviewer's face where the camera's blank lens would be, creating the illusion of eye contact. "It's an important device," Morris says. "When my subjects look at me they're looking *straight* into the lens. One of the central features of communication is eye contact. It is clear it is wired into our brains, it is *fundamentally* wired into our brains."

These days, besides continuing his work on TV commercials, Morris is putting together a half-hour television show about unusual characters. "Not every interview I do can turn into a long ninety-minute film," he says of *First Person,* which will run on Bravo and Britain's Channel Four. Morris can't give a straight answer about potential guests for the show. "I'm not being coy here, but—to the extent that I'm capable of sincerity?—it could be *anybody*. It could be a political figure, it could be a person in prison, it could be a housewife, it could be an inventor, it could be a television personality . . . I'm looking for anything. Anyone is welcome to apply." Besides obsessions, Morris has a fondness for regionalism and Americana—expect a symphony of great accents. "So what interests me? I like stories about how people see themselves."

Morris protégé David Schisgall, who has worked on the director's last three films and whose own eccentric documentary, *The Lifestyle: Group Sex in the Suburbs*, comes out this March, says he's had to correct some misconceptions about Morris while speaking to the show's researchers. "I told them it wasn't about *weird*—if you didn't find in the story something that illuminates an issue that you'd deal with in a first-year philosophy class, then you haven't found the story yet."

The only subject Morris will mention is Ron Popeil, the rags-to-riches founder of gadget company Ronco, who took the carnival pitchman's spiel onto late-night TV and has become the nation's most famous slicer-and-dicer. Morris describes him, with his usual bemused fascination, as "the son of the inventor of the Pocket Fisherman, and he himself the creator of the immortal spray-on hair and the immortal Sublimator. I love the Sublimator! You attach the Sublimator to your TV set, and it filters out all of those hidden subliminal messages that are coming out." It's hard, of course, to figure out which freshman-year philosophy point this American original will illustrate, but knowing Morris, anything's possible.

***

Morris's guiding obsession these days is clearly self-deception. "I wonder if I keep talking about it because I feel particularly self-deceived at the moment." He goes into more detail at the LACMA, discussing his own personal theory of the Book of Genesis. As God was kicking Adam and Eve out of the Garden of Eden, He began to feel guilty and came up with a way to make it go down easier. He gave mankind self-deceit. "Things will still be really, truly grotesque out there," the director says, "but they'll never notice." Big laugh; Morris walks off stage.

Van Pelt remembers Morris sitting in a seedy hotel lobby near Auschwitz with a strangely innocent grin on his face, despite the fact that the place was the sort of low-grade concrete-block Polish hostel that doubled as a whorehouse. "And I said, 'You're really like a boy, a naughty boy right now.' What I think really makes him tick is that curiosity, delight, in crazy things. Errol is still there, somewhere between seven and nine, where you simultaneously start to devour an encyclopedia and discover the library but can still be fascinated by two animals killing each other, two beetles devouring each other."

[*New Times LA*, December 23, 1999]

THE ROMANTIC EGOTIST

WHEN MOST NOVELISTS GO TO PARTIES, they don't have to worry about being threatened, challenged, or decked. But that's the way it was for John Rechy, back in the days when he haunted parties in and around Hollywood.

"At the time, I was very well-known," says the author of *City of Night*, the groundbreaking 1963 chronicle of gay hustling. "Basically, someone would come up and say: 'You think you're really hot shit! Somebody would get a little tipsy and they'd want to take me on—arm wrestling or something. 'You think you're such a stud.'" One of these challengers was Peter Orlovsky, the Beat poet and Allen Ginsberg's boyfriend, who accosted Rechy at a party in San Francisco's Nob Hill, sizing him up and asking him how much he could bench-press. "And my answer was always the same: 'Look, I don't *care* how strong I am. It's that I *look* like the stronger man.'"

It's a quintessential Rechy response, the dismissive words of a man whose life and career have been devoted to the beauty and mystery of surfaces, artifice, and the power of ego over any and all obstacles. His books have been placed on the short-list of classic Los Angeles novels, alongside Nathanael West's *Day of the Locust* and Raymond Chandler's *The Big Sleep*. Rechy, an El Paso native who moved to the city almost thirty years ago, is a kind of poet laureate of the city.

Rechy has certainly not been idle since *City of Night*'s publication, especially not recently. He's served as a guru to generations of gay men, and his books still excite all kinds of readers, young and old, gay and straight. He's won numerous prizes and became the first novelist to win the PEN/ West Lifetime Achievement Award in 1997. His writing workshops, offered through USC's graduate school and privately, are widely acclaimed, and he's taught some of the West Coast's sharpest authors and journalists.

The novelist—whose small stature, impish smile, and barrel chest lend him the bearing of a well-exercised elf—treats writing like a big fight for which he's constantly training. The mixed reviews for his twelfth novel, *The Coming of the Night,* published last summer, have brought him back with both guns blasting. Simultaneously, Rechy and his companion, a major-studio film producer, have been working on the film rights of his books and have several projects in development. Gus Van Sant, the director whose *My Own Private Idaho* alludes to Rechy's angelic street hustlers, has spoken with the two about making a film of *City of Night.* With the April release of a remarkable CD-ROM produced by USC's Annenberg Center, *Mysteries and Desire: Searching the World of John Rechy,* the author's fans will get an "interactive memoir" of his life that will allow them to read old reviews and watch computer-generated gay men cruise in Griffith Park. Whatever the reception for his latest work, Rechy is now more visible than he's been in years.

Rechy himself could be a character in an Evelyn Waugh-style satire about contemporary LA. A gay bodybuilder of mixed Mexican and Anglo blood, a proud narcissist who's worked hard to keep himself looking twenty years younger than his actual age, a lover of California's light and glamour and movies; Rechy, sixty-five, embodies much of the city's best and worst features. Life, he says, is a performance—if done right, a grand performance.

Rechy still has an enormous following, especially among gay men. But his detractors say he's superficial, a writer of limited gifts coasting on his early successes, a throwback to the gay world of the pre-AIDS sixties and seventies who hasn't matured or adapted. He's both a gay hero and a gay outlaw; and as such, his battles typically begin—rather than end—when a new novel is published.

Not everybody who meets Rechy, truth be told, wants to arm-wrestle him or praise his prose. For years, most of the people he met—the men, at least—wanted to have sex with him. And most of them did. Rechy worked the streets of New York and Los Angeles—Pershing Square, Selma, and Hollywood boulevards—from the late 1950s to about 1980, as both a hustler (who was paid) and a cruiser (who wasn't). "I remained on the streets longer than anybody in the world," he says, letting out the kind of knowing laugh with which others might recall hard-drinking fraternity days.

Rechy wove his early years on the streets into the novel *City of Night*, which is still considered his greatest achievement. The book began as a breathless letter written to a friend about the sadness and joy of Mardi Gras; when Rechy found the letter, crumpled and unsent, he sent a clean draft to the *Evergreen Review*, where it was printed as a short story alongside Beckett and Kerouac.

The novel, published in 1963 by the maverick Grove Press, became an instant best-seller and, due to its glimpse of the gay demimonde during a far less candid era, a publishing phenomenon. It drew the same kind of breathless, gauntlet-throwing jacket copy as *Naked Lunch* and *Last Exit to Brooklyn*. "Rechy tells the truth and tells us with such passion that we are forced to share in the life it conveys," wrote James Baldwin. The *Washington*

Post called the novel "one of the major books to be published since World War II." *City of Night's* impact went way beyond book review pages: Jim Morrison intoned its title in The Doors' "LA Woman," and rocker David Bowie, painter David Hockney, and director Van Sant have all spoken of its inspiration. Van Sant, in fact, says he gave Rechy's book to Keanu Reeves and River Phoenix, his street hustlers from *Private Idaho*. "I gave them both *City of Night* and said: 'If you want to know the life of a street hustler, this is the place to start.' Later, I found that Keanu had bought all of John's other books."

But something else happened when the book was published. It began a feud, mostly within the gay intelligentsia, about Rechy's worth as a novelist. Was he a great literary writer or just a hustler who wrote a book? The *New York Review of Books* ran a mocking, dismissive review under the title "Fruit Salad."

The article became a seminal event in Rechy's life and not just for internal reasons: Others followed the *New York Review's* lead. All over the press, critics speculated that a mere street hustler could not have written a book like this, that it must've been Tennessee Williams or James Baldwin using a nom de plume. Rechy, uninterested in having his private life examined, dropped out of sight; he read, from the safety of Caribbean beaches, about glittery Manhattan and Fire Island parties at which the white-hot young writer John Rechy appeared.

City of Night remains a remarkable and influential novel, and its spontaneous style and powerful rhythms echo Whitman, the Beats, and early Elvis Presley. It also established the pattern that some say Rechy has adhered to too closely in the ensuing four decades. We hear a lot about what happens to this "youngman"—Rechy jammed words together and often shattered syntax—as he roams from city to city, but we never really get to know him. Arthur Little, a professor at UCLA who loves the book, points out: "You spend hundreds of pages with the narrator, but you never know his name. So *City of Night* becomes an elaborate one-night stand." Some of the richness in the book, and in Rechy's later work, comes from its religious imagery. It's got more Catholicism than a Scorsese film—the book is dripping with ritual, holy iconography, a yearning for heaven, and prostitutes who look like "fallen angels." Its first line captures its tone well. "Later I would think of America as one vast City of Night stretching gaudily from Times Square to Hollywood Boulevard—jukebox-winking, rock-n-roll moaning: America at night, fusing its darkcities into the unmistakable shape of loneliness."

The appeal of *City of Night* reached beyond gay men. Henry Turner, a young writer and filmmaker who helps run the Slamdance Film Festival, picked the book up while wandering around Europe years ago and was struck by its emotional directness. "I'm not gay; I didn't read it as a gay book. But *City of Night* seemed to be the most honest expression of the adolescent male experience that I'd ever read." Turner is now one of Rechy's many devoted students. "He talked about narcissism, about being interested in appearance, he talked about the father. The male literary tradition is mostly about *concealing* emotion. It blew my mind—it really blew my mind. There were times when I was yelling out."

Many of Rechy's characters are aloof and withholding, and Rechy's childhood friends say the same about him. He writes of being an isolate who drove wildly into the deserts around El Paso or stretched out on mountains above the city, staring at the Texas sky. But the Rechy now alive and well in a tasteful Mediterranean apartment in Los Feliz is anything but a standoffish brooder. He's a man, instead, of almost incomparable personal charm.

***

A smile seems always to be playing around the corners of his mouth. But he's less cheerful when discussing the reception of his new book.

"I've never doubted my work—never, never doubted my work," he says, leaning forward on his couch toward a table covered with crystal goblets. Others *have* doubted him, though, and he admits that his straight readership has been eroding for years. It's been six months since the release of *The Coming of the Night*, which looks at one sex-drenched day and night in Los Angeles at the dawn of the AIDS epidemic, and he's still angry at *LA Times* reviewer Gary Indiana. The gay, often curmudgeonly *New Yorker* trashed the novel, comparing it to "middle-to-lowbrow fictions of a Jackie Collins." ("Rechy may be more 'shocking' to the still-shockable, but Collins is a lot more fun," he wrote in his front-page review.) Step into Rechy's writing workshop, ask him he's how he's doing, attend one of his speeches, and he'll unload on Indiana, calling the reviewer—whose name he sometimes pretends to have trouble recalling—a victim of "penis envy."

The games Rechy played with anonymity early in his career have given way to what he calls "a very dignified demand for attention. Besides letters to recalcitrant editors and critics, Rechy is writing an article about the *New York Times*'s failure to review the new book. He speculates that he's on a blacklist at the *Times*—"I've been done in by someone in the lower echelons," he announces to a Monday-night class—but the slight is only part of a larger problem. "I really want to get to the damn issue of *the ignoring*. And I also want to deal with the warning that every writer hears—from publishers, editors, and everything—that you do *not* protest. And my question: *Why not?* Why do you have to take shit?" His article, he says, will deal with his many victories—apologies from papers, Web sites, reviewers—even an apology from the poison pen of Gore Vidal.

"My point is: What do I have to lose? Being silent has never been effective for anybody. And I feel writers get maligned that way. We're actually inhibited. 'Oh, they'll mistreat you in the next review.' *Bullshit!* At least be heard. I have to uphold my dignity—that's the whole thrust of the thing. So fuck 'em."

As Rechy continues to fight, his novels are drawing attention from Hollywood. For years, he turned down the few offers he got, figuring his stories would be exploited. But his boyfriend, who now owns the rights to the books, has been working to bring them to the attention of directors and movie executives. Rechy has written screenplays for *City of Night, The Fourth Angel,* and *Marilyn's Daughter,* and he has several projects in development besides the potential Van Sant film. Rechy and Mexican director Arturo Ripstein, for instance, have scouted locations for a film treatment of the well-received 1991 novel *The Miraculous Day of Amalia Gómez.*

Rechy explains his recent currency in Hollywood: "I'm going to tell you *unabashedly,*" he says with a puckish smile. "Because I have refused to lay down, I've refused to be knocked down. I'm telling you, I have fought for the kind of respect that I deserve. And I have not quit. I'm still doing it. And I'm seeing the [payoff] now—the Lifetime Achievement Award, the cover of the *LA Times Book Review.* And I feel triumphant about this. When I first appeared, I battled that fucking review from the *New York Review of Books.* That son of a *bitch,* man. He wanted a knockout punch— he really wanted to destroy me. And they all followed suit—the *Village Voice,* the *New Yorker,* Richard Gilman. And they were wrong. The Book of the Month Club—'Our readers don't enjoy this sort of stuff'—and then years later they're issuing *City of Night* as one of their books." A pause. "But I feel good about it. It still stings, but in a triumphant way."

Though Rechy gets frustrated when the press fixates on his years on the street, he exudes pride, even nostalgia, when discussing his days and nights hustling. When talking about how the scene changed from the fifties to the seventies, for instance, he becomes a Proust of Pershing Square, wondering if one can recall experience without romanticizing things past.

Rechy's career on the streets began in the mid-fifties. He'd served briefly in Germany during the Korean War, but the Army granted him early release so he could attend Columbia University. He went to New York nearly broke and took a room at a YMCA. There he met a merchant marine who bought him hamburgers and told him how to make fast money hustling. Instead of graduate school, he headed for Times Square.

He writes in an autobiographical essay: "On Times Square, which the merchant marine had told me about—arousing a cacophony of terrified excitement, strange magic—I study other idling youngmen selling their bodies. From them I learn quickly how to stand, look—as if I had *always* known. A middle-aged man approaches and says, 'I'll give you ten dollars and I don't give a damn for you.'" Instead of being insulted, Rechy was gratified. "Two needs of my time then: to be desired powerfully, and not to be expected to care."

Rechy's approach was always the same—to look tough but available, to wait for men to approach, to remain aloof and play dumb, to slip off into alleys and houses for privacy.

Soon after the success of his first books, though, he left the street and moved back to Texas. "I had an idea in El Paso, to open a gym for intellectuals—and I discussed it with an investor." (When asked what he would offer to attract these intellectuals, he responds, laughing, "Myself, as an example.") But this idea, however auspicious, was not to be, because in the early 1970s Rechy got a call from a friend at Occidental College asking him to teach. Soon after moving to LA and taking up his professorial duties, he started hustling and cruising as well.

The world around him had changed drastically. As the era of Elvis and Little Richard gave way to David Bowie's Ziggy Stardust, the sexual types on the street reflected the evolution. "Earlier, we always had the so-called studs and the queens," says Rechy, who was the former. "And then, when I came back, there were the very androgynous young men. And I suppose that's why I was able to make a comeback, because I was sort of retro." He gives a self-deprecating laugh. "One person said to me: 'I haven't seen one of you in a long time.'"

His confidence was low when he returned to the streets after years of living with his mother in El Paso. "I was actually terrified to go back to the streets. I mean, Goddamn, I wondered if I'd survive." He began to body build with even more fury, to make sure he had the strength to protect himself, and went out after the sun had set so his age wouldn't show. But here, as in everything, his ego buoyed him through. "Word got around that I had once been a famous *model*," he says, laughing. "This was Santa Monica Boulevard, so this was the *most* they conceive. And they meant a body model, not even a fashion model. There was *awe* around me."

Though part of what sparked his return to hustling was financial, Rechy emphasizes that he went back by choice. That made him even more unusual among his peers on Selma and Santa Monica. "It seemed that in my time there was much more pride about being a hustler. Because now I think it's very, very, very sad—I think a lot of the kids who hustle have to. It's terrible. I believe that young people should choose what they want to be, and if one chooses to be a hustler, fine—but not *have* to be one because there's nothing else. I don't think anybody should be forced to be a doctor, either."

In both the fifties and seventies, while he was developing aspects of his street persona, Rechy worked to cover up the fact that he was a writer or even a reader. Any signs of intellect would scare off his "numbers." Sometimes he'd see his books in the homes of the men who picked him up and keep his mouth shut. Other times, his aesthetic side would take over. He would often begin an evening at the LA Public Library, reading Camus or Milton, before heading out to Pershing Square to hustle. One night in San Francisco in the fifties, at a cruising theater on Market Street, Stanley Kubrick's World War II movie *Paths of Glory* came on, and Rechy's eyes were so drawn to the film that he sat down, overpowered, and forgot about sex altogether.

"Once when I was leaving an orgy, someone said, 'Aren't you the author?' And I said, 'No, but I must look like him.'" As he taught at local colleges, it became more difficult for Rechy to stay entirely anonymous. Once, during his stint at UCLA, Rechy was on Santa Monica Boulevard at about 3 a.m., with no shirt and an oiled chest, and a car made a U-turn. Its window came down as it approached. "Good evening, Professor Rechy", a young man said. "Are you out for an evening stroll?"

Could the decades spent hustling have anything to do with Rechy's narcissism? The novelist has no problem admitting so, explaining that his exhibitionism, early feelings of rejection, and love of approval all came together when he was in "that arena." "I felt a rush of desire coming toward me, and I suppose a lot of it had to do with the repression of my childhood, its mixture of Catholicism and restrictions."

In the years after 1977's *The Sexual Outlaw*—a book of almost kaleido-scopic promiscuity, in which male bodies are linked together in combina-tions that recall human Rube Goldberg machines—Rechy started to worry. Young gay men, he concluded after visits to sex clubs and warehouse orgies in New York, might be going too far. He began to write and speak in tones of caution. "During that time, nobody foresaw AIDS. But a careful reading of my books, especially *Rushes*, will indicate that I was very worried about what was happening, and I became very controversial and unpopular for a time. I was worried that we were moving beyond sex, that it was no longer sex, just sensation, the sensation of pain and humiliation—we were just bludgeoned. I thought it was a dead end." The gay community, he says, treated him like a betrayer.

If Rechy has been targeted, it hasn't been by homophobes but by other gay men. "A faction of gay people," he says, "have been my most vociferous and venomous attackers." The novelist dismisses his negative reviews as the product of hostility and envy, but there are substantial and interesting arguments contained in these pieces.

Alfred Chester's argument in the *New York Review of Books*, in particular, is often overlooked—it's usually described in the press only by its offensive headline, "Fruit Salad," as if it were just a burst of Old World homophobia. Certainly, it's a little bitchy. But one can admire *City of Night* and still have to concede that at least half of what Chester—who was openly gay—said is true and has become even more true of Rechy's recent work. Chester, who died in 1971, argued that the book is unmusical and self-consciously literary ("that disgusting rhetoric that Rechy pours all over everything like jam"), and derivative of half a dozen writers, among them Genet and Capote.

But the biggest problem, Chester wrote, came from the narrator, who's a stand-in for Rechy himself. The hustler protagonist offers "absolutely no real, living response" to all the chaos and hedonism, leaving much of the book emotionally dead, and he's just another self-hating gay man who's afraid of commitment. That's not to mention all the "heavy," simplistically Freudian ideas that Rechy serves up alongside the inflated rhetoric.

Indiana's review, similarly, is far more than character assassination. Indiana praises Rechy's early work lavishly before describing the decline marked by *The Coming of the Night*. "Each of Rechy's later books lacks some vital ingredient of his robust early talent; this is puzzling, because what he does well in one book he does badly in the next, and vice versa."

And while Rechy and his fans argue that he's been penalized for being outside the Northeastern literary establishment, it's not only New York critics who are frustrated with his work. Greg Sarris, a UCLA professor and novelist, teaches *The Sexual Outlaw* in a lesbian and gay literature course. "I find the students—lesbian, gay, and straight—dislike it. They feel that he's stereotyping. They feel he's brutal to his fellow man. He puts down S&M, but he's sadistic toward those whom he's supposed to love and support. The women—lesbian or straight—can't believe they have to read such things."

Sarris is disturbed by the arrested adolescence and worship of youth in Rechy's books, and by the novelist's eroticizing of dark, forbidden spaces like back alleys, sending gay men the message that sex is exciting only when it's illicit.

Rechy's main failure, he says, is his inability to grow from an Eldridge Cleaver figure—driven by anger and the energy of protest—to a writer like Toni Morrison, who can look at the contradictions of relationships and the difficulties of outgrowing oppression that has seeped into a minority culture. "Where is something like that in gay literature?" Sarris asks. "Gay writing has to do what African-American literature has done since the sixties. We've been too busy celebrating ourselves. We're still being silly and funny and celebrating the fact that we fuck. Now that we're out, we want to love. Where are the stories of real relationships? In his work, Rechy doesn't see any way that we could be defined by anything but sexuality."

Why do so many of these arguments come from other gay men? Rechy has a theory. "I've said this and it sounds flippant, but a lot of it is actual penis envy. It truly *is*. Look, Gary Indiana is not an attractive gentleman. Alfred Chester was a *monster*. Which is irrelevant. Except, what I represent is a kind of envy to them. It is a curious thing—it finds its parallel in the straight world—that the *desirer* and the *desired* are different entities. The desirer is intelligent, perhaps rich. The desired is just physically attractive. And when the desired become identified as being intelligent, then you have *transgressed*. It's the *Blue Angel* syndrome in heterosexual terms—the blond bimbo."

While Rechy's books are usually, and often enthusiastically, reviewed, and a writer named Charles Casillo is researching a book-length study, there is very little serious critical work. Juan Bruce-Novoa, a professor at UC Irvine who has taught an entire class on Rechy's work at a German university, explains why Rechy has been critically ignored outside of gay studies. "People say you can write about anything you want now, but it's not true. John, in his best writing, is telling you to live the way the existentialists told you—a risking of life in every moment. And a lot of people don't like the fact that he urges an outlaw life." His writing, too, has gotten more sexually explicit with almost every book, which scares people off. "He's always trying to go one step further."

***

The "youngman" of *City of Night*, like most Rechy heroes, launches himself on a quest to substitute sex and pleasure for an infinitely distant heaven and absent God. By book's end, the young hustler realizes he's less young than he was, and no less lonely. He's traveled the country, scoring and getting paid, without allowing anyone to make an impact on him. But in New Orleans, in the book's final pages, he meets "a well-built, masculine man in his early thirties, with uncannily dark eyes, light hair." The two begin a thirty-five-page dialogue on reciprocal love versus fleeting, anonymous sex. In the end, despite pleas from his "intensely, moodily handsome" suitor to settle down, the hustler decides he prefers his freedom.

It's a moment—with its rejection of commitment and embrace of hedonism— that defines virtually all of Rechy's writing, but only partly defines his life.

It was during the first flash of the AIDS epidemic, around 1980, that Rechy met a young man from the Midwest, and they came together after an argument about Buñuel. (The author does not want his companion's name used, though the two are a visible couple.) Then in his mid-forties, Rechy took this opportunity to leave the streets. He now finds himself in an ironic position: the icon of gay promiscuity, who's written novel after novel about the swirling, psychedelic beauty of anonymous sex, creator of characters who fight commitment at every turn, settled down like a suburban dad. The two live in adjacent apartment buildings but—after years of commitment—are looking for a house together.

But while he can't say enough good things about his relationship and endorses the idea of gay marriage, he thinks gay men should fight the now fashionable implication that they need a spouse. "I don't think it's necessary to have a relationship. It's very much like the 'old maid' syndrome, the way a woman would be judged if she wouldn't get married. And the same thing is happening with homosexuals. I think one can live a perfectly decent life by oneself."

Rechy once compared gay men who have sex on the street to Rosa Parks' refusal to sit in the back of the bus, calling both revolutionary acts. He continues to champion gay sexuality.

"When you first discover that you're gay, there's a whole pressure on you to conform," he explains. "And if you pressurize anything, it finds release. We come out of a heterosexual union, so in a sense we're born into the enemy camp. Out of a heterosexual union comes this stranger. *There* begins the outlaw, for God's sake. Not later, on the streets." Add the movies and billboards that beam images of heterosexuality at gay men, combine it with religion, and you've got enough pressure for an explosion, Rechy says. The fierce dedication of gay male sexuality is the result. "It's what we have and it's what we've converted, to our credit, to something very rich—very, *very* rich.

"But let me ask you this, if you knew of a park where very attractive women, not prostitutes, hung out, and sex was easily available, right off the road, in the bushes, or wherever, would you take a peek at that park?" He pauses. "I know a friend whom I met in Griffith Park a long time ago, who said, 'This keeps me from suicide.' And that's one of the themes of *The Coming of the Night*. For a long time sex kept us going."

Rechy has always felt very close to his mother, and when she died in the early seventies, he began an intense period of mourning and drug abuse. He began seeing a psychiatrist but only began to heal when he realized how he'd let his body go, how his face had gotten gaunt. "Well, whatever narcissism may be as an illness," his shrink told him, "it *saved* you."

***

Narcissism, like Los Angeles, is one of Rechy's great causes; he calls himself "a champion of good narcissism." Pride about one's looks, achievement—they're nothing to be ashamed of. Crafting a novel, a sculpture, is not morally higher than crafting one's body. "I *hate* when it's called a neurosis," he says. "It's a very, very curious thing. If you say that you're a son of a bitch, people consider you saintly and humble. But *somebody else* can say you're a son of a bitch—why should *you*? And if you feel genuinely good about yourself—and you know, I do, it's not a pose; I feel good about my art, about my affections, and my physical being—then I feel qualified to extend myself. And I *like* physicality." He proudly points out that some of his students begin to work out when they take his class. They dress better; they lose weight.

Rechy doesn't hide his love of appearance. At one of his Monday-night classes, he unloads on his favorite punching bag: "If you see Gary Indiana on his Web site and then see me on mine [www.johnrechy.com] you'll see who's jealous of whom, you'll see what it's all about! And he has a very small penis—he really does—very tiny!"

In the Greek myth, Narcissus was a slender, beautiful boy who was pursued by the nymph Echo. Proud and aloof, Narcissus repeatedly rejects Echo's pleas, as he has rejected the adoration of many before her. Stopping by a lake one day to take a drink, his eyes fell on his own reflection, and he froze, in the words of Ovid, "like a fallen garden statue, Gaze fixed on his image in the water . . . Falling deeper and deeper in love with what so many had loved so hopelessly." He turns into the flower narcissus.

Rechy tells a similar, if Freudian, story near the beginning of *City of Night*: "From my father's inexplicable hatred of me and my mother's blind, carnivorous love, I fled to the Mirror. I would stand before it thinking, I have only Me! . . . I became obsessed with age. At seventeen, I dreaded growing old."

But these days, Rechy doesn't have to look into a pond, or a mirror to see himself—and *his* narcissism hasn't slowed him down. He sees influence all over—on fashion, rock stars, other authors.

"Believe me, I was a—fuck it if it sounds awful—I was a *pioneer*," he says with a guilty laugh. "I walked through downtown Los Angeles, in a genuine motorcycle leather jacket—I still have it, an honest-to-God classic motorcycle jacket—and no shirt. And oh! Wow! Was that startling. And I was the [first] one to brazenly walk down Hollywood Boulevard with no shirt." He speaks of his invention of the scoop shirt—a T-shirt with a stretched-out neckline—and his use of odd capitalization and exclamation points years before Tom Wolfe. "You know that Tom Waits was influenced by me. Hockney. Bob Dylan called me from San Francisco the night before his motorcycle accident to tell me how much he liked *City of Night.*"

Some of Rechy's students find his narcissism amusing or distracting. But others say that his immense self-regard is an important part of the wisdom he passes down to them. "He has the idea of a writer having a sense of dignity and developing confidence within yourself," says Jocelyn Heaney, an editor at Larry Flynt's *Barely Legal* magazine and an enthusiast of John Cheever's tweed-jacketed short stories. "It might seem kind of silly, but it's about not letting anyone take away your dignity as an artist. It's a great lesson to give your students."

It's a cold December evening when one of Rechy's female students rushes into his Los Feliz apartment, apologizing for showing up a few minutes late for his writing workshop. "Oh, it was worth the wait, darling—and I love your hair windblown like that," he says as she takes her seat beneath an enormous photograph of Garbo. "I tell my students that they'll not only come out better writers," he says, "but they'll look better. *Look* at you all—a couple of you came in looking rather dowdy."

Rechy's writing workshops are an opportunity for the novelist's talent as a showman. He has an instinctive command of the theater, and the inherent comedy, of even this most academic of social gatherings.

Later the same night, he'll ask a student to remove his sweater, knowing that he's wearing a hideous Hawaiian shirt under it, and use the shirt as a running joke throughout the rest of the evening. He does the same with any student who writes a clunky line or phrase—coming back to it repeatedly for laughs. Throughout the evening he goes back and forth between serious literary talk and his campy, one-man show. Another night, he'll ask a woman to stop chewing gum, explaining that it distorts her features.

It would seem like Rechy's emphasis on appearance, and his teasing of students, would leave some feeling bruised. But somehow it works. Says private workshop student Henry Turner: "He compliments the women, and he insults the men. And it's funny. He likes to exercise his sense of timing—he'll say something and leave the punch line half said, and then he'll get back to it, finish it a minute later." "And he times it perfectly," says Nichole Morgan, a young fan of Raymond Carver and Sylvia Plath who studied with Rechy at USC. "He gives his jokes just enough room without letting them get out of hand—but they're a relief from the intensity." Morgan has since followed him into two private workshops and hopes to take more. "He's very perceptive of people's thresholds—he has a sense of who he can jab and who he can't." This said, no man who's averse to helping women off with their jackets or walking female students to their cars should take Rechy's class.

The workshops involve more than sartorial advice. Some courses are built around novels like *Don Quixote* and *Ulysses*, others on what writers can learn from films like *Sunset Boulevard, Persona,* and *Gone with the Wind.* (This last is Rechy's favorite, and he once told the *New Orleans Times Picayune*: "The only thing that scares me—and I'm terrified of it—is dying a tacky death. Slipping on a banana peel or something perverse. I want to go out with grandeur, like Melanie in *Gone with the Wind,* and get Max Steiner to do the music.")

Rechy's students speak of the direct and practical impact his classes have had on their writing. Like his many friends, they're remarkably loyal. Unlike famous writers who do little more than lend their name and reputation to their courses, Rechy really puts out for his students, offering remarkably attentive criticism and publishing connections. He's as dedicated and perceptive a teacher as anyone could hope for.

He's taught Kate Braverman (*Small Craft Warnings*), Sandra Tsing Loh (*Depth Takes a Holiday*), Gina Nahai (*Moonlight on the Avenue of Faith*), and a number of journalists, including two upper-level editors at Larry Flynt Publications. "It helped me more than anything I've done," says Allan MacDonell, a former *Hustler* executive editor and one of the key players in Flynt's attack on hypocritical politicians. "I've been an editor for a long time, and I've been working on other people's writing for a long time, and he really ups your game." Says Loh, known for her comic one-woman shows: "I found him really incredibly useful and developed a lot of material for *Aliens in America* in his workshop. His sense of language is so precise."

Rechy's relationship to one of his most successful former students shows just how combative—or is it playful?—he really is. Michael Cunningham is the author of 1998's *The Hours,* a meditation on Los Angeles and Virginia Woolf that became both a best-selling novel and winner of the

Pulitzer Prize. Rechy treats Cunningham, who studied with him in the late seventies and now lives in New York, as an ungrateful son, someone who disavows all connections to him. "Michael actually *lies*," Rechy accuses, "says he never took a writers' workshop other than Iowa." Rechy talks about Cunningham furtively whispering his thanks—when others were out of sight—at an awards banquet. Last month at UCLA, giving a speech about the Los Angeles literary tradition, Rechy spoke of a novelist—never named—who erased all LA ties, even taking his first book out of print so the East Coast literary establishment would not hold his California roots against him. Rechy gets a laugh when he says that this is the first novelist in history to have two first novels. He's talking about Cunningham.

So how does this unappreciative punk respond when asked if he ever knew or studied with John Rechy? Without hesitation: "I don't think I've ever had a teacher who taught me as much before or since." Cunningham goes on and on, talking about Rechy's courtly teaching style, his skill at creating a healthy atmosphere for criticism in the class, and calling him "hugely intelligent, hugely respectful." In other words, he does anything but dodge his associations with the novelist.

When told about Rechy's words for him, Cunningham sounds partly confused, partly hurt, wondering where he might have failed to give credit where it's due. But what about that other matter—burying your LA roots? Why is that early book about California, *Golden States*, out of print? The reason, Cunningham says, is simple: It's just not very good.

But he asks, even after hearing about Rechy's frustration with him, "If you speak to John, please give him my love."

There's a curious contradiction to Rechy. He's a man of almost electric intelligence who can discuss Joyce and Stein, Bergman and Buñuel, and serves as literary godfather to some of the nation's best young writers. At the same time, he sometimes produces flat, cartoonish characters and writes interminable descriptions of their physical appearances and workout routines. These are, for example, some of the first lines from *The Coming of the Night*: "Jesse—the kid—woke with one thought in his mind. Today he would do something wild to celebrate one glorious year of being gay—and it *was* great to be gay and young and good-looking and *hot*. Of course, his designation of 'one year' was not exact. He had been gay from the time he became aware of sex . . ." Rechy talks about revising his books—even the spontaneous *City of Night*—more than a dozen times, but some of his writing seems dashed off. And his reputation outside the gay world is still unsteady: Rechy concedes he loses readers, gay and straight, when he departs from gay themes, as he has with books like *Our Lady of Babylon*, a novel about wanton women through the ages, and *Marilyn's Daughter*, the imaginary chronicle of Marilyn Monroe's forgotten child. He feels he's been typecast.

Rechy remains a hero to gay men but has publicly denounced the category of gay writer. "I resent the labels. I'm a writer. And for a long time I was a gay writer. And I wasn't a Chicano writer, because Goddamnit, you can't be gay and Chicano. No, really, those discussions were held by a gentleman at UCLA. Then I was a Los Angeles writer. Jesus Christ, I'm a *writer* and one of the *best* for God's sake, so I hate the characterizations because they limit the art. That's why I resent it—the ghettoization of literature." He's simply not a joiner. He thrives on exile, exiled even from his own subcultures.

Cunningham, the prodigal son, thinks Rechy's reputation has suffered because gay literature has become its own world away from the mainstream. "I think John is one of the casualties of the ghettoization of gay literature," he says. "I think history, the final arbiter, will vindicate John's work." Its best quality, he says, is its vitality. "Which is part of what turns people off—it's just so juicy and alive and sensual. The work makes people too nervous. There's a long, long history of work that made people uncomfortable, that fifty years later became part of the canon," he says, referring to D. H. Lawrence and Henry Miller.

The novelist sees himself the same way—as someone too dangerous for the mainstream. Rechy is nothing if not competitive—he struck up a rivalry with one of his own characters, trying to outscore the young stud in *Numbers*—and he speaks sometimes as if Rechy the writer were in competition with Rechy the sex icon. Oscar Wilde once said that he poured his talent into his work, but his genius into his life. Rechy would never say the same thing about himself. Part of what makes the John Rechy CD-ROM—which includes interviews, live-action footage, old letters, even the "Fruit Salad" review—so interesting is that it gives his family, his physical style, and his literary battles equal weight with his writing.

"I don't mind saying this: I know what's what," he says. "I'm one of the best of our time, best of my generation. I certainly rank with Norman Mailer. I certainly outshine Philip Roth." Same with Gore Vidal. "I know I rank with them, and that's my rightful place. And not as a gay writer, not as an ex-hustler, not as a sexual outlaw."

When assessed simply as a novelist, though, Rechy's work leaves something to be desired. Some of his books since *City of Night* are strong, some aren't; even that first book has deep flaws alongside its brilliant energy and lyricism. Writers since Whitman have spoken of the need for raw, lived experience—all kinds of it—to power good writing. Rechy has taken this manifesto further than almost any living writer—perhaps too far. While he's certainly been a writer first, his greatest creations are not his novels but his rich personality and his wildly varied, vulnerable, and defiant life itself. If living well is the best revenge, Rechy should be a happy man indeed.

[*New Times LA*, February 2000]

INDIE ANGST

The most striking film in months comes from a 30-year-old British-born Angeleno who's making a habit of tight, baffling movies that work like puzzles. Starring Guy Pearce (*LA Confidential*) and Carrie-Anne Moss (*The Matrix*), *Memento* is a contemporary noir that follows a nowhere man with a rare brand of amnesia that keeps him from making new memories: He lives life as if writing on cellophane—nothing sticks. As the film starts, he's just killed a guy, and he's wondering who and why and taking a Polaroid for reasons that are not immediately clear.

Oh, one more thing: The film plays backward, telling its story in 10-minute sequences and then jumping back to the events that preceded it.

Perhaps it goes without saying that *Memento*—like *Following*, Nolan's debut film of two years ago—is an unusual viewing experience. But it is a strangely intimate one as well. We're weirdly tied to the film's main character, Leonard (a bleached-blond Pearce, donning a pale, ill-fitting suit). Because we haven't seen what just happened; we're as confused as Leonard, who doesn't remember what just happened. Both viewer and protagonist are pulled along in a dazzling train of disorientation.

Christopher Nolan, the film's director and screenwriter, enjoys this sort of bewilderment. "You know what this has that I love," Nolan says, slipping Radiohead's eerie CD *Kid A* into his stereo and sitting down to discuss his film. "I have a very good visual memory—I need one to do my job—and I've seen the film thousands of times. But if I walk in to a screening, 25 minutes in, I don't know what scene comes next. The whole idea was to make a film that bled into the mind a little bit, spun in your head, that you constructed very much yourself. And when I listen to this album, no matter how many times I listen to it, I don't know what comes next."

Nolan, who lives in an apartment on a quiet street near the LA County Museum of Art, could be a newly appointed lecturer on philosophy at a British university; he relishes discussing issues like ambiguity, perception, the difference between objective and subjective reality. But you don't have to be a philosopher, or a Radiohead fan, to enjoy his film, which builds to a crashing climax that seems to explain everything. Or does it? *Memento*—cinematic fragments and amnesiac narrators and all—adds up to the most intriguing spin on film noir since *LA Confidential*. "I loved it," announces Peter Farrelly, the writer and director of *There's Something About Mary*, running into the hotel room where Nolan is speaking with the press, to offer congratulations. "I was watching this and thinking, he'll never be able to pull this off. It blew my mind! I felt like I did when I saw *The Usual Suspects*."

The film has also drawn the praise of Steven Soderbergh, who's become Hollywood's most vital director by fusing the mainstream and independent film aesthetics with his recent films *Out of Sight, The Limey,* and *Traffic*. "*Memento* is extremely impressive, both in its conception and its execution," says Soderbergh, who calls during shooting for *Oceans 11*. "He knows what to do with actors, what to do with a camera, and he knows how to structure a story. Selfishly speaking, it's the the kind of stuff I like, because he's interested in fragmenting his narratives. I liked *Following,* but *Memento* is a quantum leap forward for him."

Memento becomes even more startling at its conclusion, where most contradictions in the plot resolve themselves. If this movie makes money, it will be in the repeat viewing that many people will find hard to resist. The movie's storytelling and style seem the natural outgrowth of Soderbergh's statement that *The Limey* was an attempt to make the gangster film *Get Carter* using the techniques of French New Waver Alain Resnais (*Hiroshima, Mon Amour* and *Last Year at Marienbad*). This yoking of the experimental to the pulp has produced an innovative strain in American indie film that was in evidence at least as far back as Quentin Tarantino's first movies. Nolan takes it to the next level. *Memento* shows a new freedom in American film—a flexibility and brisk confidence with narrative—as young directors borrow the techniques of the postmodern novel and the French art film and apply them to pulp and genre material. This freedom has developed even as the independent film establishment grows more conservative.

Not surprisingly, *Memento*—despite its success on the festival circuit and the advocacy of an influential filmmaker—has had trouble getting distribution. It has been taken on by Newmarket Films; a small LA company that hopes to do for it what the Shooting Gallery did for Mike Hodges' *Croupier.* (Newmarket, which has funded films from *Topsy-Turvy* to *The Mexican,* was also *Memento*'s financier, and chose to deflect offers from distributors. It's a little like Dick Cheney heading George W. Bush's vice presidential search and then suggesting himself for the job.)

Memento not only plays with noir convention; it also picks up a longstanding literary and cinematic lineage of amnesia. The film works in—and subverts—a tradition, perhaps several traditions. The real strength of

Memento isn't in the way it echoes off the world of other films and novels, but the way it draws you—pulls you—into its own.

Nolan grew up split between London and Chicago, the son of a British father who ran an advertising firm and an American flight attendant mother. He started making films at the age of seven or eight, borrowing his father's Super 8 camera and shooting little movies with action figures and kids in the neighborhood, including, as it happens, the Belic brothers, who would go on to make the acclaimed documentary *Genghis Blues*.

"Some of my earliest memories are of Chris making movies," says his brother Jonathan, a 24-year-old writer who calls himself Jonah and who came up with the idea from which *Memento* bloomed. "Of asking my brother to be in his stupid little stop-action movies, asking if I could be an extra. You know how you're supposed to have a character arc in a screenplay? My brother would not make a good character. There's no arc. There's a straight vector line, straight out of the womb: *Filmmaker*. Didn't waver, didn't wrestle with any of the doubts that plague the rest of us."

Nolan studied literature at University College London, because of a long interest in fiction. A passion for Raymond Chandler led him to James Ellroy, and, looking into Ellroy's influences, he was especially struck by pulp poet Jim Thompson. Nolan says he's learned a lot, especially about narrative and chronology, by reading contemporary novels. "I got into filmmaking purely as a means of stringing images together, scenes. Then I came to understand narrative. Studying English was a very good way to give myself more grounding in the word." And he began thinking about one of his favorite novels, Graham Swift's *Waterland*, the haunting story of a mysterious death in rural southeastern Britain. "What [Swift] does, which absolutely struck me, is apply a series of parallel time lines, and jump between them," the director says. "It's a wonderful way of reimagining a story." He was also able to borrow equipment from the university's film society on weekends in order to make short films.

As he studied literature, he saw that a tale could be told from any angle, in any order. "The only useful definition of narrative I've ever heard is 'the controlled release of information.' And these novelists and playwrights—they're not feeling any responsibility to make that release on a chronological basis. And the more I thought about it, the more I realized that we don't feel that responsibility in day-to-day life." He draws a parallel with the way we tell a story in conversation, sometimes leading with the conclusion and backing up, just as newspaper stories back up from the headline to fill in background.

It was this sense of narrative—as something infinitely flexible to the artist's demands—that Nolan brought to *Following*. The 70-minute film, about a disheveled young writer who follows people for sport and then becomes, almost accidentally, the companion to a genteel housebreaker, seems to be told in a straightforward way until it twists brilliantly.

It's hard to watch the film and not be struck by the inventiveness, the polish, the sense of menace it maintains so well, the way Harold Pinter does in his plays. It's the kind of movie that announces, quietly, the arrival of a sharp and unusual talent. All this for a film rehearsed and shot on weekends while its writer-director was working nine to five making corporate training videos—a task that could numb the soul. Because of the expense of 16mm film stock, the movie was mostly first and second takes, though it's hard to see it: in the finished product. "*Following* hasn't a hint of amateurism, technically or aesthetically," *New Times's* Andy Klein wrote when the film opened.

Though obscurely released, the movie was well reviewed—the *New Yorker* said it "echoes Hitchcock classics" but was "leaner and meaner"— and helped Nolan earn support for the new film by proving he could pull off an unconventional narrative. But he bristles when people say *Following* was just a stepping-stone.

"When people talk about 'calling-card films' and things like that, I get a little bit irate," he says. "If you want to make a calling card, go to Kinko's. You don't spend four years slaving over a storyline—you would never!" To make a good movie takes commitment, dedication to the art for its own sake; he grew frustrated when people asked him when he was going to make a "real" movie. "I had no expectation for what that film was going to do in practical terms, none whatsoever. I had hopes and ambitions . . . But what I said to everyone involved is, let's just have fun making the film, do it because we're going to enjoy the experience."

He explains his passion a bit further. "For me, making a no-budget film *is* filmmaking. It doesn't make any difference what level it's at. It's very satisfying filmmaking, because the only sacrifices are practical ones. The filmmaking process in my head, the imaginative process, was identical to making a film for millions of dollars. When I made a film with a bigger budget, I realized it's the same thing. You've just got more trucks."

Nolan got the chance to work on a larger scale thanks to a fortuitous long-distance drive. In summer 1997, he flew from London to Chicago to meet up with Jonah and drive their father's old Honda Prelude to Los Angeles. Nolan's wife, Emma Thomas, had gotten a job at a film company in Los Angeles, and Jonah, a junior at Georgetown University, volunteered to come along. Recalls Jonah, who is as American as Chris is British and loves Melville and Homer: "We'd sort of run out of things to say to each other, as brothers do." So he told Chris about the idea for a story he'd had, inspired by a survey class in general psychology.

"He said his concept was this guy, Chris remembers, who had trouble making new memories, who was looking for revenge on the guy who had given him the condition and killed his wife. And he'd taken to using his body to record information, with tattoos."

This immediately struck Chris as a good idea. Though the car's timing belt broke two weeks later and the vehicle was sold for scrap, the idea was born. The story—a short mood piece that Jonah says is not typical of his more black-humored work—appears in the March issue of *Esquire*. The film opens tomorrow.

Part of what's interesting about *Memento* is that it works firmly and faithfully in the noir tradition without being a self-conscious pastiche of trench coats and fedoras. Nolan treats noir as a living tradition instead of as a fossil or museum piece with fetishized, self-referential surface details.

"When you look at what film noir was, and what it's remembered as, you see that those are two very different things," Nolan says. "And I get very annoyed when people refer to this as a retro noir. It's not a retro noir—it's a *film noir*. It's contemporary. We have the dark shadows, but we don't have the guy in a trench coat in the alleyway. If you look back at *Double Indemnity*, you see everybody was wearing fedoras—that wasn't an unusual thing for guys in those days. There are scenes in a supermarket, scenes in a bowling alley, in that film. No one remembers that."

Nolan went looking for the contemporary equivalent of the noir cityscape: "This fringe urban could be the edge of any midsize town, the gas station and the motels." It turned out to be Burbank. "You're talking about the setting for a story where a character wakes up and doesn't know where the hell he is. There's a widespread American story about trying to place yourself in this very anonymous environment. That's kind of exciting. To me, that's like a guy out of film noir."

Nolan takes noir's stock icons—the motel room, the gun in the drawer, characters who may or may not include a white knight driven by vengeance, a femme fatale, and a cop gone bad—and throws them into a valley of the mind, wraps them into a tale told by an amnesiac. "I took those familiar tropes," Nolan says, "and combined them with an unusual point of view."

Nolan, of course, is not the only contemporary artist to extend noir—a film tradition that, somehow, has failed to produce moneymaking films despite decades of creative ferment. The movie *Blade Runner* (and the Philip K. Dick novel on which it was based) put the stoic, isolated private eye in a futuristic Pacific Rim city teeming with runaway robots. Walter Mosley's novels, beginning with *Devil in a Blue Dress*, took Raymond Chandler's conventions to 1940s black LA; Paul Auster animated his *City of Glass* trilogy with postmodern theory and linguistic trickery. More recently, Jonathan Lethem's novel *Motherless Brooklyn* made its questing Philip Marlowe a foul-mouthed hood with Tourette's syndrome.

Amnesia, too, has long served as the basis for fiction and film. A new anthology on memory loss—*The Vintage Book of Amnesia*—points out that the device is used everywhere from old *Mission Impossible* episodes and the purplish noirs of Cornell Woolrich to literary fiction by Martin Amis, Walker Percy, and Donald Barthelme. (Noir writers may have been drawn to amnesia for the same reason they set their stories on the West Coast: A person with a short memory is like a city with a short history, perfect for false identities and deceptive appearances.) It was this literary heritage—and learning about anterograde memory loss in his psych class—that piqued the interest of Jonah Nolan. "It's almost a whole genre unto itself," he says of amnesia. It was this tradition he hoped to invert as surely as his brother inverted the film noir.

The idea for the story started with a visual image: "A guy who wakes up in a motel room, and looks in a mirror. And has tattoos all over his body. And he sees a tattoo that says 'John G. raped and killed your wife.' The typical noir conceit," Jonah says, "is that he's an ordinary guy who's been wronged. And it's the standard amnesia story, you wake up covered in blood. Here he woke up covered in tattoos. It suggests you've missed a whole chapter of your life."

Thanks to a strong showing at festivals—Venice, Toronto, and most recently, Sundance—and the success of its European release, a critical consensus has already formed around *Memento*, and the film has developed a reputation as "this year's *Being John Malkovich*." But like *Croupier*, the entrancing Mike Hodges mood piece that was eventually picked up for release by the Shooting Gallery company, the film has been passed over by the major indie distributors.

Soderbergh stated in a recent issue of *Film Comment* magazine that "when a film like Chris Nolan's *Memento* cannot get picked up, to me independent film is over. It's dead." The director is certainly onto something: that independent film, especially since *Pulp Fiction* introduced the indie blockbuster, has been less risky, more conventional, and far safer than it should be. (Soderbergh himself suffered from the genre's constriction early in his career.) Despite *Memento*'s settling into a secure distribution deal, Soderbergh is hardly more sanguine.

"It makes me concerned that independent distributors don't want to work hard," he says. "They're searching for the indie equivalent of a slam dunk. I know that on every level now it's more expensive to release a movie, even on the independent level. But I think there's always a way to sell a good movie. And this one is not esoteric—it's a murder mystery!"

The ever cool Nolan is not troubled by his film's outcome. He doesn't feel stung that a buyer with deep pockets—or a distributor that could move the film more widely—never showed up: "I have never looked for any kind of external validation for the filmmaking process; if I had I would have given up a long time ago. The point is to get the film made, get it out of my head, get it off the page, get it on the screen." It's important to find the right people to work with, he says, so once the deal with Newmarket was made, "I breathed a tremendous sigh of relief."

Joe Pantoliano, a veteran character actor (*Risky Business, Bound, The Matrix*) who plays Teddy, the wormy friend of Pearce's amnesiac, is still burned. Last year, he says, he was at the Independent Spirit Awards—the indie Oscars—and was besieged by compliments from people at major independent distributors, including Miramax, New Line, Dimension, and USA Films. "People were coming up to me and saying, 'We just saw *Memento*, it's your best work, it's a fantastic movie.' I said, 'Are you gonna buy it?' They said, 'No.' They thought it was a movie that would never find an audience." In other words, it was exactly the kind of film an indie would have snapped up 5 or 10 years ago and tried to break.

"The independent film thing is bullshit," says Pantoliano. "They [the studios] all want to find a five-dollar bill, buy it for a dollar, and sell it for ten." The cheapness of indie studios, he says, comes from their having lost money on hyped Sundance movies such as *The Spitfire Grill* and *Happy, Texas.* "There were fights in restaurants over these movies," he says.

Nevertheless, now that *Memento* has been picked up by Newmarket, people like Peter Broderick, president of First Look Films—the Independent Film Channel affiliate that helped fund *Following*'s last stages—sees reason for hope. The best thing for a filmmaker, Broderick says, is to find a good fit with a distributor—whether a micro-distributor like Newmarket or a traditional indie—that can push a movie with passion and creativity.

"If *Memento* does well, in the same way that *Croupier* is doing well, it says to distributors, 'This audience is out there. We have to find a link to those enthusiastic viewers.'" Nolan's movie, he says, could come from left field the way *Crouching Tiger, Hidden Dragon* and *The Blair Witch Project* did. "When a *Memento* comes along and gets the press attention that it has, and the business I think it will get, it's a hopeful sign. It says that formulaic studio movies are not the only game in town. It means that people can make the distinction between something tired and something fresh. It's reassuring."

Memento's cast and crew have lost countless hours arguing over what really happens *in* the movie. "I've seen it five times," says Carrie-Anne Moss who is, after all, *in* the movie, "and I've seen it differently each time."

Nolan, for his part, won't tell. When asked about the film's outcome, he goes on about ambiguity and subjectivity, but insists he knows the movie's Truth—who's good, who's bad, who can be trusted and who can't—and insists that close viewing will reveal all. "What you're seeing here," he says, passing his hand over his blank expression like a magician who's made a swallow appear in a top hat, "is my poker face."

Nolan wrote the script straight through—beginning with the first scene, which takes place last in time, and ending with the last, which takes place earlier—and was never tempted to lay the film out chronologically. "People were asking me to do that, and I always refused," he says.

He has all kinds of theories about film technology shaping film art. He was deeply influenced, he says, by growing up in the early days of VHS. "We're the last generation who remembers a time when you couldn't record television, you couldn't control time like that," he says. "We remember that shift. So I was very conscious of it growing up, and very conscious of it now that I see movies multiple times."

He's not, he says, the only one. Other filmmakers of his generation choose a story's structure more freely, finding something that best suits the story "rather than always insisting on chronology." Nolan points out that narrative trickery goes back at least as far as *Citizen Kane* (1941) but that storytelling became a flat, straight line for decades afterward.

"That was an *enormously* adventurous movie," he says, slipping into animated-professor mode. "What the hell happened? I think what happened is TV. TV is the most intensely linear format, and it's become the primary ancillary market for motion pictures. So you've got to create something where someone can start watching 10 minutes late, and still absorb the whole thing over an hour on TV."

But now, not only are people likely to watch movies repeatedly, they'll do it on forms like DVD and other new technologies, which audiences can manipulate. "A director of my generation is much freer to jump around, and give people information in short bursts." This, he says, is only fair since he has years to work on a film while an audience has only two hours in which to watch it. "So it should have layers," he says. "It should have a cinematic density that rewards subsequent viewings."

Soderbergh isn't the only young director fragmenting narrative, he says. "Ten years from now," says Nolan, "it's going to be pathetically obvious what we're all doing." Broderick mentions David Gordon Green's unconventionally structured *George Washington* as proof that Nolan is in good company.

Curiously, though Nolan's reputation is as a no-budget director, he sees himself as a mainstream filmmaker in the line of Alfred Hitchcock and Nicolas Roeg. In fact, as he waits for the American release of *Memento*, he is in

Vancouver shooting a Warner Bros. remake of *Insomnia*, a 1997 Norwegian thriller that stars Al Pacino. He's also set to direct another mystery, *The Keys to the Street*, for Fox Searchlight, which he's adapted from a book by the popular novelist Ruth Rendell. Nolan doesn't intend to spend his entire career making crime films, but thinks the genre suits him—and not just because it is so naturally visual. "For a young filmmaker it's a great genre. It draws on your real-life neuroses, your real-life paranoia, your real-life fears," he says. "And extends them and takes them to the realm of melodrama so they become universal. I think particularly it's a good genre when you're younger—unless you want to make films about college grads looking for a job, or trying to get into the film business. Which I don't particularly."

One of the keys to Nolan's success, clearly, is his way with actors, and the atmosphere he creates on set. "He's incredibly calm and relaxed, and appears confident," says Moss; his comfortable tone made her and the other actors trust themselves to take chances. Pearce—slight, shy, and puckishly Australian in person, more a Dickensian cutpurse than a Hollywood heartthrob—echoes Moss. "Chris is a highly intelligent guy, very respectful of what actors do," he says. "I've worked with directors before who think you're a piece of meat, and I think, 'Ah, I don't have the technical ability to do this.'" Pearce appears in nearly every scene of the film, in a very demanding role. "I thought it was going to be a really wonderful challenge. And I bashed my way through it and boggled my way through [the script], making sure Chris and I were on the same page. And when I came out the other side of it, just after we started shooting, it felt quite buoyant. It just flowed."

Soderbergh, whose *Sex, Lies, and Videotape* in 1989 made him one of the first independent auteurs, thinks young filmmakers should be wary of getting pigeonholed as indie guys. "In this day and age it's becoming increasingly difficult to maintain a career doing only independent films," he says. "And if you do, you become marginalized very quickly. There are fewer independent distributors, and those that are still around are more and more conservative." He could see Nolan going in any direction. "I think he's very pragmatic—and he's interested in engaging an audience, on his own terms."

Says brother Jonah: "I think he's enjoying being able to make movies on a grander scale. But he would make movies no matter what. He's the only person I know who's doing what he said he would be doing at eight years old. It's great that he's being celebrated. But if his luck dries up he'll keep on making films."

[*New Times LA*, March 15, 2001]

HIGH-TONE TALK

To OPTIMISTS, THE CITY HAS BECOME an enormous radio: voices everywhere speaking, echoing, reflecting on matters cultural and civic. Of course, you have to know where to look, when to listen, in this city of vast distances and discontinuous neighborhoods. But series at bookstores, universities, museums—not to mention smart talk shows on public radio, ideal for commuters stranded in cars—have never been more plentiful in Los Angeles. The city, some say, is experiencing a renaissance of talk. Think intellectuals and artists are gentle people? The Los Angeles County Museum of Art, not long ago, became the site of a conversation about art that turned ugly. The scene was a panel about Made in California, the museum's unconventional survey of the Golden State's art and pop imagery over the last one hundred years, which engulfed nearly the entire museum during its five-month run, was heavily attended by the public and roundly assaulted in the press. For the panel, seven art professionals—scholars, curators, an art critic, and an artist—got together to offer attack, defense, or postmortem.

The discussion almost immediately turned diffuse and frustrating: To an onlooker, it was like watching seven different conversations in seven different rooms. The speakers came down along predictable lines, with the academics offering cheerily "inclusive" points of view, a *New York Times* critic defending (sometimes eloquently) traditional standards, and a self-described Chicano artist hinting that the notion of quality was code for elitist racism. The debate circled central points it never fully engaged. In the audience, anger rose like smoke.

When it came to the question-and-answer period, many in the crowd forgot Made in California and simply insulted the panelists. One questioner, asked to keep her query "pointed," insisted that there were no rules forbidding her opinion, which was far from congratulatory. UC Irvine professor Jon Wiener stood up and denounced the panelists' discussion as "pedestrian." The more criticism, the more the audience cheered and egged the assailants on. At event's end, as attendees and participants filed out to a friendly cocktail reception on the patio of the LACMA West building, it was clear that the discussion had gone nowhere and shed light on nothing.

"I think it was a disaster," says Paul Holdengräber, the impresario behind the evening. "A real disaster—but from the hundreds of messages we're getting, and from the fact that internally, within the museum, people are talking, the fact that it did happen was really important."

Holdengräber, who is the head of the Institute for Art and Culture, which sponsored the event, aims to offer "rigorous and lively debate" through his more-or-less monthly series at the museum, but he admits that this one delivered neither rigor nor liveliness. "I've gotten so many comments from people saying it was one of the best conversations they've heard," he says. "And I feel very sorry for these people. Like it's really too bad: 'I'm so sorry, what can I do to help?'"

Holdengräber, a pan-European educated in Paris and at Princeton, a self-described "linguistic monster," wants to get people thinking, speaking, engaging with high culture. He wants to reawaken the childlike sense of wonder, to sharpen minds without the usual academic pomposity. "The only way I remained awake," he says of his years in academia, "was by looking at other people fall asleep—that movement of the head that we can identify. And I do not particularly care for the lecture hall."

Despite Holdengräber's tangible goals, not everything he tries works out: An event last October with the intentionally tacky title "The Healing Power of Art" involved Russian satirists Komar and Melamid and comic writer Dave Eggers. The evening was intended to make arts mavens look at their own conformity and pious assumptions. To many who attended, though, the event was pointless and inane, lacking the spirit of laughter it promised. Holdengräber calls the appearance by abstract painter R. B. Kitaj, speaking about Van Gogh, "the Kitaj disaster" for its enormous preshow mess: 1,200 people showing up for an event that could only hold half that many, with actor Michael York holding a sign identifying himself, as if he were trying to jump a red velvet rope on Sunset. (The Institute has since begun a reservation policy.) But none of these events got as completely muddled as the Made in California panel—which left many in the audience as frustrated as did the LACMA exhibit itself. "You have to know how to fail brilliantly," Holdengräber says with an accent almost comically European. "And I did so just magnificently."

Fail or not, Holdengräber has put together the city's most in-demand intellectual series, one that books up as quickly as a Springsteen concert. "Paul is one of the great mad hatters of Los Angeles," says Michael Silverblatt, host of KCRW's literary interview show Bookworm. "His way with an event is to leave it free to succeed or fail. This is a great virtue. Usually you go to an event, and you know exactly how it will turn out. There's no excitement. Paul's things are exciting in mysterious ways. At the beginning of the series you didn't know if you were going to get in. There was an enormous sense of anticipation. He's an intellectual who wants to be a sideshow barker, or a sideshow barker who wants to be an intellectual."

Holdengräber has directed LACMA's Institute—a two-person team, plus a host of volunteers, that orchestrates the speaking series as well as internal museum events—for just over two years. In that time, he's brought Susan Sontag to discuss her novel *In America*, director Tim Robbins to interview lefty oral historian Studs Terkel, and polymath memoirist Richard Rodriguez (*Days of Obligation*) to interview himself. ("He paced back and forth," Rodriguez recalls of his host, "like I was the pregnant wife and I was delivering.") He's hosted Jamaica Kincaid discussing Thomas Jefferson's relationship with his African slave, and writer Pico Iyer recounting the week he spent living at LAX as a metaphor for the human condition. Beat poet Lawrence Ferlinghetti appeared and drew a crowd of 2,000, way more than will fit into LACMA's Bing Auditorium. In March, painter David Hockney, discussing his discovery that painters as far back as the Renaissance used optical devices to aid their work, drew an enormous crowd as well. Coming up on May 31, jazz photographer William Claxton is scheduled. At each event, Holdengräber moderates as much as he thinks necessary. Though he constantly riffs on his favorite poets and philosophers, Holdengräber comes across like a big kid full of enthusiasm—a twelve-year-old on a sugar high—instead of a stodgy academic. He speaks six languages, four of them well, and slips from one to another to find the root word for whatever he's discussing. "What I like about him is that he's quite mad," says Rodriguez. "He's one of the very few people I know in the whole world who's in love with ideas, in love with language. And you can tell—it spills out of his mouth. It's wonderful to be with someone like that, impossible to love them, because they're always talking, they never shut up. But it's wonderful. He's sort of the last European in America."

Holdengräber is fond of saying that institute is a verb and not a noun, and that his goal is "to initiate, to instigate and, yes, to irritate!" He wants to leave his audiences with one impression: "Thinking is a pleasure."

He lived up to his ambitions nor too long ago with a lively, illuminating evening around conductor Esa-Pekka Salonen and opera director Peter Sellars. The trio discussed the legacy of composer Igor Stravinsky: to Salonen, the artist of the century; to Sellars, a self-promoting monster who "looked through the trash and found God." The conversation, both high-minded and colloquial, managed to speak to many issues—the city's impact on artists, the rootlessness of modernism, fascism and folk culture, and, most memorably, exile. Holdengräber's genius was mostly to lie low and let the high-cheekboned conductor and the spike-haired director go at it. "Everybody there could take something from the evening," Holdengräber said later, "without it becoming populist, banalized, dumbed down."

It's evenings like this, and evenings like the angry and unfocussed Made in California panel, that show the difference between Holdengräber's efforts and a conventional speaking series. Like the guests he favors—Iyer, Rodriguez, Salonen—he's an exile, a polymath, someone who combines his backgrounds and travels in a way more fruitful, more provocative, than the usual multicultural cliches. "My motto," he says, "is rigorous and playful debate. Both of them can go together marvelously." Or, it turns out, terribly.

"People," he's fond of saying, "are hungry for substance." The Institute fills a vacuum, he says, satisfies a hunger. But to some Angelenos, the city's awash in public conversation—from Andrea Grossman's Writers Bloc series to readings at bookstores to lectures at UCLA and USC and the Getty. Ralph Tornberg, the philanthropist who sponsors the Institute, also helps fund series at two other museums. And besides all the private salons cropping up in the lavish homes of rich Westsiders, the city hosts groups like the Los Angeles Institute for the Humanities, whose members, including *LA Times* book editor Steve Wasserman, author Susan Faludi, and poet-playwright Luis Alfaro, gather for monthly discussions. But there's no series as well-known or as longstanding as the program at New York's 92nd Street Y.

What's unique about Holdengräber's program—besides the heat it's generated around town—is its wide-ranging eclecticism and mix of high-tone discussion with a rare accessibility. The series is free, and while it helps to be on the Institute's mailing or email list, anyone who calls during the appointed reservation hour can get in, LACMA member or no.

Iyer credits Holdengräber with splicing different traditions together in a way that duplicates LA's wild diversity. "We're used to thinking of intellectuals, especially from the East Coast and Europe, as dour, skulking, downturned figures," he says. "And some people think of excitement as a sign of folly. But Paul, to a rare and heroic degree, manages to combine high spirits with high intellect, and to flood the book-lined study with light and spirit."

Author Carolyn See says he's gracious and charming and has a "civilizing influence." And Douglas Messerli, publisher of Sun and Moon Books, considers Holdengräber, and others like him, important to the city's evolution. "There's not quite a vacuum, but there's been a real lack of discourse. Sometimes when there is exchange people are baffled. I remember going to dinner parties when I first moved here, and if you had a spirited discussion, people were frightened."

Dissenters concede that Holdengräber is smart, and charming, but also sycophantic, covering his subjects in endless and rambling flattery.

"In eighteenth-century English literature there were these characters who were really well-versed in current chitchat," says one Angeleno, calling Holdengräber a creature of affectation and pretension. Others suspect him of fraudulence, wondering about the Austrian accent on this Texas native, this intellectual Barnum who seems to come alive around famous people. "What's in it for Paul Holdengräber?" they ask.

Holdengräber learned to argue almost before he learned to talk. "I grew up in a family where arguing was part of what you did," he says of his childhood in Mexico City, Switzerland, Vienna, Dusseldorf, and Brussels. "We spoke about everything. Everything was an object of discussion and debate and difference of some kind." Holdengräber's parents were Viennese Jews who fled the Nazis in the late 1930s, leaving Austria for Haiti, where they met as members of a small community of exiles. His father, a vegetable farmer and later a textile merchant, was an especially strong intellectual influence on Holdengräber, who was born in Houston. By the time he was four, they had left for Mexico. "Whenever we were having lunch and something came up that I didn't know he would say, 'Look it up!' When I was growing up, eight and nine, I had to write reports for him on books I read. I had to underline every word I didn't know. And that would make me go to the dictionary." Holdengräber and his father, he says, have been engaged in a vigorous but good-natured struggle all their lives. "When I was ten years old," he says, "my father thought I was already late because I had not read the complete works of Goethe."

Holdengräber went to college in Louvain, Belgium, where he was taught by pugnacious Jesuits, then to graduate school in Paris, where he studied with Michel Foucault and Roland Barthes—for better or worse, two of the most influential intellectuals of the last forty years. After taking a doctorate in comparative literature at Princeton in 1993, he taught at Williams College in western Massachusetts, a pretty place that lacked the grit and friction he wanted. Academia fostered an environment "that put boundaries on the imagination . . . where you write an article for forty-two people," he recalls. "My appetites are greater." By 1995 he was a postdoctoral fellow ("a jolly good fellow" is the phrase he can't resist using) at the Getty; he worked, over the year following, at the Getty Research Institute. In 1997 he came to LACMA to assist Stephanie Barron, chief curator of modern and contemporary exhibitions.

With Barron, he helped moderate some of the early elaborate planning meetings for Made in California, and moonlighted in the graduate school at Claremont College, teaching cultural studies. A few months later, he took the Institute—an idea already hatched by museum director Andrea Rich, but barely—and ran with it. The first event he orchestrated was anthologist Jerome Rothenberg performing prose poems by Picasso. "It's not as if we had a program in place and the Institute led a national search for someone to head it," says Barron. "The Institute took off in a way beyond anyone's expectations." Holdengräber's energetic, chaotic temperament and pro-gramming are not typical of the museum staff, Barron admits. "There are people who like it, and who prefer that things be a little more planned out," she says. "You couldn't run an entire institution this way."

At the end of the Made in California panel, a local art critic came up to Holdengräber to tell him it was one of the worst things his ever witnessed. "It was nearly as bad as the show," the critic said. Recalls Holdengräber: "And I wanted to talk to him about it, and he left! If you have grievances, express them!" Can conversations make a difference? Some come and go with no record or impact. Some become venerable institutions, like the series at the 92nd Street Y. Still others, like Socrates' often drunken discourses about sex and politics, alter the whole course of a civilization.

"I'm always surprised that Los Angeles doesn't have more forums like this," says Richard Rodriguez of Holdengräber's efforts. "It is clearly one of the great cultural capitals of the world, yet my sense as a Northern Californian is how little conversation at the civic level is happening in Southern California. And that means magazines, newspapers, television shows. Here you are, the pop media capital of the world, yet there is this kind of silence. So my sense of Paul from the beginning was that he wanted to get Los Angeles to focus on conversation."

Holdengräber is not the first Southlander to try to bring disparate members together for a dialogue about the city and its direction. In 1929, when Los Angeles had recently passed San Francisco in population and was beginning to feel its oats as an intellectual capital, a few dubious experimenters launched a journal called *Opinion*. From left to right, from anarchist to aesthete, the group centered around a charismatic poet and bookstore owner named Jacob Zeitlin. "Had satyrs been permitted in ancient Israel," Kevin Starr writes in *Material Dreams*, an LA history that documents the circle, "they would have resembled this small, dark, curly-haired, hawk-nose sensualist hierophant."

Though Zeitlin's journal folded—*Opinion*'s editors, reputedly, had too many opinions—it helped instigate a movement of culturally ambitious men striving to build a regional culture outside the movie industry. With a zeal for book collecting developing in this still-provincial city, Zeitlin's bohemian group, along with others like the California Art Club, began to lay down an intellectual infrastructure for the city. Zeitlin, writer Carey McWilliams, and others helped bring serious authors and serious classical music to the city, and began important modern art and photography collections. They also took the direction of their city personally—in marked contrast to the reckless boosterism and development being urged by the *LA Times*.

Like Zeitlin, who hitchhiked from Texas to California, hoping to bring Chicago-style literary populism to Los Angeles, Holdengräber aims to conjure the spirit of 1890s Vienna in the City of Angels by "bringing the arts to live together again, while at the same time making people less afraid." He's probably never appeared in public without quoting Oscar Wilde: "Either you make the arts popular or you make the people artistic."

Rodriguez thinks such efforts are important, especially in a state fragmented by so many languages, creeds, and competing myths. "I think something will come out of California," he says, "beyond the bolshevism of Mike Davis and the despair of Joan Didion. And it will spring in relation to Paul's dream."

Holdengräber's intellectual hero is Walter Benjamin, a German intellectual (1892–1940) whose most famous photo shows him brooding behind an enormous moustache. Holdengräber wrote his doctoral thesis on the scholar; he can barely get through a conversation without quoting him or referring to one of his essays. Though Benjamin is best remembered today for pessimism and nostalgia, for committing suicide at the French border for fear of capture by the Gestapo, he was also a champion walker. (With Charles Baudelaire, he was strolling's poet laureate.) Some of his most famous essays are about the flaneur, a figure of inspired, nineteenth-century aimlessness who walked to catch glimpses of passersby and "who demanded elbow room and was unwilling to forgo the life of a gentleman of leisure." The flaneur sought streets full of crowds but uncluttered by horse-drawn carriages. (Around 1840, they were known to take turtles walking along city avenues.) "To endow this crowd with a soul," Benjamin wrote, "is the very special purpose of the flaneur. His encounters with it are the experiences that he does not tire of telling about." A century and a half after the stroller's heyday, Holdengräber is driving down Fairfax Avenue, seeking to recapture the experience of which Benjamin wrote. But there are no crowds, no cobblestoned pavements, no ferries sighing along the Seine; instead of a few carriages, Fairfax is crowded with beat-up Chevys, street construction, and SUVs. "Los Angeles is not particularly a city for the flaneur," he says as he cruises past the 99 Cent Store, "because flaneury presupposed rubbing shoulders, catching glances." He refers to a story of Poe's, a poem of Baudelaire's. "And here we are caught up in our cars, our own little universes." A little farther up Fairfax: "The security of this Park LaBrea, of all gated communities, is something I fear, somehow."

Holdengräber's indifference to the automobile goes way back. At sixteen, he hiked 170 miles across the Swiss countryside, and he claims to have walked every street in Paris from one side to the other. "When I was eighteen years old, instead of getting a car I asked my father for ten pairs of shoes, which I got. And I walked. I loved walking. I didn't like cars; I thought they changed people's relationship to the world. I feel lucky to have a father who was fearless about the world. He felt that his son should do what he did, which was hitchhike around the world. So when I was eighteen years old I came to the United States and hitchhiked around twenty-nine states. I was everyone's lost son. It teaches you how to entertain people with stories." An ambulance screams by.

Now he's approaching street construction, and tiring of driving. It clearly doesn't suit him. (He carries a cell phone almost exclusively so he can call his wife, Barbara Wansbrough, a Hollywood set decorator, when he gets lost, which is nearly every time he climbs into a car.) When he first moved to town, he only found his way home to Santa Monica by getting to Sunset and driving west to its end. "Do you know the famous lines of Benjamin's, from 'Berlin Chronicle,' where he says, 'To find oneself in a city is easy—to lose oneself is an art'?"

Holdengräber gets out to walk, but there's no crowd. A few homeless men, a scattering of kids in backpacks getting off from school, but none of the charge, none of the random glances or serendipitous meetings that Holdengräber imagines from Benjamin or Baudelaire. He surveys abandoned side streets; his spirits droop. He drops into a dusty, delightfully obsessive Yiddish record store and comes alive again. "Our compatriot from the art museum!" says the shop's owner, Simon Rutberg, extending his hand. They discuss a Connie Francis version of "Havah Nagila" that Holdengräber wants to buy for his wife.

"I'm trying to get Mel Brooks to the Institute, to the museum," Holdengräber says, spotting one of Brooks' records on the counter. "What, does he paint?" says Rutberg, sweeping his hand over the wall behind him as if holding a dripping roller. "Two coats!"

Despite all its private pleasures, Los Angeles is a city in which the concept of "public" may be as dead as anywhere in the civilized world. Whether it's public spaces, public architecture, public schools, or public transportation, Los Angeles keeps to itself, favors the private—especially compared with cities such as London or New York, established in more civic-minded centuries past. What LA has always needed is institutions that can knit the private factions together and instill in people a sense of living in a community. It's unlikely that Paul Holdengräber, in a monthly speaking series that accommodates only a few hundred, can pull off such a feat single-handedly. But he's setting a tone that the rest of the city can follow, however hard that may be. "I think sometimes that he doesn't know how rough-and-tumble this place is that we call California," Rodriguez says. "And in that sense how difficult his job is going to be. To get a conversation here is really going to be something. Because we're fragmented—not only physically and geographically, but in the ways we understand each other. For a city that is quite so confusing and confused as LA, I find his fragmented intelligence to be quite thrilling and appropriate."

Says Silverblatt: "What I would like to see is the museum leave these things completely in Paul's hands. He's got ideas about how to stage an event, but the institution doesn't want anything unpredictable to happen. When you've got a person as inventive as Paul, you should trust him. I wouldn't like him as much if I didn't think him capable of both the wonderful and the terrible."

Holdengräber has bigger plans than the series, though. He'd like to do more events each year, and to bring Hollywood talent like Warren Beatty, Curtis Hanson, Steven Soderbergh, and Susan Sarandon out to discuss issues that go beyond their next movies. "I want to connect in a meaningful way with the movie industry," he says. He'd like to become a full-scale public intellectual, to spend more time on the radio and in other media, to host a public television show modeled on National Public Radio's Fresh Air, to put together a mammoth event at the Hollywood Bowl.

In a city full of charlatans and false surfaces, where high culture often seems like an invader from another, older world, Holdengräber is that rarest of things: He is what he claims to be. What he claims to be, though, is a kind of intellectual huckster, a creative anarchist. "You don't get to be P. T. Barnum without the accusations of humbuggery," Silverblatt points out. "Is it a real bearded lady or is it a fake?" Holdengräber doesn't deliver each time out, but he's building an important forum in which people can dream, fight, argue. Says Iyer, "He marries exuberance to sophistication."

Here's Holdengräber, looking forward to an upcoming show: "When the line wraps four times around the Bing and five hundred people are terribly angry, and I get one hundred letters: 'How dare you! I am such and such!' . . . " Holdengräber pauses to laugh. "It's fine. The whole world should have this problem!"

[*New Times LA,* May 2001]

HITTING A NERVE

CONSUMERISM AND THE COUNTERCULTURE collide hard on Telegraph Avenue, where political posters fill the space between chain stores. Three kids in hooded sweatshirts crouch on the sidewalk: "Can you spare some change . . . for pot?"

Away from the clamor, inside Cody's Books, a few dozen people have gathered to meet a reserved young man who could be a chemistry T.A. with a good haircut. He's discussing *Optic Nerve*—his chronicle of lonely, good-looking Bay Area denizens who hold down negligible jobs and struggle to connect. Adrian Tomine, who lives nearby and seems dressed for anonymity, has spent twelve years producing a comic that has more in common with the spare, disillusioned short stories of Raymond Carver than with Batman and Robin. Visually, his style is not far from that of Dan Clowes, whose *Ghost World* comic was made into an art film last year: a mix of the clean lines of 1950s magazine ads with touches of film noir and a careful, almost documentary realism.

This summer, Tomine released a hardback, *Summer Blonde*, that collects his last four issues, tales of a harried telemarketer who meets her dream guy while making prank phone calls, a nebbish writer who returns home to seduce an old crush's less appealing sister, and a smooth ladies' man who's unceremoniously humbled. The only character rendered without sympathy is Carlo, a guitar-toting Casanova who would not look out of place at SkyBar or Erewhon. "He's just the sort of young, good-looking... extrovert that makes me sick," a rumpled character tells his shrink. Despite the jaded tone of the work, the frames are drawn with an intense concentration and meticulous detail.

Comics and "graphic novels," as non-superhero comics are sometimes called, have been discovered lately by the intellectual mainstream, from Michael Chabon's Pulitzer-winning novel, *The Amazing Adventures of Kavalier and Clay*, the tale of two comics creators, to the *New Yorker*'s recent Comics Issues. The critical success of Terry Zwigoff's *Ghost World* made the reclusive Clowes a cultural hero rivaling Robert Crumb. And films like *Spider-Man*, *Road to Perdition*, and *Men in Black* all originated in comics. Comics are reaching out of their subculture like they haven't in years, and Tomine's work is one of the reasons. Obscure rock musicians have even begun to take notice. "He really has the best taste of anyone I know," says Eels leader Mark Everett, who's hired Tomine to draw record covers.

As the Cody's crowd stares longingly, the thoughtful, self-contained, and coolly detached Tomine, twenty-eight, has no trouble stepping back from his own life, from his work, from his upbringing. "I think there was part of them," he says of his parents, both academics, "that would've preferred me to be outdoors and making friends and stuff." Of his very short, frustrated career drawing *Optic Nerve* as a studio art major at the nearby UC campus: "They were waiting for me to put some ironic spin on it, like I was commenting on lowbrow culture or something." Laughter. Of the arduous, solitary life of a cartoonist: "It's not like *Chasing Amy*," he says of the Kevin Smith movie, "where your drafting table is up against your best friend's, and you're giving each other high-fives over the table." More laughter. "It's why cartoonists go crazy in old age."

Few cartoonists have hit this hard this young. Perhaps as a consequence, Tomine is both beloved and hated in the comics subculture; the letters page in his comic book is a gallery of hatred, fawning, and almost academic close-reading.

With 16,000 copies of his latest issue of *Optic Nerve*, Tomine is one of the five top sellers among alternative comics and the bestseller for Drawn & Quarterly, his Montreal publisher. He's also one of the best regarded in the business, along with Clowes, Art Spiegelman (*Maus*), and Chris Ware (*Jimmy Corrigan: The Smartest Kid on Earth*). Besides releasing *Summer Blonde*, he's included in the new, Dave Eggers-edited *The Best American Nonrequired Reading*. And starting this month, Drawn & Quarterly's comics will be distributed by Chronicle Books, allowing Tomine's work to get outside comic shops, where it seems increasingly uncomfortable.

After the reading, the cartoonist sits at the head of a long queue of admirers waiting to get their books signed. For the most part it's a well-behaved crowd—Tomine is all too familiar with fans who are physically trembling, who come to act out in public or to pass on a strange, deeply personal artifact. But a good third of the crowd seems to want something from him, from a corduroy-clad guy who puts out a comic about erotic spanking, urging Tomine to revive a favorite character, to a well-coifed man with a French accent who wants to interest him in creating work for cell-phone screens. Tomine, who may be the only writer in America who exudes a tangible fear of spelling his devotees' names wrong, handles them all with cordial distance.

Not everyone in Cody's tonight is a fan. Two skinny blond girls, about eight years old, wander by; both seem to be recovering from recent perm and dye jobs. "Why do they want him to sign their books?" one, in a Princess University T-shirt, asks dismissively. "Oh," responds the other. "He's some famous author guy or something."

Feeling like an outsider

Tomine grew up all over the West Coast, splitting time between a psychology professor mother who moved every few years and his engineering professor father in Sacramento. As a teenager he lived in Germany, because of his mother's teaching stint, though he never learned German, and he felt like an outsider even in the places he lived the longest.

"A lot of cartoonists have that in common," says Tomine, sitting in a cafe surrounded by students. "It's like the life of an Army brat; you never make any strong connections with people." Tomine says the cartoonists he knows—Clowes and Richard Sala (*Evil Eye*) are among his best friends— all have similar temperaments: "kind of soft-spoken and reticent, pretty cynical, black sense of humor, a fascination with human foibles. We're all kind of more observers than participants." As he put it at Cody's: "My friends and I say, 'Never trust a socially adept cartoonist.'"

Tomine's high school experience, he says, was rigged by his moving with his mom to Sacramento a few weeks before his freshman year began. He started with no friends and gained little ground from there. Tomine remembers the other students as affluent white kids; he drove a yellow van to school that backfired so loudly it set off the car alarms on his peers' new BMWs.

"A lot of the things that made me unhappy as a kid led to things that make me happy now," he says, with characteristic even-handedness. "In high school all I wanted was to have a lot of friends, or to go on dates with girls, and because none of that was happening, I had a lot of time at home. Speaking now, at twenty-eight, I'm grateful," he says, the rare artist who lives entirely from his art, along with illustrations for the *New Yorker* and indie-rock records. Had he been presented with a choice—misery now and artistic success later, or teenage glamour with an uncertain future—the cute girls and convertibles would've won in a second. "I would've said, 'Forget the art, no contest.'"

When he started drawing a comic book at fifteen—after years eavesdropping on the corny superhero comics his older brother, Dylan, brought home from 7-Eleven—he was in a vacuum, not even sure where to get pens and paper. In 1987, he stumbled upon the Hernandez Brothers' *Love and Rockets*, one of the first alternative comics with its combination of magical realism within an LA punk-rock setting, and saw that the medium didn't have to concern superheroes in tight costumes. He kept his interest to himself. "It was bad enough as it was. I certainly wasn't going to be, 'And by the way, I like comic books!'"

But soon after creating *Optic Nerve* and selling photocopied editions at a local shop, he began to hear from other readers, and the attention spurred him. He got letters describing his debt to Carver, and picked up his stories for the first time, responding to their emotional bleakness, unresolved tone, and "the tiny, small things charged with some kind of emotion."

High school's trial behind him, Tomine headed to Berkeley, where he intended to become an art major. "It didn't take me long to totally hate it," he says, explaining how his comics were dismissed while a wooden box filled with a feather and news clippings was deemed politically charged high art.

"The thing that had the strongest impact on me, over my life, is *Peanuts*, which looks nothing like what I do. People sell it as if it's this uplifting, fun-loving thing. But if you read it, it can make you cry. I still can't quite understand how such a neurotic, original person like Charles Schulz became the most mainstream, widely embraced figure of all time."

Tomine is known as a "literary" cartoonist. "He's the guy who creates comics as though he's a mainstream novelist," says Clowes. "He really thinks in those terms." Switching his studies to English, he was drawn to thorny work—Nabokov, the Bible, Chaucer—and enjoyed the rigor they required. "Peeling back layers, seeing what's beneath them. That's how I felt when I had *Lolita* taught in a class, that there's this whole other art beyond constructing a plot or creating interesting characters." About this time, as a college sophomore, he hooked up with Drawn & Quarterly.

"Adrian is kind of an anomaly in alternative comics," says cartoonist Sala. "It's almost straight from the Art Student's League circa 1950. His work is that disciplined and, in a way, conservative. There is a total absence of expression or cartoon-y experimentation in his latest work, which is ironic because it makes his art so individual and instantly recognizable."

Tomine used color imaginatively, and his drawing captures the surfaces of West Coast post-graduate life, but the best thing about *Optic Nerve* is its storytelling. Like a songwriter, he works in miniature, finding gestures and phrases that define his characters, who are almost instantly recognizable. He also gets loneliness and disconnection pitch-perfect.

Dan Raeburn, the Harold Bloom of the comics world, praises Tomine in an essay in "Summer Blonde" that reads like a manifesto from 1919 Paris. "He's a very shy guy," says Raeburn, who calls Tomine's style collegiate noir. "I'd describe him as nice. He tries as hard as he can to be as outwardly normal and average."

Spartan and disciplined

Standing in his immaculate apartment, Tomine is surrounded by books by Tobias Wolff and Chekhov, walls lined with intricate, retro comics and vintage *Peanuts* paperbacks. His exacting taste led Clowes to describe him as "a very picky guy, at a very early age." While he's known in the often nostalgic cartoonists community as the scribe least likely to own a big stack of 78s, he still seems stuck in time.

"I think my natural tendency is to be like a vampire and to steal material from people's lives," says Tomine, who's considering his own, in part thanks to his tenth high school reunion so his thoughts about it kept him up all night. He feels thirty approaching and has reached a plateau with a following, a serious girlfriend, and more illustration work than he can handle. While some artists might plan to dive into screenplays or TV, Tomine's dedicated to *Optic Nerve*, which requires so much work that he averages a page a week. Spartan, disciplined, he's a comic-book ascetic.

With eight issues and three books behind him, Tomine's planning his next *Optic Nerve* as part of a larger cycle, three or four issues, with Asian American characters; he wants to appease fans who've suggested he was ignoring his Japanese heritage.

His goal, Tomine says, is to mature without going soft, to take criticism without pandering, to escape the trap of those who become too successful too young. "Not that I was ever that huge a Michael Jackson fan," the cartoonist says with his usual flatness. "But here's someone who could definitely use some input from the outside world."

[*Los Angeles Times*, October 28, 2002]

MARS IN APOGEE

RAY BRADBURY IS THE FIRST LOS ANGELES WRITER many people read. He's also the first reasonably serious writer—someone concerned with political and moral themes—many encounter. His early science-fiction novels and story collections have drawn readers, especially intellectually ambitious teenage boys, for a half-century now. Many of these Bradbury fans become lifetime readers, moving into all kinds of weightier fare, from the darker, more complicated science fiction of William Gibson, Ursula K. Le Guin, and Philip K. Dick to mainstream literary work without end. He's the ultimate gateway drug.

Bradbury Stories: 100 of Bradbury's Most Celebrated Tales is a new anthology of work selected and introduced by the author, one that does not overlap with an earlier collection from Alfred A. Knopf. First, the good news: The stories included here from *The Martian Chronicles*—first printed in magazines in the late 1940s and later published as a story cycle inspired by Sherwood Anderson's *Winesburg, Ohio*—remain powerful, even at times rhapsodic. With their combination of lyricism and quiet gravity, these stories are so different in tone and effect from the rest of this volume that they could be the work of another author entirely. Perhaps they're best attributed to the writer Bradbury briefly became and perhaps could have remained. Here's the opening of "February, 1999: Ylla":

"They had a house of crystal pillars on the planet Mars by the edge of the empty sea, and every morning you could see Mrs. K eating the golden fruits that grew from the crystal walls, or cleaning the house with handfuls of magnetic dust which, taking all dirt with it, blew away on the hot wind."

The setting is so strange that it can take a while, as it does for the Earthmen who arrive and struggle with the planet's thin atmosphere, to adjust to the author's cadence and imagistic marvels. Here's the second sentence:

"Afternoons, when the fossil sea was warm and motionless, and the wine trees stood stiff in the yard, and the little distant Martian bone town was all enclosed, and no one drifted out their doors, you could see Mr. K himself in his room, reading from a metal book with raised hieroglyphs over which he brushed his hand, as one might play a harp."

This graceful, morally serious book marked not only the author's mainstream breakthrough—thanks in part to a rave by Christopher Isherwood, who brought the kind of respectability to Bradbury that W. H. Auden would later bring J. R. R. Tolkien—but a triumph for the science-fiction genre itself. Before long, *Time* magazine was hailing Bradbury as "the poet of the pulps," and suddenly science-fiction authors were appealing to a mainstream, sometimes even intellectual, readership.

Bradbury Stories includes five pieces from *Chronicles*, which began a debate among science-fiction fans about whether the author was part of their club. Detractors called him an anti-science-fiction writer, since he was suspicious of technology and often seemed to lack interest in science altogether. The genre, in those days, prided itself on its "hard" nuts-and-bolts science and was more masculine and far less literary than it became in the late 1960s, when the "New Wave" writers of England and America brought psychology, feminism, liberalism, and the social sciences into the mix.

Parochial debates like this are best left to the purists. What Bradbury does is often closer to a blend of Edgar Allan Poe and Aesop's fables than the now-forgotten authors of space operas: He creates myths, or metaphors, that express universal human truths by slightly displacing them. At their best, they're ambiguous, resonating equally into the past and the future.

The Martian stories, for all their high-tech settings, are rooted in the Bible and Nathaniel Hawthorne's Puritan allegories. With its pioneering Earthmen who discover a culture they can't understand and aim to recreate Old World lives, the book echoes backward to the conquistadors—and LA's Ohio-born settlers—and forward to "Apocalypse Now."

In their way, "The Martian Chronicles" are nearly as good a guide to the history of Southern California as the histories of Kevin Starr. The final story in the "Chronicles," "The Million-Year Picnic," not collected here, may still be the truest and most poignant description of becoming a Californian. Of the stories collected here, Bradbury's combination of moral seriousness with understatement and irony works best in "June 2001: And the Moon Be Still as Bright," which takes its name in part from a poem of Byron's. After landing on Mars, years after several failed expeditions, one of the Earthmen gathers some wood and watches it burn.

"It wouldn't be right, the first night on Mars, to make a loud noise, to introduce a strange, silly bright thing like a stove. It would be a kind of imported blasphemy. There'd be time for that later; time to throw condensed-milk cans in the proud Martian canals; time for copies of the *New York Times* to blow and caper and rustle against the lone gray Martian sea bottoms; time for banana peels and picnic papers in the fluted, delicate ruins of the old Martian valley towns."

Bradbury may be the last visible survivor of the Midwestern Protestants who once dominated Los Angeles, the "folks" who made the city over as a sleepy Iowa village decades before the city re-imagined itself as a high-tech, Asia-facing, multicultural metropolis. Famous for writing of rockets while refusing to drive a car, Bradbury embodies a contradiction: He's associated with his stories of the future, but his values are nostalgic, yearning for, and calling from, the past.

Raymond Douglas Bradbury was born in Waukegan, Ill. He was weaned on comic books, magic shows, Jules Verne, circuses. In 1932 his father lost his job as a telephone lineman, and after two difficult years, the family moved to Los Angeles. Despite difficult high school years as a bespectacled dreamer, Bradbury loved the city. He became a serious autograph hound, walking miles to film lots to beg signatures from W. C. Fields and Burns and Allen. While still in high school he joined a science-fiction fan club and met writers including Robert Heinlein. He was soon editing his own fanzine, placing fantasy stories in pulp magazines and breaking into the "slicks." The 1950 publication of *Chronicles* was followed in short order by *The Illustrated Man*, *The Golden Apples of the Sun*, and *Fahrenheit 451*, famously written at UCLA, where the author fed dimes into typewriters in the basement carrels.

By now, Bradbury was a success, a man who boasted of writing every single day, who was, as the author Tom Disch put it, "America's Official Science Fiction Writer, the one most likely to be trotted out on State occasions." He became a literary celebrity, often photographed in the turtlenecks, heavy glasses and floppy hair that gave him the look of the producer for a

West Coast psychedelic band. He inspired movies and plays; a lunar crater was named for one of his book. But as a writer, he was losing his magic.

The pieces the author has collected in *Bradbury Stories* show a writer of sporadic gifts and limited curiosity. He doesn't seem to really know, or care, much about individual people. While some of the stories are strong, the volume reveals a deeply uneven writer who can't separate his most evocative, soulful work from what's flat and dashed off. The ones that don't connect are like little machines, built of premises that don't pan out, rigged for punch lines that don't punch, surprise endings that don't surprise. Because the stories are one-dimensional, lacking convincing characters or realized settings, they thud audibly when their machinery tires.

When Bradbury leaves Mars, he loses his bearing. The anthology includes Midwestern vignettes, apocalyptic but slight stories set in rural Mexico, mossy Irish tales, and Gothic sketches. His 1953 trip to Ireland, to develop the script of *Moby-Dick* for John Huston, seems to have equipped Bradbury with material for endless stories, all offering permutations on steady rain, heavy drinking, and driving fast. Some of the Illinois stuff reads like a Pepperidge Farm commercial.

A few of the volume's stories come from Bradbury's lifetime fascination with carnivals—"seedy, fleabag things that live off the edges of people's lives"—the best of which is "The Illustrated Man," a well-known tale that retains its power to chill.

The weaker stories often begin with a clever premise: An actor playing Hitler is really a Nazi, an alien is really Christ, kids are planning to take over the world. But the tales don't develop, and their characters serve only to drive the conceit. "The Pedestrian," for instance, is biographically interesting because it was inspired by the author being stopped by police while walking on Wilshire. The story envisions a world in which people don't walk and then fails to take it anywhere.

Some of the gee-whiz stories may be more appealing to children than adults, though the best Bradbury—like much of Tolkien, J. K. Rowling, Isaac Asimov, and H. G. Wells—appeals equally to each, even if different generations hear the prose in different keys.

A few of the horror stories, some of which were collected in 1955's underrated *The October Country*, fare better, as little gems of atmosphere and setting, though the characters are as flat as ever. Two of the best are the engaging tale of a writer who quits early, "The Wonderful Death of Dudley Stone," and the disturbing "The Dwarf," which echoes the Frankenstein legend.

In the introduction to *Bradbury Stories*, the author describes the background of these pieces: "Writing, for me, is akin to breathing. It is not something I plan or schedule; it's something I just do. All the stories collected in this book seized on me at the strangest hours, compelling me to head for the typewriter and put them down on paper before they went away."

Bradbury has spoken elsewhere about how writing should be unconscious, Zen, like the opening of water flowers—news that surely reassures struggling writers everywhere. But writing enduring work—stories that can stand up in a collection fifty years after their penning—has little in common with the rituals of a New Age retreat. Art that lasts—whether *The Martian Chronicles* or the poems of Wallace Stevens—comes from enormous labor and from unrelenting self-criticism. Bradbury seems to know this in his best stories, which are polished and fully realized. But the less successful writing collected here seems driven less by his earlier passion than by merely a "high concept."

Either way, this prose magician and elder statesman has found the common denominator between the Red Planet and Southern California. But he hasn't left us, like a major writer can, with a body of work that takes in all the world.

[*Los Angeles Times*, August 3, 2003]

THE CULT OF GLENN GOULD

It BEGAN, UNPROMISINGLY, with music written to put you to sleep. But when the dashing twenty-two-year-old Glenn Gould recorded a little-known piece Bach had come up with to soothe an aristocratic insomniac, the pianist's ecstatic, ferocious playing kick-started popular interest in the composer. Few had heard him performed this way: as a living, almost modern, force.

Just as important, Gould's 1955 recording of "The Goldberg Variations" ignited a career that would make him one of classical music's last culture heroes. Gould would become not a New York insider like Leonard Bernstein, nor a middlebrow regular-guy like Van Cliburn (or later, Yo-Yo Ma), but a rebel angel from the Canadian wilds who drew both disdain and comparisons to James Dean and Jimi Hendrix. Like theirs, his reputation seems only to have grown since his death.

During his life, Gould revolutionized the way we hear eighteenth-century music. Now, more than twenty years after a stroke felled him in 1982 at just fifty, he has one of the decade's best-selling serious piano records. Last fall's three-CD set *A State of Wonder*, which collects two versions of "Goldberg Variations" with a disc of interviews and outtakes, has sold nearly 60,000 copies since its release. Those numbers are astronomical for a classical release—the set dwarfs the sales of any single CD by Rubin-stein or Horowitz, including Rubinstein's legendary version of Chopin's "Nocturnes." (Scores of Gould albums remain available, and a collection of him playing Romantic music, called ... *And Serenity*, is due this fall.)

He's also the rare classical figure who appeals to rock musicians, Gen-Xers, jazz pianists, and Net-heads, as well as artists, writers, and folks with little interest in other classical music. It's no surprise he's inspired a play, a film, and at least one novel. For some, Gould's records are the first of many classical purchases.

His disparate devotees include maverick filmmaker John Waters (*Pink Flamingos, Hairspray*), the actress who played the wisecracking Flo on the sitcom *Alice*, even a young guitarist who tours with the Allman Brothers.

"I can put him on for hours—he's like nobody else," says Waters, who owns ten books on Gould, hunts for anecdotes on him, and gives his CDs as gifts. "He was the ultimate original—a real outsider. And he had a great style, the hats and the gloves and so on."

Much of Gould's support, of course, comes from the classical cogno-scenti. But Gould has unparalleled powers to reach outside them. In some ways, he's a man of the 1950s and 1960s—perhaps the last era when an undiluted high culture figure could become a media star. But in a broader sense, the idiosyncratic Canadian, who disdained fashion and called himself "the last Puritan," has become—with his interest in publicity, technology, and pop culture—a man for our time.

Touchstone film

Sometimes, it starts with the movie. Jason Moran was a high school kid in Houston when he took a date to see *Thirty-Two Short Films About Glenn*

Gould, an unconventional 1993 picture by Francois Girard that focused on the pianist's eccentricity.

Electrified by the film and by Gould's intense dedication and stunning technique, Moran couldn't help notice that his sixteen-year-old companion was sinking into her seat. "That never happened again, me and her," says Moran, now twenty-seven and a leading New York-based jazz pianist signed to Blue Note. "If you can't deal with Gould, then maybe you're not my type."

Moran became a serious Gould fan, reading about him, seeking out his music, watching the film again and again. He saw Gould as a parallel to his hero Thelonious Monk, both eccentrics—jazz great Monk was as famous for his wild hats as Gould was for wearing overcoats in August—who approached music with a "reckless abandon."

Born middle class in Toronto to a furrier and an amateur musician, Gould became a prodigy who at fourteen played Beethoven's Piano Concerto No. 4 with the Toronto Symphony, but he neither entered nor won the contests that have since announced the emergence of a virtuoso. After his first American recital, in 1955 in New York, an executive from Columbia Records heard Gould and signed him immediately.

His playing was marked by its clarity, its accuracy, and—often and controversially—its speed. In his Bach, he avoided the pedals, so the notes aren't sustained or shaded as they can be with other interpreters: The result is a dry, clean style, each voice articulated clearly, that some listeners find lacking in emotional nuance.

While he's best known for his Bach, Gould was unusual in recording both the overlooked Jacobean composer Orlando Gibbons and twentieth-century atonalists like Schoenberg, Berg, and Webern. By contrast, he mostly avoided the twentieth-century masters—Chopin, Schumann, Liszt—who make up the meat and potatoes of the piano repertoire. When he recorded them, he skipped well-known pieces, favoring obscurities. He's considered an intellectual player especially attuned to a piece's structure, to producing what one critic called "an X-ray of the music."

Why, then, the broad appeal?

"Musically, he represents a kind of purity," says jazz pianist Brad Mehldau, thirty-three, a former Angeleno who discovered Gould at age eleven through Brahms recordings at his local library. "It's an uncompromising pursuit of the aesthetic in and of itself. He approached the music head-on, with a kind of emotional baldness that shocks you."

Gould's single-mindedness, Mehldau says, makes him a hero to musicians of all kinds. "Gould's Bach is like watching Bach with 3-D glasses."

"One of the things that makes him speak to us jazz musicians is his unbelievable time," says Bill Charlap, another jazz pianist in his thirties. "He's really a swinging piano player when he plays Bach. The playing is so clear, so rhythmically vital, so extemporaneous."

Besides Gould's purely musical side, he continues to generate followers for his ideas and the strange way he managed his career.

In 1964, two years before the Beatles quit concert performing to make intricately crafted records with George Martin, Gould stepped down from the stage—where he'd developed a formidable reputation—because he found it demeaning and craved the ability to edit and manipulate his work. (His decision came, as it happens, after a concert in Los Angeles.)

Gould spoke and wrote frequently about his withdrawal from the stage, and of his fascination with technology and its ability to transform art and culture. Appropriately, fellow Canadian Marshall McLuhan was a frequent conversation partner of Gould's. In contrast to the often technophobic world of classical music, Gould was almost a figure from the Internet age.

"Any dedicated thrift-store hound stumbles upon that Byronic, pretty-boy edition of the 'Goldberg Variations,'" says Drew Daniel, a San Francisco electronica musician with the group Matmos. But Daniel's drawn to Gould's technological side—specifically to his experimental radio documentaries like *The Idea of North*, in which the pianist interviewed people and mused essay-like on philosophic themes—more than to his Bach.

"I just couldn't believe what he was doing as a sound editor," Daniel says from Portugal, where he's in the midst of the European leg of a tour with Bjork. "It was this bizarre polyphony: Everything slowly ramps up and dissolves into everything else. He had so much trust in the ability of the ear to follow two voices at once." Daniel has given a copy of *North* to the Icelandic chanteuse.

Gould resonates with sound-art aficionados, he says, because his fierce playing offers an alternative to what Daniel calls the "Novocain for the elderly" programming on most classical music stations.

"He's one of their validating figures," UCLA musicologist Robert Fink says of the appeal of Gould to electronica musicians. "Because he theorized the idea of the studio as better than live performances, an ethos of the studio as a tool. If you think [Brian] Eno's cool, Gould has exactly the same ideas."

A restless recluse

Otto Friedrich's biography describes Gould—rumored to be one of history's worst drivers—speeding in his Lincoln Continental through the Canadian countryside one day, waving his arms wildly inside the car. When a policeman pulled the pianist over, Gould told him he was driving under the influence of a Mahler symphony that had so consumed him he was conducting it with both hands as he drove.

Anyone who's seen the captivated way Gould played, live or on film, will understand why the judge who heard the case let the pianist off.

His legend wasn't all about fast cars: Gould was known as a recluse who spent most of his time in a dreary suburban hotel because it offered twenty-four-hour room service, who wore not only overcoats but gloves in August, packed dozens of pills and lived, as he put it, in "horror of catching colds." Restlessly intellectual, he called friends and associates all over the world for long, wide-ranging discussions.

"He would always call me person-to-person, and we'd have these two-hour conversations and he'd get billed four dollars a minute," says Tim Page, the *Washington Post* critic who edited *The Glenn Gould Reader,* a fascinating collection of the pianist's writings. "He'd continue calling people till seven-thirty or eight o'clock in the morning, which was his bedtime."

Gould usually wanted to talk about theology, film, philosophy— anything but classical music, Page says. The pianist's wide-ranging mind was in contrast to most musicians', says UCLA's Fink. "It's like talking to a figure skater," he says of conversations with virtuosos. "There is a cloistering effect to classical music, a narrowing of the intellectual horizons." Not everyone liked Gould's playing. He was dismissed by some early-music purists for playing the music of Bach (who composed for the harpsichord and organ) on the piano. And Gould—who said he recorded a set of Mozart's piano sonatas to demonstrate how bad they were—was considered musically brash and unlovely, too free and easy with a composer's work.

In 1962, Bernstein actually warned the New York Philharmonic audience when the pianist came to perform a Brahms concerto, with "Don't be frightened." The conductor all but disavowed Gould's glacial approach to the piece, and reviews were dismissive.

Many listeners, now as then, can't abide the pianist's loud humming over his own playing. But even this annoying mannerism helped fuel the myth: One puckish Web site advertises "the Glenn Gould Devocalizer 2000," an imaginary item calibrated to remove Gould's moans. Filmmaker Waters calls the humming a sign of Gould's subversive individualism.

Gould's star eventually rose, Page says, because of "a younger generation of critics who took what he was saying as seriously as what he was playing. Glenn's real legacy has been posthumous."

The pianist was also oddly, sometimes comically, obsessive. In *Glenn Gould: The Alchemist*, a 1974 documentary released on DVD this past spring, Gould describes the battered, sawed-off chair on which he performed all his concerts as a member of the family. When his bespectacled French interlocutor, incredulous, asks if the chair could be as close to him as the music of Bach, Gould deadpans: "Oh, much closer, actually."

Unlikely followers

The pianist's legend resonates outside the world of musicians. "It's like a secret world, Glenn Gould fanatics," says Waters, who calls *Thirty Two Short Films* one of his "five favorite tasteful films" and listens to Gould almost every Sunday.

"He's definitely crossed over," the director says, noting that he doesn't typically obsess over classical musicians. "But to what kind of people? Extreme people in the other arts. Inspiring a cult from beyond the grave— I'm all for it!"

Gould, who had a natural sense of the dramatic, has long compelled actors. Among them, says Page, are Barbara Feldon, who played the sultry Agent 99 on TV's *Get Smart*, and Polly Holliday.

Holliday is best known for playing Flo, a saucy diner waitress on the series *Alice*, where her signature exclamation was "Kiss ma grits!" But since leaving the show, she's become a huge Gould fan.

While shooting a TV series in Los Angeles in 1995, she found a biography in a bookstore, was intrigued and then picked up a copy of the 1981 "Goldberg Variations" and played it over and over. "Having not heard music for years, I was absolutely stunned," she says. "I remember that day so clearly because that's all I did that whole day."

Despite not having listened to or played music for decades, Holliday now practices Bach on the piano every day, goes to concerts and underwrites a New York chamber music series. "I'm more interested in music than I have been in my entire life. It seems like music has just invaded my life since I played those Glenn Gould tapes."

Some musicians who follow the pianist are equally unlikely. Derek Trucks, twenty-four, a Florida-based blues guitarist who plays with the Allmans, is another Gould freak. "I'm always drawn to people who create their own worlds," he says, praising the pianist's dynamic range and comparing Gould to jazz visionary Sun Ra.

"The classical world is a forbidding world to an outsider, and any welcome is welcome indeed," says Sean O'Hagan, a member of two British rock bands, Stereolab and the High Llamas, that evoke Kraftwerk and Brian Wilson more than J. S. Bach. "I don't think Gould was comfortable in the classical world, and that immediately sends out a positive signal to those who are anxious to know about the music but shy away from the culture of the structure that surrounds it."

More than his quirks

The early Gould got a lot of mileage out of being a mad artist. "There's also the fact that he was kind of beautiful," critic Page says. "He seemed kind of autoerotic. When you see him playing, there's this sense of someone making love to his music."

While pop culture elements—television, fashion, a media star's mystique—fueled Gould's fame, his cult is not a passing pop fad like pianist David Helfgott, whose uplifting tale of surviving childhood abuse inspired the film *Shine*, or famously blind opera singer Andrea Bocelli. Take the biography away and Gould still turned out sturdily great music.

"He helped me define what I call the peak moments in music, the mountaintop experiences," says Charles Enman, a Canadian classical music critic who was transfixed, at ten, by one of the pianist's television appearances. Gould's playing, Enman says, offers "a sense of stepping outside time: He was the first musician of whom I remarked that quality." It's a quality he still seeks to find in other performers.

"Part of the hook for getting people into Gould is the fifties maverick angle," admits Jon Brion, the LA pop musician and producer who provided the music and sound design for the films *Magnolia* and *Punch Drunk Love*. "It's easy to focus on the eccentricities. But when you hear the music, you hear what it was all for. The part that spoke to me was his commitment."

A Gould cult flourishes in Russia (he was the first Western classical musician to play the USSR) and Japan. It's irresistible to think of Gould fandom spreading to other planets, thanks to his recording of Bach sent on the 1977 Voyager spacecraft.

The ability of art to move people decades and centuries after the death of the artist is one of culture's strangest mysteries. It's hard to imagine what will come next in the world of pop music and youth culture and what taste will be like in twenty or thirty years. Yet chances are Gould's music, personality, and penetrating ideas will speak to that time as vividly as it does to ours.

[*Los Angeles Times*, August 10, 2003]

HIS BACK PAGES

One night this fall, Benedikt Taschen was planning a modest dinner with the editor in charge of his Los Angeles office. Something in Koreatown, he figured, or maybe Tom Bergin's, perhaps a drink later at an old Hollywood haunt like the Formosa Cafe. Although he runs an international empire and favors expensive suits, the German publisher makes it a point of pride to eat only at restaurants with a B or C health rating.

But Taschen, it turned out, had scored invitations to a fashion show at Armani, and soon he and editor Jim Heimann were standing in frustration behind a roadblock on Rodeo Drive. Beverly Hills looked poised for an invasion, its streets patrolled by young people wearing sleek black clothes and headsets.

Taschen and Heimann have become, over the last two decades, innovators in a new kind of publishing, one that brings the humor of pop culture to high art and some of high art's seriousness to kitsch. It was Taschen, a friend of fetish photographer Helmut Newton, who published Newton's collected works in a $1,500 coffee-table book that came with its own coffee table.

None of this, though, helped with the burly guards on Rodeo. Clearly not used to being detained, the publisher stood seething until a shapely blond Englishwoman apologetically escorted him and Heimann to the Armani store's entrance, terming the scene outside "very uncivilized."

"Yes, it is," Taschen intoned.

Pouty models were soon marching down a red carpet as music pounded, and Steve Martin appeared to praise and tease a smiling Giorgio Armani. Then Taschen was off to a Vanity Fair after-party, where he sipped a pomegranate martini and shook hands with Macy Gray, Samuel L. Jackson, and Armani himself.

To some, it would have been a big night out. Heimann, who drives Taschen around when the publisher's in town and acts as what he calls "court jester," seemed to enjoy the display of flesh and star power. But his boss was unimpressed, calling the party OK and Armani's clothes "completely overrated."

"I'm not that social," Taschen said over dinner later at Mr. Chow. "I'm more private."

In a crowd of his own assembling, by contrast—as at a party Monday—he's so much looser and more effusive that it seems as if his very DNA has changed.

Just who is Benedikt Taschen? His late night after the Armani show offered a sort of analogue of his career. From scrappy origins—as a teenage comic book merchant in Cologne, Germany—he has wandered casually into a world of glamour and sexuality. Now forty-two, he runs offices in six countries, employs 150 people and sells fifteen million books a year, mostly on his own whims and hunches. These volumes often anticipate cultural trends. They allow buyers to live vicariously, to play voyeur—in Neutra houses, German art museums, Japanese sex hotels.

For a certain kind of retro-minded sophisticate, Taschen books are the gold standard. Even expensive, lavishly packaged tomes spotlighting the experimental Case Study House program and rare early photographs of Marilyn Monroe sell rapidly. Taschen's success, with generally low prices, huge print runs and taboo subject matter, has rival publishers scrambling to keep up.

Outside Mr. Chow, Taschen paused to admire one of Hugh Hefner's limousines. He himself has a reputation as the Hefner of the art book, a jet-setting maverick in frog-skin shoes.

In September 2002, the company moved its US offices from New York to Hollywood, which has led to a new emphasis on Americana and pop culture and the hiring of Heimann, fifty-four, a graphic artist and author steeped in LA history. While once Taschen changed the world of the art book, now Los Angeles has begun to change Taschen.

Last week, an "Old European," mahogany-and-brass Taschen store, designed by Philippe Starck, opened in Beverly Hills to showcase the imprint's books and provide a space for lectures and events. It will be for Taschen what the Playboy mansion is for Hefner, a way of packaging, and bringing to life, a mystique—an idiosyncratic blend of art, kitsch, nudity, and international capitalism.

Eclectic range

Sharp suits and cool taste aside, Taschen makes an awkward figure of glamour. Though he's tall, his heavily bagged eyes and weak chin give him the look of an introspective tortoise, always on the verge of retreating back into his shell. Often reticent or cryptic in conversation—when asked which American women he fancied as a boy, he responds, "Besides Minnie Mouse?"—he speaks most loudly through his books.

The catalog Taschen puts out twice a year is among the oddest, least predictable publications on Earth. Last spring's edition, for instance, announced a book about *Jaybird*, a late 1960s/early 1970s nudist magazine that showcased hirsute, liberated young people frolicking in pastoral settings—California as Eden.

In the same catalog was a book that captures Eden more literally: a facsimile of the 1534 Lutheran Bible, printed in Germany, bound at the Vatican and featuring scores of flaming chariots, rolling hills, and pious shepherds in full-color woodcuts.

With typical Taschen aplomb, the catalog imagines a riot involving the characters in both books—"The naked protesters and the Protestants marched hand-in-hand to the Crossroads of the World where they staged their protest at the Taschen offices"—and calls the 1534 volume, which launched Protestantism, "the first bestseller in world history."

Sex and God don't mark the limit of the house's taste. The same catalog offers the latest installment of *All-American Ads*, this one on the 1950s: a huge, heavy tome of magazine advertisements where suburban moms swoon beside Frigidaires, and lantern-jawed, snap-brimmed dads earnestly pilot sedans. Despite a fascination with the goofy exuberance of American capitalism, fall's catalog leads with a book of Chinese propaganda posters, in which Chairman Mao appears as "the Communist superhero."

The scale of Taschen's books ranges almost as widely as its subject matter. A new line called Icons boils down everything from contemporary architecture to old travel posters to female genitalia into small books priced at nine dollars and ninety-nine cents. And the house is perhaps best known in publishing for democratizing the art book with its cheap volumes on Dali, Picasso, and twentieth-century photography.

Increasingly, Taschen also turns out projects like a gargantuan book on Muhammad Ali, an eight hundred-page compendium of photos and text that will retail for $3,000; one thousand "Champ Edition" copies will cost $7,500 and include a sculpture by artist Jeff Koons. In part because Taschen, unlike most publishers, has worldwide distribution, many copies of the book (called "GOAT," for "Greatest of All Time") are already spoken for, though they won't ship until spring. If "GOAT" has the same success as 1999's "SUMO"—the Helmut Newton volume   it won't grow old on bookstore shelves.

Early biz savvy

By the time he was twelve, Taschen was already a seasoned entrepreneur, with his own mail-order business selling comic books.

He was born in 1961 in Cologne, a large Rhineland city, Gothic in style, with a reputation for tolerance, mercantile savvy, and serving beers in small glasses instead of massive steins. The youngest of two doctors' five children, young Benedikt actually started shilling when he was eight, with a booth on the fringes of an art fair where he peddled his vampire drawings. "At the end of the fair, he had eight hundred deutsche marks in his pocket," says Veronica Weller, the publisher's personal assistant. "Which made him more successful than some of the artists inside the tent."

Taschen also developed a passion for American comic books. "I fell in love with this artist, Carl Barks," he says with gravity of the creator of Donald Duck. He loved "the psychology" of the comics as well as their Technicolor glow, so different from the prevailing grays of German culture.

"I learned so much about American capitalism, about all these big shots, Donald Duck and Uncle Scrooge. It was a major influence. I thought I would be the only one who was interested in this stuff."

On the contrary—as his mail-order company soon demonstrated. By eighteen, he had opened a store in Cologne called Taschen Comics and begun to publish his own.

In 1983, still in his early twenties, he teamed with a friend to buy forty thousand remaindered copies of an English book on the surrealist painter Rene Magritte and doubled their investment reselling them. With his new nest egg, Taschen published similar artist monographs, most priced under ten dollars. Tired of waiting for clerks to fetch art books from glass cases, he aimed to make his books as accessible as comics.

Angelika Muthesius, a Bonn native who had just earned her doctorate in art history, remembers going to the Frankfurt Book Fair in 1986. "I saw all the serious art publishers," she says, making the face of a long-suffering pedant. "It was too dry. Like, 'Don't touch me!' I was twenty-six, I wanted to have some fun. Even though I'd gotten a PhD, I was never an academic person. My fantasies were much more crazy. And I saw Benedikt's booth— they were young people, they were laughing, they were drunk."

Muthesius wrote to Taschen, asking for work, and within two months she was an editor in the Cologne office. A tall, thin, outgoing woman, she became the second Mrs. Taschen in 1996. (The publisher has three children from an earlier marriage.) More clearly embodying a mix of intellectualism and sexuality than her husband—she stood nude in a now notorious magazine ad while he sat beside her fully clothed—she edits books on art, design, and interiors.

Taschen Books experienced tremendous growth during the 1990s, beginning with the purchase of a three-story Cologne mansion, outfitted with Donald Duck door handles and pornographic photos, to serve as a new office. Taschen set his mind on world domination: As the decade wore on, communications technology made working in multiple cities possible, expanding his company's reach.

"In the last fifteen years," Taschen says, sitting in his Hollywood office below a Nazi-themed Mike Kelley painting, "art books have become an international market. Before that, you had a book's publisher in America, one in Spain, you had five different jackets, and so on. Our idea was to make it so we never sold any rights to anybody. Keep 100 percent control. I saw that the market wasn't Germany but the world. So we released each book with the same cover and look, under the same title."

Taschen also offered his artists unusual contracts, with a big payment upfront and no royalties. "There's not an artist alive who doesn't like getting a chunk of money," says William Claxton, the photographer of the 1950s West Coast jazz scene. "Instead of waiting for accountants to send you little checks over time."

The house's business style is unorthodox: It prints twenty thousand or more copies of most books, distributes them itself, insists stores take a minimum number of copies if they want a title and refuses to take returns.

"In cases where I've disagreed with a book's approach," says Glenn Goldman, owner of the Sunset Strip emporium Book Soup, "I'm almost always proven wrong. I thought the Newton book was beautiful, but I questioned whether it would sell at $1,500. It sold extremely well."

The company guards its financial information closely, but some estimates have sales quadrupling in the last decade, to about $40 million annually.

"We're a private company. We can do whatever we want," Taschen says. "That's why artists like to work with us. They're the most important ones. Any book has to represent the artist without any compromises."

Another area where Taschen doesn't compromise is books about sex, which are usually a bookstore's most explicit volumes. Some look at mores in the past—Taschen was into Victorian nudes years before the Brooklyn Museum—while others are contemporary and depict not soft-focus "erotica" but actual sex. Dian Hanson, Taschen's "sex editor," says every time she walks into Book Soup she sees publishers ripping off Taschen's work. "But they don't get it right, because they're not thinking with their groins."

Naked as a Jaybird, with a text connecting hippies to the German nudists of 1900, is one of Taschen's favorites. But he insists these books don't keep the ship afloat. "I only do the sex books because they're supported by the art books," he says, explaining that volumes about sex account for about 10 percent of sales.

"There's nothing wrong with sex," he adds, confused by American puritanism. "There's a lot wrong if you don't have it."

The new guy

When he first saw California, Taschen says, he half-recognized it from "Donald Duck" and reading Raymond Chandler and Charles Bukowski. In 1998, he bought the $1-million, flying-saucer-like, John Lautner-designed Chemosphere House off Mulholland Drive and, after renovation, began to live here part time.

An important aspect of Taschen's MO during his Los Angeles years has been to cultivate friendships with older artists—father figures like architecture photographer Julius Schulman and director Billy Wilder. The first book about film he put out was a $200 tribute to Wilder's *Some Like It Hot*. That was followed by volumes on Fellini, Kubrick, and other masters.

"Benedikt reminds me of an old-time Hollywood figure," Wilder told *Vanity Fair* in 2000, two years before his death. "A studio head, someone who is in firm command and has his hand in everything. And I know when I tell people that I know him, it is always a feather in my cap. He's very popular in Los Angeles—all the artists want to know him."

Claxton, another father figure, recalls dinners at the house with "an incredible group of people: Billy Wilder, a porn star, a few writers, someone who'd worked with Andy Warhol, saxophonist Benny Carter. After a semiformal dinner, the evening would burst into a dance party. Benedikt would play jazz and dance on the table. Everybody would dance, including his chef."

Despite the publisher's comfort in Los Angeles, the company's move here took many by surprise.

Says his assistant Weller: "That step was much criticized: 'This is a mistake. He will regret it.' 'It's a known fact that New York is where the media are, the intellectual and publishing worlds.' But LA reflects his interests much more than New York. He fits in much better here—he hates the noisiness, the rain, in New York, and doesn't like formality or conventions."

Still, a few months after the opening of the Los Angeles office, Taschen and Angelika separated. They have since divorced. That awkwardness—he now stays at a hotel off Sunset when he comes to town—and the consuming nature of the Ali book have made him scarce for the last year. (She continues to edit for the press and live in LA much of the year.)

His staffers attribute changes to Taschen—a "going native"—despite his limited sojourns in Southern California. They say he's tanner, more relaxed, into convertibles.

"His style of dress has completely changed," says Hanson, who came to the press after fifteen years at *Leg Show*, which she proudly calls "Benedikt Taschen's favorite men's magazine."

"He's more tropical. Benedikt has become quite buff and muscular recently, and I think that comes from lifting his own books."

His urge to make everything bigger and better probably can't go on forever, though. William Drentell, a small publisher in Connecticut, points out that the Italian art book publisher Rizzoli opened stores around the US during a period of expansion but recently retreated, laying off staff and closing all but a single outlet.

"It starts to be a little more like the movie business," he says. "If your blockbuster doesn't sell, it's a major loss."

No pigeonholes

Taschen's associates say that he keeps his finances to himself and that it's hard to guess what he's worth because of a lifestyle both extravagant and frugal. "One side is very glamorous because he's a jet-setter," says photographer Claxton. "He could be in Indonesia tomorrow and then at a party in Miami the next day."

"He's pretty thrifty in a lot of ways," says editor Heimann. "If he's gonna spend money, it's on art, or on Eames chairs or something."

Heimann says Taschen's favorite haunt in Cologne is a brewery dating from the nineteenth century that serves sausage and sauerkraut and where the bill comes on a coaster marked with a grease pencil.

People who know Taschen seem to agree on one thing: He's driven. Yet even his closest friends—and he inspires a powerful bond—have a hard time explaining that ambition.

"Oh, my God, it's unbelievable," Newton says. "I don't know what drives him. He puts an enormous amount of time and energy into it."

The Ali book is especially baffling. "I have my interpretation, but I don't want to share it," ex-wife Angelika says with a laugh. "Because what Benedikt puts into it, his energy, and money-wise, it's more than any book he's ever done. I think he's an obsessive person. When he goes for something, he goes for it."

Claxton sees Taschen as a Chandler-esque figure. "He's an amazing detective. He knows how to seek out people who have valuable and maybe obscure information on a subject. To me, that's his greatest talent."

Hanson says her boss is always racing to keep from falling into a rut, becoming predictable. "He reinvents almost as often as Madonna," she says.

"I think Benedikt, like most great men, is somewhat alienated from society. And he really doesn't care what other people want or like. He follows his own inner directives. We're doing a big *Playboy* book, for the fiftieth anniversary, and that was exactly Hefner's formula. He just did what he wanted, and he had absolute confidence that this was going to work."

Private eye, Madonna, Hef? Who is the real Benedikt Taschen?

"I want to have a happy life," he says. "You see, I am very simple-minded."

[*Los Angeles Times*, November 23, 2003]

MUSIC ON THE EDGE

ALL MUSIC CAREERS ARE RISKY. Becoming a chamber musician is riskier still. Instead of collecting a regular paycheck and following a conductor, a member of a chamber group enters a complicated partnership that promises musical freedom and the chance for a strong voice, but few other guarantees. The audience may be more dedicated, in thrall to a repertoire of unmatched intimacy, but it's definitely smaller.

Yet at an age   their early twenties—when many of their recent USC classmates are aiming for life in a symphony orchestra, and some of their generational peers are forming rock bands, Ben Jacobson, Andrew Bulbrook, Jonathan Moerschel, and Eric Byers are beginning to taste success doing something curiously in between.

Two violinists, a violist, and a cellist, together they make up the Calder Quartet. Their lives entail not only playing difficult music requiring extraordinary discipline but also some of the same creative tension and frequent travel (if not the groupies and trashed hotel rooms) as life in a rock group.

Second violinist Bulbrook, twenty-three, who holds an economics degree and often speaks in financial similes, compares the Calder to a small business. "I've heard orchestral playing likened to corporate life," he says, "versus chamber music, which is more entrepreneurial."

The challenges go beyond the economic. Peter Marsh, the USC music professor who first put the four together, says the most difficult trick for chamber musicians can be putting up with one another. "Some people say it has all of the disadvantages—and none of the advantages—of marriage."

To fans, chamber music has an intensity and human scale that orchestral music can't touch. In this view, it represents a composer's finest work: The small number of voices results in more purposeful expression than an eighty-piece symphony. And the proximity of audience to performer means the musical push-pull, the tension and release, of the players acquires an almost physical force.

Jacobson, twenty-three, is one of these true believers. "The repertoire is unparalleled," says the elfin first violinist, who loves Beethoven's knotty late quartets and Janacek's folksy small pieces. "There's nothing like it in other genres of music."

"It's also music that goes out on a limb," says Bulbrook. "Did Beethoven write anything more out of sight than the 'Grosse Fugue'?"

Despite their strange calling, the Calders—whose choice of mobile artist Alexander Calder as namesake hints at their playfulness—come across as fairly ordinary guys. They're all into pop or rap music; Byers, twenty-three, the soft-spoken cellist, once played drums in a reggae band and took a semester off from USC's Thornton School of Music to live in a van and rock-climb with a friend.

They see the jocks and rock fans they went to school with as their natural audience. They joke about finding a signature as good as that of the band Guided by Voices, whose lead singer guzzles beers onstage in a parody of rock-star excess.

Whatever lies ahead, the year just ended brought the group to a turning point. Last spring, all four graduated from USC. In the summer, they began a two-year residency at LA's Colburn School of Performing Arts, the institution's first, which offers them financial stability. In the fall, they made their New York debut, and now they have signed with a manager.

At the same time, their progress was shadowed by the illness of violist Moerschel's wife. In September, she succumbed to the cancer she had battled for several years.

So far, the Calders say, all this has made them a stronger unit.

But because chamber musicians' rapport, and their understanding of any given piece, tend to deepen with time, the life of such a group is a kind of endurance test. The longer and deeper the commitment, typically, the more sublime the music they can make.

"I've had sociologists just fascinated," says Marsh. "How can it possibly work?"

Down to business

It's the day after a concert at Colburn's Zipper Hall, and the Calders are in unusually relaxed moods. They're in Bulbrook's apartment, across the street from Colburn. Apart from an almost alarming cleanliness, it's a typical post-college pad: nothing on the walls, one plant, velvet Elvis, big TV, simple blond wood furniture that could have come from IKEA.

Bulbrook is making coffee for his bandmates, though he's clearly had enough himself. "The day after a concert, I'm so excited that I can drink coffee again that I go nuts," says the thoroughly wired violinist, who worries that his bow will shake on held notes if he tanks up before a performance.

This day they're discussing their new manager and considering which quartets to learn next.

A chamber group is defined by the pieces it plays, and certain quartets have a strong commitment to a single composer, era, or national tradition. The Calders go for Austro-Germanic mainstream with a bit of flair: Beethoven, Mozart, and Haydn, with the odd contemporary piece like a dark-hued Christopher Rouse quartet. They encore with a strange and difficult movement of Bartok's Fourth Quartet—a crowd-pleasing frenzy of plucking and strumming to rustic Magyar melodies.

At Bulbrook's, some of the Calders, decked out in jeans and sandals, have brought sheet music and are trying out various pieces. Byers has spent the last few months listening to all 68 of Haydn's quartets, and introduces one he's fond of.

"This is one I like to call Opus 64, Number 6," he says, slipping into Grand Ole Opry patter.

Bulbrook picks up the Southern accent: "It goes out to all the ladies in the house."

Throughout the afternoon, they'll run through pieces, rejecting some, taking to others. Though each has his preferences, minor disagreements usually turn into consensus without much trouble.

When talking business, they're serious but sometimes mischievous too.

"Hey!" shouts Jacobson, while looking over a page of halls their manager works with. "I don't see the Playboy mansion on this list of venues."

The Calders, though, are serious about chamber music. Their rehearsals involve assessing one another's strengths and weaknesses—from details like articulation and tempo to the general character of playing—but little shouting. Indeed, the life of a chamber quartet probably includes more listening than either talking or playing.

"I always view criticism as something that's not negative but aimed at the greater good," says Jacobson, who as the group's leader says he tries "to keep the diplomacy flowing."

"They have a commitment to what they're doing," says Ronald Leonard, the USC professor who coaches the group. "There are a lot of groups who get together, play well, but they don't plan to make this a major part of their life. It takes an unusual dedication to say, 'This is what's going to come first.'"

Besides a three-hour rehearsal each weekday, the Calders practice by themselves three hours a day. Two are taking a music theory class, and their residency requires them to lead sections within the Colburn's chamber orchestra. For the last few months, they've had a concert virtually every week, which can mean traveling to the South Bay or the northwest of France. When flying, Byers buys a ticket for his 230-year-old cello.

What really drives them is performing: They love the challenge of winning over a crowd.

"I think the chamber music audience in general is a little more informed," says Moerschel, twenty-four, "while with symphonic music, it's more of a social thing: get dinner and see a concert."

Even by the graying standards of classical music, chamber fans tend to be more gray, coming to the form only after years of listening. "It's definitely more subtle," the violist says. "Orchestral music is big and loud, and you've got someone waving his arms around."

In mid-December, a black-suited Calder Quartet played at the Los Angeles County Museum of Art. Even without waving arms, and with tension induced by a radio broadcast, they were able to bring much of the sizable audience to its feet.

Complex relationships

Like the music they play, the personal dynamics of a quartet are a delicate balance—the kind that can benefit rather than suffer from creative disagreement.

The Calders first got to know one another as friends, but they spend less time palling around now that the group has become a full-time job. Around Thanksgiving, they took a week off and didn't even meet for a friendly beer.

In a 1988 documentary about the Guarneri Quartet—a Calder favorite, esteemed for its warm romantic tone—the Guarneri players discuss how they maintain an appropriate degree of proximity after heavy touring and hours of brutalizing rehearsals. Partway through a tour, three of them arrive in Tampa, Fla., for a concert. When the fourth, violist Michael Tree, gets there, he's asked by the hotel concierge how close he'd like to be to his bandmates. "Put me in St. Pete!" he responds, referring to a city twenty-five miles away.

After observing the group's range of personalities—from swan to bulldog—negotiate, quarrel, and make up, it's clear that Tree is not really joking. But the founding Guarneris lasted from 1963 until 2001, making them the United States' longest-standing quartet with all original members.

Though its profile remains far lower than that of orchestral music, chamber music—music for small groups, with a single player to each part—predates symphonic music by roughly a century. Originally performed in the homes of aristocrats, often by amateurs, chamber music thrived in an era when musician and audience were not separate categories.

"The music was conceived to be performed in a small room where people are very close to you," Moerschel says. "You've got these bare-bones ensembles and pieces with an incredible depth."

"And a lot more pressure too," says Byers. "Because you're it, always. You can't just blend into a section. You're always exposed, and people always hear what you're doing."

In the early days, the audience was small to nonexistent: This was something people of a certain class did for fun, the way corporate executives play golf.

By the late eighteenth century, when the homes of wealthy merchants were displacing the salons of the gentry, chamber music began to take on its contemporary form as Haydn brought the string quartet to maturity.

Originally driven by a regal first violin with the other instruments accompanying, the quartet went on, as revolutions flared in North America and France, to parallel the move toward democracy: By late in Haydn's career, the best quartets demonstrated a dynamic interplay among the four instruments.

In the hands of nineteenth-century romantics like Beethoven, Schubert, and Brahms (whose small pieces Schumann called "symphonies in disguise") and in the rugged twentieth-century excursions of Bartok, Elliott Carter, and Shostakovich (who saved his private feelings about Stalinism for his quartets), chamber music deepened further.

For all the evolution, however, chamber music still carries an effete, aristocratic connotation, says UCLA musicologist Robert Fink. "It evokes people in wigs sitting around with candles," he says. "America has embraced the symphony orchestra, with its technological know-how and mass appeal. A large orchestra fits in better with a large country with a large middle class."

At the same time, chamber music has been—since the 1960s mini-malists—the area in which composers do their most radical work, and the Kronos Quartet, for one, has concentrated on risky music for young audiences as no orchestra could. Chamber music now is played in private homes, in churches, in rock clubs.

Despite the aesthetic triumphs of chamber music, the Calders felt as if they were going against classical music's very grain when they formed their group in 1998. "Teachers will even say, 'Let's face it, a lot of you won't ever have a solo career, so you'll be making your living playing in an orchestra,'" says Moerschel. "I had to tell people, 'No, this is what I want to do, even if I'm not going to make much money at it.'"

Something to rely on

In early November, the Calders played a luminous concert as part of an eleven-piece group at USC's Newman Recital Hall. The concert, of Bach's double and triple keyboard concertos, was so packed that people crowded the aisles and doorways to hear it.

Many in the audience, like the musicians, were assembled in honor of Eugenie Ngai, a pianist and USC doctoral student who had died two months before. She was also Moerschel's wife.

"I think it changed us all," the violist says now.

Three years ago, he had to go with the group to Colorado while Ngai—whom he married late in 2002—was hospitalized. "She insisted that I go. It was really hard. I was calling back and forth ten or twenty times a day. It was very hard to focus. It was difficult because the quartet really depends on me. If I was in an orchestra, they could just pick up someone else."

Of the four Calders, Moerschel is the most cautious, the least whimsical; even his smile has a hint of resignation. He describes his personality as fitting the viola—reserved, not show-offy. It's perhaps no coincidence that while the other Calders live downtown, he's half an hour away in Pasadena.

His sense of distance includes his handling of his wife's illness. "I didn't want to involve the quartet any more than I had to," he says.

"When she was in the hospital, we were debating, 'Should we just find a sub so John won't have to worry about this?'" Byers says. "But John was really adamant about wanting to play. He would just spend the night in the waiting room and rush home for a few minutes to get a nap" before or after rehearsal. "I was amazed at how dedicated he was to her—but also to the group."

"John kept an amazingly optimistic attitude the whole time," recalls Jacobson. "We never really knew the gravity of the situation; it was only when she actually died that we fully realized just how serious the whole thing was. We knew she was ill, but we always thought she was getting better."

When she was at her worst, last August, Moerschel had to ask the group to go to France with Peter Marsh subbing for him.

"They live somewhat carefree lives, and my life has been very full of worry and stress for the last few years," Moerschel says. "But I don't get nervous playing in front of people anymore. It's a reflection of what's happened. It put things in perspective.

"I don't know how it affected them," he adds. "But I know I've been very thankful to have the group to play in, because if I didn't, it would have been very hard to get myself to do things. I went on a trip with them to Chamber Music Sedona not long after Eugenie died, and that was a godsend for me. It was great for me to get out of LA and do something different."

Staying together

One of the biggest threats to any group is not bad times but unevenly distrib-
uted good times, especially if a member gets offers to perform as a soloist.
A whole group can collapse when a single player leaves. The London-based
Amadeus Quartet made a vow that if one player left, they would disband.
Forty years later, after the death of violist Peter Schidlof in 1987, they did.

To remain intact, the Calders plan to seek a residency to follow their
gig at Colburn—in this area or elsewhere. "Los Angeles needs a resident
quartet," the *LA Weekly*'s Alan Rich wrote after a Calder performance in
September, adding, "on the strength of this one hearing, the Calders are
worthy of consideration."

If they stay, they'll be following in the footsteps of groups like the Hollywood String Quartet, 1940s studio musicians who played with a telepathic
rapport, and the Angeles Quartet, a long-standing group that broke up in
2002, soon after recording all of Haydn's four-part works.

"What often happens," says MaryAnn Bonino, who's run the local
concert series Chamber Music in Historic Sites for three decades, "is that
groups go to New York and get major management. You'd think with the
Internet and so on you could run a career from anywhere. But it all boils
down to travel: If you want to go to Europe, you're better being in New York."

"At times, this feels out of place, because of Hollywood and everything,"
the Ohio-bred Byers says of pursuing a livelihood in LA "And California
is so new, compared to Haydn, or Europe. But we're proud of the fact that
we've stuck together in a place like this."

What's to keep individual Calders from straying once they taste the
glamour of soloing?

"I feel like the greatest repertoire is the quartet repertoire," says Jacobson. "You're still completely exposed and have the ability to make yourself heard like you would as a soloist. And in a quartet, you have the camaraderie all the time, the input from the others, that I think can keep you a little bit more grounded."

Earl Carlyss, a longtime Juilliard Quartet violinist and a Calder mentor, says it's important they keep their dedication.

"You should always be searching," he says. "You're never finished with this music. Some musicians feel, 'We've played it twice. We never want to bother with it anymore.' I've seen this and it's poison. This music is always a lifetime search."

[*Los Angeles Times*, January 4, 2004]

RETOOLING FORM AND FUNCTION

IT'S TEMPTING TO CALL ANY YOUNG COMPANY that works on a small scale the "garage band" of its genre—but in the case of one Echo Park architecture firm, it's almost literally the case. Benjamin Ball and Gaston Nogues—both scruffy, intellectually driven young designers—really work out of a garage: In a space filled with electric saws, lathes, and sanders and next to a home cantina that pokes out of a neighbor's house, they hack through plywood and dream up concepts as they blast Internet radio.

Unlike most young Los Angeles architects, they are rarely designing houses.

"There's a lot of work out there for innovative design that's not exactly architectural but that's architectural in its preoccupations and architectural in scale," says the blond, vintage-clad Ball. "Exhibition design, installations, events, sets. That's the wave we're riding now."

This kind of work allows them to retain more creative freedom than peers who are drafting shelter projects, says Nogues, a lanky, cap-wearing Argentine who once designed furniture for Frank Gehry. And that's a good thing: "We're both," Nogues says, "obsessive-compulsive control freaks."

Mavericks though they are, Ball, thirty-seven, and Nogues, thirty-eight, are part of a larger movement of young, tech-savvy designers who have skipped the traditional paths for Southland architects—a long apprentice-ship at a big firm or decades of designing homes, then the slow building of reputation in late middle age—and moved into an alternative path called fabrication.

This involves designing objects as small, and practical, as the prototype for a watch and as large, and whimsical, as a wide, funnel-shaped canopy of tinted Mylar meant to emulate a black hole that Ball and Nogues put together for an outdoor space in Silver Lake last summer. In the same spirit, there was the groovy bar-reception desk the firm Gnuform designed for a Beverly Hills cable TV station, and the serpentine exhibition design for "Dark Places," the current Santa Monica Museum of Art show, rendered by the globe-trotting architecture collective servo.

Their work, these breakaway architects say, isn't just about making products or museum pieces but defining spaces or designing new ways to construct familiar objects. It's a twilight zone between sculpture and architecture.

There have always been architects interested in breaking through the field's hierarchical structure, whether out of simple restlessness or to realize their own vision. What's new, says Charles Lagreco, associate dean of USC's architecture school, is a new wave of technology that is "transforming the field," and that allows some practitioners to control their work as well as their destiny.

The stars of this movement are mostly New York-educated designers in their middle thirties who came to LA and took advantage of the region's concentration of digital technology, Hollywood set facilities, and auto and aerospace technology.

Like nonconformists in any field, they sometimes express a disdain for their more conventional peers. Ball, a former set designer, points to fellow

SCI-Arc grads who landed jobs with big firms but have "taken about ten years to design anything that's an expression of their interests . . . There are people in our classes who are drafting toilets now."

While they differ in manner—the stocky, cigar-chomping Hernan Diaz Alonso resembles a mad scientist, servo's David Erdman is cerebral and hip, Gnuform's Heather Roberge is crisply academic and rail thin—they all talk about creative freedom, about sticking to work that's "research-based," about their fascination with unusual materials. They're also keenly aware of one another's work.

Not surprisingly, they are not all beloved.

"If you ask other architects about these people, they hate 'em," says Greg Lynn, forty-one, who taught many of the fabricators and remains a kind of older brother. "Hate 'em, hate 'em. 'They're self-promoting, using technology to get famous, have academic affiliations . . .' and so on. You hear complaints about them from the country-doctor-type architects. What's encouraging is that they haven't killed each other—they still remain friends and competitors."

Quicker out of the chute

Architecture may seem increasingly glamorous, even youthfully cool, to the culture at large, but most of the field's really successful practitioners are over fifty—in some cases well over. The years between graduation and late middle age can be a hard road, and the profession has a history of eating its young.

"There's this horrible thing that happens to an architect," says Jenna Didier, thirty-six, a willowy fountain designer based in Silver Lake. "They have all these wonderful, beautiful ideas. But they get out of school and go through a hazing process: It squelches their creativity and anything that was ever interesting about them."

To fill this awkward gap in an architect's traditional career path, Didier and thirty-three-year-old partner Oliver Hess, who exudes a monk-like calm, put on exhibits by some of these young designers at an outdoor space along Silver Lake Boulevard. She calls Materials & Applications, as it's known, a showcase for "the frustrated artist inside every architect." The first exhibit was by the fabricator Marcelo Spina, thirty-five, who teaches at SCI-Arc; the most recent was Ball and Nogues' Mylar vortex, "Maximilian Schell." (A new installation, "Here There Be Monsters!," involving water and a bamboo footbridge, went up last week at M&A's location at 1619 Silver Lake Blvd.)

M&A's space is not the only outlet for fabricators: Architects have been doing fabrication, one way or the other, for decades. (Gehry, whose rise to prominence came when he designed his own Santa Monica house in the late seventies, also worked in exhibition design.)

What's new is that the rise of digital technology, and the infrastructure of industry in place in the Southland, makes it a feasible way not just to channel creative energy but to build a career.

It's also allowed ambitious architects to reach outside the straight-line bounds of the form. "What in architecture seemed very alien was not so strange in the worlds of car design or movies or airplanes," says Diaz Alonso, thirty-six, who is best known for an almost science-fictional sculpture installed last year in the courtyard of New York's P.S. 1. (Fittingly, he grew up wanting to be a filmmaker and is interested in "the beauty of the grotesque.")

"I always thought architecture was about form and geometry, so this was a natural evolution for me," since digital fabrication is "not so much based on Cartesian order but on other rules—on motion and other things."

Another factor in the emergence of this band was the struggle of universities to keep up with increasingly important design software. "There was this gap in the academy," says Roberge, thirty-five, who runs South Pasadena's Gnuform with Jason Payne, thirty-four. And these younger architects stepped in "because there were not older, more established professors able to teach these emerging technologies."

Teaching earlier—most of these fabricators have positions at UCLA, SCI-Arc or Columbia University—not only frees up an architect to do noncommercial work but orients even a very young designer toward independence, she says. Old-fashioned dues paying, as an apprentice in a large firm, suddenly makes less sense.

So might the other most common route: forming a residential firm soon after graduation, which can ensnare even the most imaginative. Says Lynn: "To build up a small practice in LA is a real trap, because there are so many houses to build. Once you do twenty houses, you're a residential architect. And the museums don't call you. The concert halls don't call you."

That makes it hard, says Lynn, to get where most ambitious architects are trying to go. "It's most satisfying to have an effect on the public realm—deep down I think it's what every architect wants to do."

Los Angeles architects have typically defined themselves through residential architecture, and the house has long been used by auteurist architects here to create works of art. Richard Neutra, R. M. Schindler, and Charles and Ray Eames did much of their most distinctive work with single-family homes, and the most famous experimental series in LA history was the Case Study House project. That makes the flourishing of fabrication here, of all places, striking.

Erdman, who holds down the Santa Monica office of servo's far-flung design operation, sees his work in the lineage of risk-taking Southland architects Gehry, Thom Mayne, and Eric Owen Moss. "There's a legacy here of pushing traditions," he says, "innovating through the explicit resources of LA and finding other languages of architecture to play with. Traditionally that's been done through the house." But servo launched its reputation largely through gallery installations.

To Spina, a boyish, goateed Argentine native, Los Angeles is defined by "the lack of architectural history and conventions" that would inhibit these "new forms of making." The city, instead, he says, "could be more open to embracing those possibilities."

His work—all the way back to "Land Tiles," a twenty-four-by-sixteen-foot cast-concrete "micro-environment," with water running through it, that grew grass and moss over six months at M&A—in 2003—involves precision and letting nature take its course. The pieces were vacuum-formed, or shaped, at Warner Bros. film studio, a popular spot for the fabricators, and routed at SCI-Arc, where Spina teaches.

"I'm interested in using the most advanced technology," he says, "where you control every bit of geometry as well as [allowing for] the indeterminacy of the material."

And the Southland is a good place for it, he says, since artists or set designers have needed almost every conceivable material cut or shaped: The resulting local cottage industry has few parallels.

In some ways, fabrication has begun to replace another route to success for the young architect: competitions and journals. These are easy to get access to in New York and European capitals but harder in Southern California.

This distance from the architecture establishment can be an advantage. "Your career is more philanthropically guided on the East Coast," says Lynn. "But they *make stuff* out here."

Success still a gray area

At this point, the fabricators are just starting to build reputations outside the academy. Their firms are still quite new, and they have yet to get the big civic commissions that make an architect's name and fortune. Gallery installations can serve as seeds for similar, if more lucrative, commercial work, such as the exhibition space servo did for Nike on the Venice boardwalk. And most of these companies take some residential jobs if they find the right client. But some are still enduring lean months for the sake of creative freedom.

Both Lynn and USC's Lagreco compare these designers to the New York Five (which includes Peter Eisenman, Michael Graves, Charles Gwathmey, John Hejduk, and Richard Meier), a group of architects who exhibited together in 1969, shared some Corbusian principles and did some of their own construction to get work built.

Will these thirty-something fabricators become intellectual dilettantes, or will they have a real impact on the field and the city? It's too soon to tell for sure, but their importance in architecture education is not likely to change. "I think the need to keep young people in the academy to keep up with technology will persist," says Roberge, who knows just-graduated architects who already have teaching gigs.

Ball cautions that his peers have to overcome a fetishistic fascination with technology. Some young fabricators, he says, "are so computer-oriented they don't even know how to hold a hammer. A designer's 'hand' is always going to be interesting: Ten years ago there was a lot of techno on the rave scene that sounds terrible now because it was all made with digital tools. Now it's trending back."

Whether architecture trends back similarly or not, Lagreco calls the fabrication path a healthy development. "I feel it's quite within the tradition of architecture as a discipline," he says. "It might threaten certain kinds of established professional points of view—but ultimately it enriches and reinvents what we do."

[*Los Angeles Times*, March 19, 2006]

BOOM TIMES FOR THE END
OF THE WORLD

IN ONE, A THICK LAYER OF ASH COVERS EVERYTHING as a nameless man and his son push their cart through a shattered land of absolute silence and darkness without end.

In another, the world inexplicably floods, sending a watertight hospital full of sleep-deprived doctors and their young patients bobbing on the waves like a new Noah's Ark.

And in a third, the Manhattan Company dispatches a team of rogues from a mysteriously devastated Northeast to settle an untouched part of tidewater Virginia inhabited by a twenty-first century Pocahontas.

They're all recent or upcoming novels with literary heft: Cormac McCarthy's solemn and elegiac *The Road*, Chris Adrian's ironic-religious *The Children's Hospital*, and Matthew Sharpe's black-humorous *Jamestown*, respectively.

It's not just Mel Gibson, Feral House, and the *Left Behind* books anymore. Long the province of the paranoid left and Christian right, apocalypse has moved indoors, and it's going highbrow. Literary novels with end-of-the-world settings—these books and others by respected writers such as Daniel Alarcon, Michael Tolkin, David Mitchell, and Carolyn

See—are surging at the same time as serious filmmakers engage a subject most often left to B movies.

Based on P. D. James's 1992 novel, Alfonso Cuaron's well-received 2006 film *Children of Men* shows a world in which human fertility has died out and fascism reigns. Over the next year, Hollywood will release a slew of "class" films involving environmental destruction, among them M. Night Shyamalan's *The Happening,* and James Cameron's *Avatar,* in which the beleaguered planet Earth turns on its inhabitants.

The notion of apocalypse—the word is from the Greek for "the lifting of the veil"—has been with us, in various forms, for a long time. But it's still worth asking: What does it mean that the dream life of the richest, most scientifically advanced nation in history is troubled by nightmares of the end?

The simple answer is that the attacks of 9/11 and the Iraq war have brought a sense of unease and vulnerability to both artists and audiences. Growing worries about global warming and the greater visibility of the Christian right—Protestant fundamentalists, for whom the apocalypse is not metaphor, are thought to have swung the last two presidential elections—have brought the end of the world in from the shadows.

See, whose 2006 novel, *There Will Never Be Another You,* centers on chemical warfare, said that even more important was the fearmongering that followed 9/11. The worry over anthrax and other threats, she said, "lodged in a sick part of our unconscious. It turned something ordinary, like 'yellow cake' or opening a letter, into something that would kill you in a fearsome and disgusting manner."

Literary issues are also at play.

"I think to a certain extent it's a delayed reaction," said Steve Erickson, a novelist who edits the Cal Arts journal *Black Clock.* "It's been going on in popular culture for a while, whether with the Clash's *London Calling*," which imagines a nuclear attack on Britain, "or *Blade Runner*, which conveys a feeling that outside Los Angeles the rest of the world has kind of dropped off."

This new emphasis also has to do with a blurring of lines between literary and genre fiction, said Erickson. "Twenty years ago, there was still an insularity to a lot of fiction, especially work put out by the New York publishing houses. It was still doing Raymond Carver and that neorealist minimalist thing. It regarded the futurism that's kind of implicit in apocalyptic writing as kind of lowbrow."

Now, Erickson said, "there's a new generation of writers who are more involved with other things happening in the culture."

One of those writers is Matthew Sharpe, forty-four, whose second novel, *Jamestown*, comes out next week and has been getting strong early reviews.

His uncomfortably funny book was written from Wesleyan University, where he teaches, out of anxiety for the future as well as what he calls "frustration and rage" about recent US policy, he said. His bumbling settlers look for oil, food, and water in scenes meant to highlight our current short-sightedness. "One item in the writers toolkit I draw on a lot," he said, "is hyperbole, to intensify and exaggerate the situation."

His exaggerations come from historical models. When Sharpe started researching the 1607 Jamestown settlement, which was mercantile in inspiration, for his job advising middle school teachers, he "was fascinated by the sheer extremity and weirdness of it: 100 guys, and they were all guys, getting on a boat and coming to a continent they expected to be so narrow that a river would run through to the Pacific. And expecting to find, like the Spanish, gold in the ground. And then they got here and promptly started dying."

As he wrote, after the 2001 terrorist attacks and during wars in Afghanistan and Iraq, he saw parallels between English foreign policy of the seventeenth century and America's in the twenty-first. "This sense of exceptionalism, that we are the moral arbiters, that we know better than they do."

Brushing up on disaster

Sometimes the impetus for this kind of book is more idiosyncratic. Chris Adrian, thirty-six, was a medical student in the years he conceived of his well-reviewed *The Children's Hospital*. "It started out as a story about being stuck in a hospital day and night and not being able to get out. Sort of a typical story of residency," he said from his home in Cambridge, Mass.

"But after 9/11, a lot of new ideas moved in."

He was forced to rethink the book's tone, and his approach also became more concerted.

"I knew I couldn't set a story during a second flood without knowing something about the first one; I'd never read the Bible before." He found himself digging in deep to get what he calls a background in apocalypse. "There's a lot out there besides Revelation. Most of them involve a person who's had a vision that's mediated by an angel."

For a culture that doesn't like to talk about death, he said, the apocalypse may be a way to discuss the subject indirectly.

Adrian went so far into both mainstream and apocryphal books of the Bible that he's now halfway through divinity school at Harvard. "Though the difference between those books and mine," he cautioned, "is like the difference between a real mouse and Mickey Mouse."

The trick for a literary writer is to avoid the obvious, which may be one reason 9/11 has taken so long to show up in the serious novel.

"I think we're just sort of figuring out how to talk about it," said Erickson, whose next novel, *Zeroville*, comes out this fall. "It's all so immediate it risks becoming a cultural cliche before we even know what to do with it ... It took a while to write about Pearl Harbor, I think. James Jones' *From Here to Eternity* didn't come out until ten years after the attacks. The culture has to process these things."

Erickson himself felt the lure of apocalypse back when he was writing his first novel, in the early eighties, which he recalls as "a scary time" despite today's Reagan nostalgia. "*Days Between Stations* started out as a love story. And suddenly, about a quarter of the way through, I was burying Los Angeles in sand. I hadn't planned on doing that, and for about half an instant I resisted it, because I thought it was the kind of thing that happened in fantasy or science fiction."

His was not the only eighties novel set after Earth's destruction: Other notable examples included Denis Johnson's *Fiskadoro*, a mythic tale in which shards of pop culture are worshipped as religion, and Carolyn See's *Golden Days*, in which nuclear war is, for some laid-back Angelenos, good news.

Now, as then, the end of the world allows for a lot of powerful writing in a range of styles.

McCarthy's *The Road* is the bleakest of the bunch, written in raw, bitten-off utterances.

"By dusk the day following they were at the city. The long concrete sweeps of the interstate like the ruins of a vast funhouse against the distant murk. He carried the revolver in his belt at the front and wore his parka unzipped. The mummied dead everywhere ... like latterday bogfolk."

By contrast, James's *Children of Men* reaches Keatsian notes only hinted at by the film. "'The children's playgrounds in our parks have been dismantled ... Now they have finally gone and the asphalt playgrounds have been grassed over or sewn with flowers like small mass graves. The toys have all been burnt, except for the dolls, which have become for some half-demented women a substitute for children."

Adrian's protagonist in *The Children's Hospital* wonders if what she is seeing is real: "They were more likely experiencing some cruel experiment—black out the windows and blow in some aerosolized LSD and get Phyllis Diller to hide somewhere with a microphone and claim to be a sweet, creepy angel—than the end of the world."

The roots of these doomsday novels predate America's founding, according to Thomas Schaub, a University of Wisconsin professor who edits the journal *Contemporary Literature.*

These books, he said, resemble the jeremiads that Puritan ministers issued in the seventeenth century to awe-stricken audiences. "They preached the day of doom as a way of bringing the flock back to our original mission. 'The wrath of God is upon us, we have forgotten what America was supposed to be.' That's a fairly consistent dynamic in American history."

What's new, he said, is an increasing pace of change as well as an explosion of ways to bring that change to us. "The hyperawareness delivered by the media provides a sense of implosion, an immediacy, a sense of imminence."

This has led the latest wave of apocalyptic writing to have a different tone than the work of a generation or so earlier.

"In *Jamestown*, it's annihilation without the revelation," Sharpe said. "Certainly revelation is not visited on anyone in the novel. The settlers are really bumbling around, not knowing what the hell they're doing."

The work of William Burroughs, Robert Coover, Thomas Pynchon, and Norman Mailer—who credited fear of the bomb with the creation of the Beats and other subcultures—saw destruction as a chance to wipe out a corrupt order, "The System."

Instead of renewal, Schaub said, he picks up "a sense of real limits . . . and a kind of regret," from both his students and new fiction.

Have things really gotten worse? "This is the most uncertain time since the early sixties, since the Cuban Missile Crisis," said Erickson, "where it's difficult to have much confidence that things will turn out OK. If the times get any crazier, I think you're going to see more and more of this."

Said Schaub: "There's no question that the country is wealthy, but the middle class has declined since the seventies. There's a general sense of the intractability of our problems. The race problems, the religious problems, in the Middle East and in our country," and the limits offered by resources and the environment. "It's mind-numbing really."

Strikingly, given the dead-serious subject matter, some of these novels are genuinely funny. "You couldn't approach this with a straight face without seeming ridiculous," Adrian said.

Without humor, Sharpe said, "I think it would be unbearable to me as the person who has to sit there writing it every day for several years. I would pause from time to time and say, 'This is really grim, can I go on with this? Why am I writing this?'"

His answer ended up being that however nasty the subject matter, the novel and the future were important. "And I realized," he said, "I had to face up to it."

[*Los Angeles Times*, March 25, 2007]

DRAWN TO A DARK SIDE

OF THE TWO OXNARD-BORN BROTHERS who created *Love and Rockets*, the punk-era comic series that's arguably the genre's most influential work of its day, Gilbert Hernandez is widely considered the John Lennon figure—the driven, "serious artist," allergic to superficiality and attracted by ugliness as well as beauty.

But digging into dinner and joking about his childhood on a recent evening at a Valley bistro, he comes across as a well-adjusted, down-to-earth guy. It's hard to imagine him producing the kinds of characters and situations his three decades as a comics artist have led him to: the child who disappears during a solar eclipse, the father who's killed in prison fighting for a cigarette lighter, the lives full of hurt and sudden loss.

"I'm not a brooder," said the bearded and bespectacled Hernandez, fifty, in town for a recent appearance at Book Soup.

"But those dark thoughts come out when I'm drawing. Sometimes I'm criticized for sitting around and thinking of the worst things that happen to people. But that's only partly true."

His goal, he said, is always to create a compelling narrative, not just a catalog of horrors. "I do want it to be a story."

That talent has earned him a legion of fans, including the novelist Junot Díaz. "In a real world, not the screwed-up world we have now, he would be considered one of the greatest American storytellers," Díaz said.

"It's so hard to do funny, tragic, local, and epic, and he does all simultaneously, and with great aplomb."

Hernandez's latest work is *Chance in Hell*, the violent and perverse graphic novel about a vulnerable young girl found wandering in a city dump. When co-creators break up—Gilbert and his brother, Jaime, are still producing one *Love and Rockets* a year but have basically "gone solo"—their tendencies typically emerge full-blown.

At the risk of forcing the Lennon analogy, *Chance in Hell* is more Plastic Ono Band than "Imagine": It's raw and, at 120 pages uncut by Jaime's more hopeful worldview and more graceful style, seems like a lot of pain and peril in one place.

For Gilbert himself, who hopes to produce a one-off each year, the process was liberating.

"There's nothing harder than doing new stories with old characters," he said of his multi-generational cast, headed by the fiery and large-bosomed Luba, who mostly reside in the vaguely magic-realist Central American town of Palomar. "Even though these characters are part of me. But I can't do it anymore, after twenty-five years. While with *Chance in Hell*, I took the chance to deal with a character, all in one place, and say goodbye to her. It wasn't always easy, but it was freeing."

He's the kind of storyteller who's not afraid to overreach or miss completely. Douglas Wolk, whose new book, *Reading Comics*, considers the Hernandez brothers alongside other key figures, writes that Gilbert's comics "look like the work of an iconoclast—he's got the rough, wobbly line and a pervasive interest in grotesqueries, he highlights the wrinkles and flaws in everything he draws, and he's fond of one-off experiments in which he lets his id run wild on paper."

"Growing up with him, he was a normal kid," said Jaime Hernandez, forty-seven, who lives in Pasadena. "And he grew up to be a normal adult. But he's got certain demons. Gilbert's one of these artists who has to do what he does, or he'd die."

'On the high end of poor'

When Gilbert and his brothers were growing up in Oxnard in the sixties and seventies, comics were everywhere. They seemed to have the only mother in the nation's history who encouraged them to collect, and even revere, comic books rather than throwing them out. They developed a special fondness for adventure comics, Milton Caniff, *Dennis the Menace*, and the superhero auteur Jack Kirby.

"We were poor, but just on the high end of poor," Hernandez recalled. "Poor enough to know it, and poor enough not to have things, but not enough for it to ruin our future selves."

The budding Bros. Hernandez—including Mario, fifty-four, who contributed to a few issues and brought an issue of *Zap* comics into the house—were ravenous in their pursuit of visuals in all forms. "It got to the point where we'd look at a magazine, and if one of the pages was an advertisement for Uniroyal Tires, we'd try to figure out who the artist was."

The brothers got drawn into punk rock, playing in a few now-forgotten bands and designing fliers and album jackets for bands such as Dr. Know and Black Flag. They were also serious film fans: Gilbert today loves the visual storytelling of silent films, as well as directors including Fellini,

Howard Hawks, and Kurosawa, and he runs Turner Classic Movies in the background while he draws.

About the same time, the brothers started *Love and Rockets*, which was, early on, a mix of science-fiction stories and tales of the SoCal punk scene. While their work appeared in the same issues, the brothers soon found their own directions, with Jaime developing stories of two punkettes and a female wrestler and Gilbert creating an extended family in Central America that's been compared to the works of García Márquez.

It was also clear that while Jaime had the smoother, more effortless drawing style—"he'll draw in his sleep," his older brother said—Gilbert was the more sophisticated storyteller of the duo.

Perhaps because their father had died when they were young, the main characters are almost all women.

The comic came from what Gilbert describes as "a mixture of things we heard happening to people, overhearing conversations of adults talking—when the adults don't think you're listening—things we saw in the paper and on the news, and a lot from films." His literary influences, which he said include *The Great Gatsby* and some novels of Carson McCullers, are more limited.

Gilbert's work, Wolk writes, captured the tensions of post-punk Los Angeles, where the strains "of race and class and sex and language and culture were insupportable and about to erupt into flames."

It's not hard to track the influence of the series, which served as a bridge between the sixties underground and the world of today, inside the comics subculture. Probably the most respected comics artist under forty, Adrian Tomine of the *Optic Nerve* series, is lavish in his praise of Los Bros Hernandez.

The current reissues of the books in oversized trade-paperback form on Fantagraphics is only likely to increase the exposure. But the stories resonated outside the comics ghetto as well: When three former members of the gloomy English band Bauhaus started a new group in 1985 they took the name Love and Rockets. And Díaz, the author of *The Brief Wondrous Life of Oscar Wao*, began reading the series in the eighties and never stopped. Díaz praises Gilbert's ability to write about Latin America without cliché, sentimentality, and folkloric overdose.

"For those of us who are writing across or on borders, I honestly think he was, for me, more important than anyone else. The stories he was writing on Palomar were recognizable to me, who grew up in the Third World, in a way that made everything else seem shabby and familiar. And his eye is stupendous."

Hernandez appreciates the acclaim *Love and Rockets* has drawn and the growing respectability of comics. But this hasn't made it any easier to make a living as an independent comics artist, and he lives in Las Vegas with his wife and daughter largely, he said, because he couldn't afford to buy a house in Los Angeles.

In harm's way

Soon after starting *Love and Rockets*, while still living in Oxnard, Hernandez and a friend met a boy of nine or so who insisted they give him a ride. The kid sat in the back seat, playing with an army tank and talking a mile a minute.

At the time, they thought it was funny. But looking back, Hernandez realized how vulnerable kids are. "He was lucky he picked the right guys; we were the last ones to give him trouble." The new book,

Chance in Hell, takes an innocent and puts her in what he calls "a more harrowing setting."

Walking around for years with ideas that only gradually develop into full-blown stories is typical for Hernandez's way of working. But some things have changed since the days of *Love and Rockets.*

"In the old days, it was like I was writing the Great American Novel: I only worked when the muse came; I couldn't force it. Now I know you can do a lot of boring, technical stuff while you're not inspired . . . so I don't waste time."

And these days, he said, he's not afraid to be indulgent and admits that much of his recent work is "near ragged. These days I make the mistakes. Because there's an energy to the way a filmmaker or artist or writer works at the beginning."

As for Vegas, he still seems baffled by the Strip: "Once in a while I'll take a trip there with friends and go, 'Oh, yeah, this is where I live.'"

But his attraction to larger-than-life-characters in his comics may explain it in part.

"The professional fraud—the blowhard—has always fascinated me. As a storyteller, I've always liked the good lie." He's always been interested in professional wrestlers, as well as outrageous characters such as Liberace and the schmaltzy hosts of old horror films.

"People say, 'That's not true.' But I don't care—I'm in this world where the story is enough for me."

[*Los Angeles Times,* October 7, 2007]

HIGHBROW. LOWBROW. NO BROW.
NOW WHAT?

IT WAS ONLY FIFTY OR SO YEARS AGO that critics and intellectuals were busy constructing—and redrawing, and shoring up—hierarchies about what kinds of culture were good for us and which ones were bad.

Literary man Dwight Macdonald wrote a famous essay about "Masscult and Midcult"—both, he said, were degrading real, traditional High Culture. Art critic Clement Greenberg, in an influential essay about modern painting, looked at "Avant-garde and Kitsch," championing the former as essential to the human spirit and denouncing the latter as tinder for a fascist revolution.

But judging from my recent conversations with a handful of literary and intellectual types—the heirs, you could say, to the Macdonald/ Greenberg tradition—we live, today, in a pleasingly hierarchy-free, almost utopian cultural world. Most people I know share my disparate taste, enjoying *South Park* alongside Franz Schubert, the crisply plotted novels of James M. Cain as well as the philosophically searching films of Antonioni.

Do guilt or shame still play a role in shaping people's taste? The answer was a unanimous "no." What I found instead when I asked my posse what culture they were consuming this summer was a sense of good feeling, an expectation of openness—a lack of angst all around. Writer Michael Chabon, in an interview, even said he hates the very phrase "guilty pleasure."

"My reading in general is kind of heavy and pretentious," said *New Yorker* classical music critic Alex Ross, who favors modernist literary masterpieces. "But when I go to the movies, I love to see bloated Hollywood blockbusters. I never worry too much about the category that those experiences fall into."

"I'll probably go see *Hellboy II*," said the unimpeachably smart *Salon* book critic Laura Miller. "I like to see popcorn movies in the theater."

Pico Iyer, the eminent Japan-and-California-based travel writer, told me: "One highlight of recent summers for me was *Nacho Libre*; I saw it in a packed house on opening night and subsequently hurried to see it again, so carried away was I by Jack Black's impromptu hymn." Like a true twenty-first century man, Iyer likes to mix it up: This summer, his favorite has been *4 Months, 3 Weeks and 2 Days*, a grim Romanian art-house film (now on DVD) unlikely to be remade with Jack Black.

Not that it matters. "To me, high and low, guilt and innocence, masscult and midcult are as out of date now as East and West and old and new," said Iyer, who thinks globalism and the Internet have shuffled all the decks. "Many of the more interesting artists today, from a Salman Rushdie to a Sigur Rós, blur the distinctions in all kinds of ways 'til we don't know, exhilaratingly, if we're being elevated or entertained."

Miller was more sober but no less decisive: "There are still some people who are snobs about it," she said. "But they are so few and they don't have much influence on anyone but other snobs."

Fast-tracked freedom

How, then, could this melting of the hierarchies have happened so quickly and so completely?

Ross thinks his own listening—from Messiaen to Missy Elliott to Miles Davis—is pretty typical these days. "The most natural state is to have this curiosity and openness," he said, describing "a deep-seated American impulse. It was only in the twentieth century when people really tried to organize and divide different art forms off from each other."

Ross is fond of a scene that begins Lawrence Levine's *Highbrow/Lowbrow*, which describes Shakespeare performances on the nineteenth century American frontier. "There were scrambled programs," Ross said, "with a Rossini aria, then a vaudeville pianist, and then a movement from a string quartet, and then dancers, and then something from Shakespeare." That kind of mix, he said, "is very deeply rooted culturally," and today's eclecticism is just a return to the way things were before culture became sacred.

Novelist and Los Angeles magazine film critic Steve Erickson thinks the ice broke more recently. "Mass media, as much as anything else, has broken down the distinction between high and low," he said. "One of the reasons the Beatles took over the world was they came along at a certain point on the timeline," when they could appear on *The Ed Sullivan Show*, show up in magazines, and record songs that would play all over the world with a then-unheard-of speed. Thanks to their interest in classical and experimental music, they made strict highbrow/lowbrow divisions look creaky: With 1966's *Revolver* album alone, said Erickson, "The Beatles obliterated those distinctions."

Other distinctions are melting away as well. Formerly "uncool" musicians—psychedelic cowboy Lee Hazlewood, for instance, who died last summer—have become very cool today "because people have gone back to listen with fresh ears and without those cultural biases," Erickson said. "Kids today can see something on YouTube and get into it without looking over their shoulder."

But it's taken awhile for other perceived bastions of the culture to catch up. "One of the areas that lags behind the rest of the culture is literature," Erickson said, "with the *New York Times* perpetuating those high/low distinctions," in the attention it gives to realistic, purportedly "literary" fiction over genre works rooted in fantasy, horror, or pulp traditions.

This may be, but Miller, who writes often for that hidebound *Times*, doesn't think literary types worry all that much about these categories. They don't even consider pulpy work a guilty pleasure anymore. "I think most people are so proud of themselves for reading anything," she said, "that they don't make a huge distinction between high and low."

Instead, they feel guilty about things that seem to them morally reprehensible or utterly mindless.

"What people feel sheepish about is that they watch 24 and can't stop . . . It's so politically repellent, but you can't stop watching. As opposed to something that is just fluff. If I read something like a chick-lit book, I don't think I'd feel guilty. Who really feels guilty about fluff anymore?"

Americans, she said, began to see reading as "morally improving" about the time radio and movies began to dominate leisure time, and the arrival of television in the fifties made reading seem more virtuous still. As reading has been moved aside by the Internet and everything else, its connection to virtue has only increased.

Restoring some value

I wonder sometimes if we may have succeeded too well in getting rid of distinctions, though. It's hard for me to avoid a low-grade worry that we're losing our ability to recognize quality itself.

"What we seem to have nowadays is more of a hierarchy of media," said Iyer, "whereby, for example, dance, classical music, opera, and even theater and books, all of which commanded their own sections in *Time* magazine only a generation ago, are now regarded as lofty and remote subjects for only a handful of connoisseurs." Those pages, he said, are "given over now to a Britney watch or extended investigations into the new iPhone."

Instead of feeling guilty about reading pulp novels, he said, we worry that we've become "elitist" if we go see chamber music or jazz. "The culture as a whole seems to have decided which arts are elitist and which ones popular, and so made some people feel guilty to be watching European movies (otherwise known as art-house stuff) or to be reading novels not likely to be turned into screenplays."

Having some standards seems more and more important in a time when the traditional arts have lost a bit of their prestige, some of their audience, and all of their monopoly on perceived quality. As silly as the chaste, Victorian tones of the literary and high culture worlds could be in their heyday, we need a certain amount of seriousness in our lives. At least I do. If the marketplace is left entirely unfettered, we'll lose a lot of what we consider valuable—not just J. S. Bach and John Coltrane but shows such as "Deadwood" and non-chain bookstores.

In California, among the least traditional of states, we have an unusual perch. For a long time, it has had a more flexible sense of what was valuable than Eastern elites did. But California became bound up in tyrannical ideas of hipness as well as a Cult of Now. "The West Coast became a concept unto itself," Erickson said. "And things that didn't conform to that were dismissed as passe."

The great twenty-first century work seems to me to merge this promiscuous blend of pop styles with a rigor and discipline that comes from the old-school approach to serious art. So I don't just mean, say, the exuberant, 1990s-style high/lowisms of Quentin Tarantino and Beck, whose films and music, respectively, are wonderful but driven by, let's face it, an adolescent sensibility. (I'm leaving poignant, mature work such as Beck's *Sea Change* and Tarantino's *Jackie Brown* out of this.)

What I'm talking about—what I hope the demise of rigid hierarchies is leading us to—is a flowering of work that draws on the whole range of culture but with a genius of structure and sophistication as well: novels such as David Mitchell's *Cloud Atlas*, from 2004, which merges a South Seas adventure story with a seventies-style corporate thriller with a science-fiction tale into an intricate whole, or Junot Díaz's *The Brief Wondrous Life of Oscar Wao*, which rightly won this year's Pulitzer Prize for its combination of trash-talking, comic book love, and a very serious Dominican history lesson.

It's what I expect to find when I see *The Dark Knight*, which, let's not forget, was made by Christopher Nolan, an outsider (and literature student) whose first masterpiece, *Memento*, was a bizarre personal vision made with very limited connections to the Hollywood mainstream.

I'd dig those any time, any season.

[*Los Angeles Times*, July 27, 2008]

THE NOVEL THAT PREDICTED PORTLAND

SOMETIMES A BOOK, OR AN IDEA, CAN BE OBSCURE and widely influential at the same time. That's the case with *Ecotopia*, a 1970s cult novel, originally self-published by its author, Ernest Callenbach, that has seeped into the American groundwater without becoming well known.

The novel, now being rediscovered, speaks to our ecological present: in the flush of a financial crisis, the Pacific Northwest secedes from the United States, and its citizens establish a sustainable economy, a cross between Scandinavian socialism and Northern California back-to-the-landism, with the custom—years before the environmental writer Michael Pollan began his campaign—to eat local.

White bicycles sit in public places, to be borrowed at will. A creek runs down Market Street in San Francisco. Strange receptacles called "recycle bins" sit on trains, along with "hanging ferns and small plants." A female president, more Hillary Clinton than Sarah Palin, rules this nation, from Northern California up through Oregon and Washington.

"*Ecotopia* became almost immediately absorbed into the popular culture," said Scott Slovic, a professor at the University of Nevada, Reno, and a pioneer of the growing literature-and-the-environment movement. "You hear people talking about the idea of Ecotopia, or about the Northwest as Ecotopia. But a lot of them don't know where the term came from."

In the seventies, the book, with a blurb from Ralph Nader, was a hit, selling 400,000 or so copies in the United States, and more worldwide. But by the raging eighties, the novel, along with the *Whole Earth Catalog*, seemed like a good candidate for a time capsule—a dusty curio without much lasting impact.

Yet today, *Ecotopia* is increasingly assigned in college courses on the environment, sociology, and urban planning, and its cult following has begun to reach an unlikely readership: Mr. Callenbach, who lives in Berkeley, California, and calls himself a "fringe, sixties person," has been finding himself invited to speak at many small religious colleges. This month, the book's publisher, Bantam, is reissuing it.

"For a while it seemed sort of antique to people," said Mr. Callenbach, a balding and eerily fit man of seventy-nine, sitting in his backyard, which he was converting into a preserve for native plants. "They said the book is 'very Berkeley' and all that. But now that you go out into America and young society, it apparently doesn't seem that weird to them at all."

When he began working on his novel, Mr. Callenbach was a middle-aged editor of science books at the University of California Press. His marriage was crumbling, and he despaired over what he saw as an endangered environment. He spent three years writing the book, sending each chapter to scientists to make sure the science held up. Then the real work began.

"It was rejected by every significant publisher in New York," Mr. Callenbach said. "Some said it didn't have enough sex and violence, or that they couldn't tell if it were a novel or a tract. Somebody said the ecology trend was over. This was New York, circa 1974. I was on the point of burning it."

But he cobbled together money from friends—"I think they wrote me checks out of pity for my poor, about-to-be-divorced state"—and printed 2,500 copies. The first printing sold, as did the next, and after an excerpt in *Harper's Weekly*, Bantam decided to publish *Ecotopia*.

The author now calls it "a lucky little book."

But not a classic book, the kind taught along with Herman Melville in American literature classes. Set at what seems to be the turn of the twenty-first century, and told through the columns and diaries of a reporter from the fictional *New York Times-Post*, the novel is not especially literary. Its characters are flat; its prose—well, call it utilitarian. And the plot, in which the narrator drops his skepticism and settles into Ecotopian life, thanks in part to a love interest, lacks sophistication. And yet the book has managed to find its place in the here and now.

Alan Weisman, author of last year's acclaimed *The World Without Us*, a nonfiction chronicle of the planet after the departure of the human race, said the book was ahead of its time. Environmental writing in the early 1970s was not especially concerned with shortage and sustainability, he said. "A lot of it was about preserving beautiful areas and beautiful species."

In fact, like other important environmental books, the novel's impact may be lasting. Writing has a special place in the environmental movement—"a literature with measurable effects," wrote Bill McKibben, in the introduction to *American Earth: Environmental Writing Since Thoreau*, a new anthology. John Muir's essays and books about the Sierra Nevada gave the country national parks, just as Bob Marshall's writings about forestry led to the Wilderness Act, which has protected millions of acres of federal land.

So what has *Ecotopia* given us?

A great deal, thinks Professor Slovic of the University of Nevada, including the bioregionalism movement, which considers each part of the country as having a distinct ecological character to be cultivated. The green movement's focus on local foods and products, and its emphasis on energy reduction also have roots in *Ecotopia*, he said. In fact, much of Portland, Oregon, with its public transport, slow-growth planning, and eat-local restaurants, can seem like Ecotopia made reality.

"People may look at it and say, 'These are familiar ideas,'" Professor Slovic said, "not even quite realizing that Callenbach launched much of our thinking about these things. We've absorbed it through osmosis."

Daniel Brayton, who teaches English and environmental literature at Middlebury College in Vermont, plans to teach *Ecotopia* in his utopian fiction class. He sees the book's genius as its "big-picture environmental thinking," successfully predicting the big issues of today. "Callenbach got that right," he said. "He's looking at the total physical health of the social body."

Ecotopia has its critics. Feminists attacked it for its ritual war games, in which men don spears to work off their "natural" aggression, dragging women into the woods to celebrate. (Mr. Callenbach said he was influenced by the anthropologist Margaret Mead, and her idea that the sexes express aggression differently.)

Some were made uncomfortable by the way black people were excluded from Ecotopian society: most live in Soul City, which is less affluent and green than the rest of Mr. Callenbach's world. The author said he was reflecting black nationalist ideas of the time, as well as an early seventies skepticism about integration. "I probably would write it quite differently at this point," he said.

Mr. Brayton of Middlebury sees "a deep conservatism to the book," where categories like race and gender are unalterable. "In academia we call that essentialism."

Over the years, Mr. Callenbach's readership has changed, as hippies and New Agers have been joined by churchgoers. The author often visits St. Mary's College of California, a Catholic school near Oakland. *Ecotopia* is required freshman reading at the Presbyterian-affiliated Muskingum College in rural Ohio. And it's part of the curriculum at the University of San Francisco, a Jesuit institution.

Mr. Callenbach hopes the book will resonate among the greening edges of an evangelical movement. But the novel's relatively free sex and liberal politics may limit that readership. Susanna Hecht, a professor of urban planning at the University of California, Los Angeles, sees it as a counterpoint to Thoreau's more austere *Walden*.

"*Walden* is very Protestant," she said. "'This is pagan, with a Zen relationship to nature."

But to Mr. Callenbach and many of his fans, *Ecotopia* is a blueprint for the future.

"It is so hard to imagine anything fundamentally different from what we have now," he said. "But without these alternate visions, we get stuck on dead center."

"And we'd better get ready," he added. "We need to know where we'd like to go."

[*New York Times*, December 12, 2008]

WILL ANY BAND EVER BREAK UP?

THE THICK SCENT OF EUCALYPTUS AND POLLEN DRIFTS upward from a downtown Los Angeles flower shop to an upstairs rehearsal space: The five-piece band Spain, on a hot July night on a dodgy street, are launching into "It's So True," a brooding early number, following it with "Ten Nights" and "The Only One." Intricate, understated lines coil from the lead guitar while the drummer plays brushes, jazz-style; the rhythm guitar summons the Velvet Underground's spare, eerie third record, and in some of the structures you can hear the ghost of fifties country, thanks to leader Josh Haden's family roots in Missouri's Ozarks.

A good Spain song is like falling into a trance: It's a blend of disparate, vibrato-rich sounds that, when played right, sounds inevitable. It's also a sound very few people have heard lately: This band broke up more than a decade ago.

"We've kind of been in deep freeze," says Haden, a reticent guy in clear-framed glasses who seems energized by the chance to talk about the group again. After the band had seen some success in the 1990s—the song "Spiritual" covered by Johnny Cash on *Unchained*, a song in a Wim Wenders movie, a signing to DreamWorks that ended up unconsummated—they drifted apart. Haden quit music, enrolled in a fiction-writing program and was dragged into a low-key solo career by Dan the Automator. But when he spoke to fans, one thing was clear: "The feedback I got was that people wanted Spain to record a new album."

None of the four other current members were part of the original group—one heard Spain's ethereal debut album in his father's car stereo during road trips. But as the band moves through its set, they sound like they've been together for ages: Audiences in the United States have not heard much from these guys lately, but they're just back from a three-week tour of Europe that involved playing packed clubs from Norway to Italy, and headlining a 3,000-person festival in Germany.

Rock reunions have been going on for many decades now, but seem to be picking up in frequency as rock's history gets more crowded with the rubble of busted-up bands. Simon Reynolds has pointed out, in his perceptive book *Retromania*, that popular culture has become addicted to its own recent past. Reading the music magazines is a bit like walking down a city street and seeing someone in a Mohawk, another in a Carnaby Street blazer, another in grunge flannel.

At the same time, the bonds that cause people to form, and stay together, in bands can be both strong and intimate—as complex and powerful as a marriage—and sometimes the old ties reassert themselves. Australia's Go-Betweens reunited in 1999 and produced three albums that were as melodic and charming as their original work, until the sudden death of co-leader Grant McLennan in 2006. But anyone who's ever drunkenly fallen in bed with a former mate or spouse knows that reunions are fraught with peril.

Many of them have been embarrassing or pointless, whether the Eagles reuniting in 1994 (and several times since) for another mega-tour, or this year's much-hyped Van Halen reunion, which sputtered when the band canceled more than 30 shows amid reports that they'd been "arguing like mad." Even the Beach Boys—for all the death, mental illness, and bad blood in the past—are back together, sort of. The Monkees are back on the road just weeks after the death of Davy Jones. The Jackson Five reunited to tour without their most talented member—Michael.

There was a sense, at least, that bands from the alternative and indie worlds—heirs to the ideology of punk—would not duplicate the pattern of these never-say-die AOR heroes. "The idea was that arena rock sucked, and that we were gonna make it different," says Ira Robbins, founder of the *Trouser Press Record Guide*. "We live in a world with an over-glut of everything. There are very few bands that have not overstayed their welcome. I'm in favor of bands who stop while they're still good—there are plenty of other things to do with your life, other bands to be in."

Still, some of alternative music's leading lights—Pavement, the Pixies, My Bloody Valentine, the Jesus and Mary Chain, Codeine, and Archers of Loaf, for instance—have reunited for bracing tours over the last few years, without recording new songs or giving a sense that they've necessarily become working units again.

But several other groups from alt-rock's past are not only playing out again, they're releasing albums of new material. Some of them—alongside Spain, Southern jangle-poppers the dBs, New Jersey's ecstatic minimalists the Feelies, and Boston's pioneering noise-punks Mission of Burma—appear to be hitting a real second wind.

This pileup of revivals arrives at a time in which rock musicians last longer than they did in the fifties or sixties: It's as if the live-fast-die-young model has been replaced by the kind of longevity more typical of blues or country musicians. It's especially true for solo artists: Leonard Cohen—born before Elvis Presley—remains a vital touring and recording act despite the over-covering of his song "Hallelujah." Even Keith Richards, who has called a rock career as long as his uncharted territory, has survived his ravages.

Indie rock—dating back to, say, the emergence of "college radio" bands like the Smiths and R.E.M.—now has a three-plus-decade history, and a self-consciousness about it that includes anniversary reissues, concerts devoted to a single iconic album and . . . reunions that aim to recapture a "cultural moment," like Pavement or the Stone Roses.

Bands, of course, get back together for as many reasons as they break up. For all their differences, what these four groups share is that they didn't last long enough to exhaust themselves artistically. They also never got big enough for a spectacular self-destruction. And there is less pressure, financial and legal and otherwise, on their reunions than on, say, the Quadrophenia tour by two of the Who's four original members.

"We *really* were not popular when we were around the first time," says Mission of Burma's singer/guitarist Roger Miller. "People were really confused by our concerts. I remember playing a show in Cleveland, and it was just *dead silent* between songs. We could get gigs the first time around; people just wouldn't show up. We became famous for losing clubs money."

Burma, whose strong body of work since coming back together in 2002 has helped to make post-punk reunions respectable, broke up after only a single LP and some other recordings because Miller feared for his hearing. (The band's latest album, *Unsound*, came out in July.)

"We died in a very weird way," the guitarist says now. "We didn't have drug problems, we didn't hate each other, we weren't spent creatively—so it was easier to pick up again."

In Burma's case, they had turned down numerous offers—most driven by a sense of the group's long-term influence—to tour again. "Sometimes the money was really good. But we'd say, 'No, that would be stupid.'" The only way they could see doing it, he says, would be to go onstage and play cards.

But the offer to reunite for two shows in New York—soon after their inclusion in Michael Azerrad's indie-rock chronicle, *Our Band Could Be Your Life*—led to a performance at 2002's All Tomorrow's Parties. (That history-conscious English rock festival, along with California's Coachella, has instigated many reunions.) And soon they were in business again. Along with bigger halls, including 1,000-seat theaters, they played to 20,000 at Coney Island's Siren Fest.

"People's response was that it was like we had stopped in March of 1983 and picked up in April of 1983," Miller says. "Like we picked up where we left off."

For Peter Holsapple—one of the two singer-songwriters behind the dB's, a band that remained obscure despite its uncommon tunefulness and role in sparking the R.E.M. revolution—it was all for the sake of the song.

Holsapple has worked with fellow dB Chris Stamey—who left the band for a solo career after its second record—on several occasions since, and sometimes they'd start to wonder. "We tried to imagine how to treat the songs best. We had this feeling that they would sound better with Will (Rigby) and Gene (Holder) on drum and bass. We'd always been friends anyway—when you grow up together and have known each other since you were eight years old . . . The idea made sense."

Until a few shows in Chicago in 2005, though, the whole band had not played together since Reagan's first term. Several of the songs on their new album, *Falling Off the Sky* (check out, for instance, "Far Away and Long Ago"), are among the year's most perfect pop. Holsapple says they worked hard on the production—with Scott Litt and Mitch Easter—to make the album sound timeless.

Like a lot of the successful reunions, they're seeking a synthesis of old and new. "It's the same as picking up a conversation with people we've known for a long time," says Holsapple. The dialogue can involve familiar topics, but also new excursions. "I've been in a whole other band [roots combo the Continental Drifters] and Chris has recorded a lot of records as producer." (Rigby has played bass with Matthew Sweet and Steve Earle; Holder has produced Yo La Tengo and Luna.)

"I think there are people who get back together for the cash," he says. "But other bands still like being together, and still have something to say."

Some of the most beloved bands of the eighties alt-rock era became casualties of the indie boom that followed—the Nirvana era's bet that bands at home in small clubs could suddenly be pushed into expensive studios and larger tours. "The 'next level' wasn't really that comfortable for us," says Feelies singer/guitarist Glenn Mercer, explaining that the economics of signing to a major were hard on the group. "There were more people in the crew than in the band."

But over the post-breakup years, as he and fellow guitarist Bill Million, who'd lost interest in music and effectively ended the group with a sudden move to Florida in 1991 to work at Disney World, spoke from time to time, the idea of getting back together occasionally came up.

And then one day, when Sonic Youth was booked to play a show in New York's Battery Park, SY guitarist Thurston Moore's thoughts went back to a band whose crazed strumming had floored him when he was a young man. "I had this fond memory of the Feelies always playing on American holidays," Moore told the *New York Times*. "I thought, 'Why don't we get the Feelies? Do they exist?'"

Two shows at Hoboken's legendary Maxwell's, which sold out almost instantly, and other New York-area gigs proved the group's devoted following—which still argues as to whether the spikey *Crazy Rhythms* or the warm, pastoral *The Good Earth* is the band's masterpiece—still existed.

But becoming a real unit again was important for the Feelies. And while day jobs, families, and the commuting distance between Florida and New Jersey meant that new songs took a while, last summer's album *Here Before* ended up as a very fine return that merged the band's various acoustic and electric impulses.

"For us it would have been too much of a nostalgia trip to just get together to play old songs," says Mercer. "From the beginning, our first shows, we talked about writing new music." Creative vitality was not the sole reason: "We always felt more comfortable in the studio," Mercer says. "We're not really hammy people. 'Hey everyone, put your hands together!'"

Ironically, the live shows of this bashful band are reputedly among the finest in its career, and they've sold out nearly as soon as they've been announced. On the West Coast, fans are still waiting.

So some of these reunions have been successful. The Jayhawks put out an excellent record last year, *Mockingbird Time*, with the two leaders' harmonies no less sterling on tour. LA canyon-rock revivalists Beachwood Sparks have a good new record. Midwestern power poppers Shoes are back in style as well. Dinosaur Jr. have confounded skeptics with their recent tours and recordings. Mazzy Star is recording new material.

Trouser Press's Robbins still thinks the track record for rock reunions is pretty unimpressive. "Go onto any vintage band's website and they've got a record. It may not be in stores, but it's 'the best thing they've ever done.' *Please*—stop it."

It's even worse when a band was really good once, but now tours well past its sell-by date. The Rolling Stones—jeered by punk rockers as dinosaurs thirty-five years ago—draw bigger and bigger crowds each year, even as they seem more like a corporation than the band of raw genius from the sixties and early seventies. As for the Who, after the death of Keith Moon and John Entwistle: "They're a Who tribute band, with incredibly good credentials," says Robbins. Which ain't the real thing.

Part of the blame for excessive reunions goes to retro-minded rock festivals, Robbins says. "Maybe we need a festival run by lawyers, because it usually comes down to people suing each other. Sometimes it's the girlfriend or the wife. But as bands get older, it's usually about making a living, and somebody sued somebody."

With or without attorneys' assistance, the tide of revivals will likely continue with time, including groups that seemed like non-entities the first time. (Men Without Hats, of "Safety Dance" fame, have just announced a new tour.)

In the old days, when bands were together, you knew it. Publicity photographs made it seem like groups like the Beatles or the Byrds spent all their offstage time together, dressing the same and cavorting in a desert setting or in swimming pools. Founding members of iconic bands were rarely replaced, and when they were, it was a big deal. But rock culture—and the music business—has changed in ways that make a band's identity more flexible. And hologram technology could make it even easier.

"It used to be, when the singer left, you're done," says Robbins. "The industry has grown up to keep bands as 'brands.' If you go into the studio with ProTools, and knock out a couple of blues tunes, you're a band again."

It all has a direct bearing on reunions. "J. Geils band announced a tour that doesn't involve J. Geils," he says. "It's like the band version of an oxymoron."

We're back at the flower shop in LA, and Spain is starting to dig deeper into old songs like "She Haunts My Dreams" as well as new material like "I'm Still Free," driven by a soulful organ and a guitarist who loves counterpoint and chromaticism. This is not a group that's faking it. On August 28 [2012] they'll play a show at LA's Bootleg Bar with the Haden sisters backing and with former Minuteman Mike Watt opening—a record release party to mark the release of Spain's three original records on vinyl.

Vinyl reissues, of course, are a way that indie bands keep the flame alive and keep funds coming in. So, these days, is Kickstarter, but the group tried in vain to generate support for new recording.

Like most bands whose fans are past their teens and twenties, it's not easy to generate sales or attention, and the very fine new record, *The Soul of Spain*—well distributed in Europe and available on iTunes—does not yet have a US label.

So while some reunions are big business, these cult bands are mostly in it for the art, or the fun, or whatever strange combination of the two combines to form rock 'n' roll.

Holsapple is happy to have a new record that's getting a real retail push—in contrast to the way early dBs records were mishandled—and he could see another dBs record after this one, if the songs he writes seem to fit. But he has no illusions.

"I see my future as being less of a professional musician," says the singer, who helps manage the performing arts center in Durham, N.C. "We have a generation of listeners who don't think they need to pay for music. I have a family and a life and I have to think of something besides beating my head against the wall as a musician. It's sad for me." Sometimes, he says, he wishes he'd finished college and chosen to do something more practical.

But the band's return is also a quiet kind of triumph. "They're more like a broken-up couple who move in together because they want to share the rent," Robbins says. "They've learned to live together."

Nearly every artist and musician is trying to find a way to survive in a radically redrawn digital world. For the dBs, the Feelies, Spain, and Mission of Burma, the reward is in the music they make, and the souls they reclaim.

[*Salon*, August 16, 2012]

CAN UNIONS SAVE THE
CREATIVE CLASS?

Being a musician is a good job, but that doesn't mean it's okay to go broke doing it. —David Byrne

THEY'RE JUST FOR HARD HATS. They peaked around the time Elvis was getting big. They killed Detroit. They've got nothing to do with you or me. They're a special interest—and they hate our freedom.

That's the kind of noise you pick up in twenty-first century America—in politics and popular culture alike—when you tune your station to the issue of trade unions. Union membership, and ensuing muscle, have been in steep decline in both the public and private sectors. Just look at Wisconsin's "right to work" push, the anti-teachers union "reform" movement, corporate union-busting, P.R. "messaging" firms hired by management to smear striking workers, hostility from the Republican right, and indifference from a Democratic Party that's reoriented itself around professionals and Silicon Valley.

Also in decline: America's creative class—artists, writers, musicians, architects, those part of the media, the fine arts, publishing, TV, and other fields—faced with an unstable landscape marked by technological shifts, a corporate culture of downsizing, and high unemployment.

So is it time for artists to strap on a hard hat? Maybe unions or artists' guilds can serve and protect an embattled creative class. With musicians typically operating without record labels, journalists increasingly working as freelancers as newspapers shed staff, and book publishing beginning what looks like a period of compression, unions might take some of the risk and sting out of our current state of creative destruction.

"Musicians are trying to negotiate this changing landscape," says Kristin Thomson, once a guitarist for the band Tsunami and an owner of indie label Simple Machines, now a director of the Future of Music Coalition. Many musicians ask the group how to deal with today's complicated mix of outlets and platforms, or what to expect from label support. "Others saw their mechanical royalties falling off a cliff. There are revenue streams out there, but they're all changing so fast. This is a difficult time for artists trying to understand it all. And there's a lot more competition because the barriers to entry are a lot lower."

To their partisans, of course, unions don't just help the workers at a few companies; they can have a transformational effect on society as a whole. Supporters credit them with the forty-hour work week, the weekend, fair wages, safe working conditions, overtime pay—much of the edifice that built the American middle class in the mid-twentieth century. Unions often set wage standards across a field, even for people who don't belong to them; uncounted artists, writers, and musicians can pursue their craft because their spouses have union-protected jobs, like public school teachers.

"And it's because of the decline of labor that these things are going away," says Thomas Frank, best known as the author of *What's the Matter With Kansas?* "If you're worried about inequality in this country, which is just galloping along, the main cause—even bigger than the skewed tax code—is the decline of unions."

The journalist and author Scott Martelle has seen the issue from several angles. While working at the *Detroit News*, a Gannett paper, he served as a union activist during the 1995 strike, and rather than cross a picket line to work, left for the *Los Angeles Times* two years later. The locally owned *Times*, by contrast, still retained a whiff of old-school corporate benevolence: for some of that decade, the paper had employed a staff doctor on call for the newsroom, and sometimes sent writers on first-class flights to cover stories. We never formed a union, its staffers sometimes told each other, because they treated us well. (Disclosure: Martelle was a colleague of mine at the *Times*.)

But the good times didn't last. When private-equity mogul Sam Zell leveraged a buyout of the Tribune Corp.—owner of the *Times*, the *Baltimore Sun*, the *Chicago Tribune*, the *Hartford Courant*, and other papers—and drove the company into bankruptcy, waves of bloodshed for the newsrooms began. In the summer of 2008, something like 300 reporters and editors at the *Times* alone lost their jobs. Martelle was one of them. The next batch of firings came in October, and there was still no union to make the process more humane: Staffers were told they had until 5:00 p.m. to clean out their desks, and security was standing by for anyone who dawdled. (By contrast, the *Tribune* executive who steered the doomed sale to Zell, Dennis Fitz-Simons, walked away with a golden parachute in excess of $40 million.)

"In a lot of ways, the newspaper industry went along thinking it would be rich and fat forever," says Martelle, who last year published the book *Detroit: A Biography*. "And the journalists were in the same situation. So when the Tribune Corp. blew up, it was too late to organize. People get motivated to join unions because they are frustrated or scared. And ten years ago, no one was frustrated or scared."

Trade unions and artists' guilds—various bodies in which creative types collaborate politically—date back at least as far as the first stirrings of the market economy. Masons lodges, common in the Middle Ages, operated like a cross between movie studios and architecture firms. As early capitalism became a force nearly as important to artists as the church, artisans and artists joined guilds, which were less hierarchical than the lodges, and worked in some ways like contemporary unions. They asserted rules for training, apprenticeship, and journeymen, not radically different from a blacksmiths' or saddlers' guild.

"Guilds in the Middle Ages arose whenever an occupational group felt its economic existence threatened by an influx of competition from without," historian Arnold Hauser wrote in his definitive *The Social History of Art*. "The object of the organization was to exclude or at least restrict competition." These guilds could be illiberal in some ways, but they also "marked a decided step forward in the artist's freedom."

This conflict between those inside and outside the guild exerted itself frequently in these years: Itinerant entertainers like jongleurs and wandering minstrels often enraged guild groups like watchmen or town musicians, who typically held a monopoly on performing at weddings and funerals, and were beaten back by established players. Stage actors experienced similar conflicts: Some were connected to a local guild, others wandered from inn to inn to perform for a passed hat, while some, as permanent theaters began to be established in Shakespeare's time, joined standing companies and resented those who didn't.

Guilds were hardly perfect—the Meistersingers were almost comically Teutonic in their earnest love of musical rules, and guild traditionalism sometimes put them behind artistic developments. But they were important to keep amateurs from stealing material—songs, for instance—in these days before copyright or contemporary notions of intellectual property. The nature of art means that these guilds did not function as smoothly as, say, blacksmith guilds. "There never was a period in their history," British music historian Henry Raynor wrote, "when the town musicians were not engaged in a bitter struggle to preserve their monopoly."

When the culture of the Renaissance told artists that they were individuals—even, in some cases, geniuses—that their talent was inborn, and that their role was to liberate the human spirit, many painters, sculptors, and others decided they did not need some musty old medieval guild, with its years of training and numerous restrictions. But because artists have little power and influence in isolation, they found themselves soon migrating into academies of art that were more conservative and hidebound than the guilds. In seventeenth century Holland, similarly, a formidable group of painters emerged—Rembrandt, Hals, and Vermeer among them—but because artists fell on the wrong side of the supply/demand curve, and there was no guild to protect them, even the best artists struggled, some selling tulips to pay the rent, some just going broke.

Romanticism in the nineteenth century doubled down on the cult of individualism: An artist or poet was a supernatural creature destined to soar about the dull crowd. As industry came into Britain and New England, creating inhumane working conditions and belching smoke into the skies, only the most political of artists saw anything in common with the masses filing into the sooty factory each morning. Unions started up in earnest about this time, and some guilds saw a revival. But, by and large, artists were committed to an individualism either heroic (Beethoven, Wagner) or dejected/alcoholic/absinthe-sipping (Baudelaire, Poe).

The turn of the twentieth century, flanked by the Progressive era, saw a growth of unions and successes such as child-labor laws. Perhaps more than any subgroup of the creative class, musicians—classical, Broadway, and big-band artists especially—became unionized by the twentieth century, generally with the American Federation of Musicians.

"The unionization of music in the United States has a mixed history," says Ted Gioia, a music historian, jazz pianist, and former corporate executive. "Many US cities still had segregated musicians unions long after the Supreme Court said 'separate but equal' was wrong—in 1963 we still had thirty-nine all-black locals in the AFM. James Petrillo, the head of the AFM, didn't want to force the issue, and this one man had an enormous influence on what happened—or didn't happen—in American music. Petrillo was also responsible for the musicians' strike of 1942–1944, and though I'm sure he felt he had good reasons for calling a halt to recordings, many blamed the decline in the big bands to this decision. And even today, we face a gap in American music history."

The American Society of Composers, Authors, and Publishers—the songwriters' union, dedicated to protecting and enforcing copyright— also made its share of mistakes. "When ASCAP launched a boycott of broadcasters in 1941," Gioia says, "they opened up opportunities for its rival BMI, and eventually had to settle for lower rates from radio than what they started with. In this instance, the public was deprived of music and the composer ended up with a worse deal."

Of course, the most consequential event in the recent history of unions has nothing to do with art or music. When Ronald Reagan—the only American president to come out of organized labor and simultaneously an avatar of "rugged individualism"—fired 13,000 striking air-traffic controllers in 1981, he helped erase unions from the American map. "The government had never done something like that, replacing striking workers," says Frank, whose latest book is *Pity the Billionaire*. "It was a signal to striking workers, that it would side with management. It was the beginning of an offensive. For the strikes of the eighties over and over again, strikers just got replaced."

In the right circumstances, guilds could be a force for stability for artists and artisans during unstable times. But between unions and creative types sits a long-standing cultural barrier.

"A lot of white-collar employees don't see themselves as workers," says Martelle, who now belongs to the Authors Guild. "They see themselves as 'partners' or some other euphemism." Newspaper journalism has blue-collar roots, and typically the production staff was committed to unionism. "But by the seventies and eighties, journalism was more about kids coming out of college, from the managerial class."

He saw this in action while striking in Detroit: Roughly half the journalists went to work during the strike, while virtually none of the drivers, printers, or production staff did. "There were a lot of liberal journalists who talked a good game. But when push came to shove, they crossed the picket line."

These days, he says, "journalists don't see themselves as union people. The only difference is the tools we use in the trade." Reporters and editors are brought up in a culture that discourages entangling alliances—they're supposed to be impartial, which leads some to decline even to vote—and they're discouraged from joining anything.

It's nearly as true for many musicians, says Thomson. "When musicians enter this world—as a rock band, hip-hop singer, or electronica act—a larger structure like a union doesn't seem to make sense if they are still booking their own shows," she says. "For musicians it just doesn't align with how they see themselves. 'I don't have a salaried job, how can I go on strike if it's just me and my band?'"

Many of them eventually join a union, she says, and many musicians around Hollywood studios, Broadway stages, and Nashville's music factory are unionized, typically with the 90,000-member American Federation of Musicians. Even some of the rock bands come around. "It's when people see a larger career arc, or if they ever play on live television—say, as a guest on a late night talk show—as the AFM and SAG-AFTRA are almost always the conduit for payments. Or when a Canadian artist needs a visa to perform in the United States. Until then, it might never cross their radar."

Says Frank: "You're talking about people who went to college; they've been brought up thinking that unions weren't for them. This whole idea of the 'free agent society' has gone so far; I don't know how you reverse that. And they didn't just sell it to management—they sold it to workers. They think it's cool to not have health insurance or benefits!"

The key work of this movement, *Free Agent Nation: The Future of Working for Yourself*, was written by former Al Gore speechwriter Daniel Pink. "Democrats are as deep into it as Republicans are," Frank says. "The Democrats are embarrassed by organized labor, especially when they think about their future. It's professionals—that's who they want."

This isn't just a class, or ideological, problem. Artists, musicians, writers—even some journalists—go through periods of developing their individual voices, years of what jazz musicians call "woodshedding." This can take place in graduate school, or while bartending, or driving a cab—Philip Glass and Steve Reich ran a furniture-moving company—but whatever the details, it tends to reinforce a sense of individualism. Whatever a person's specific politics, the artist's path often discourages a sense of collective unity.

"Collective bargaining requires an obedient rank-and-file," Gioia says. "But is there a profession more resistant to this than art-making? I'd rather try to put the toothpaste back in the tube than attempt to get artists to march in lockstep."

One of several groups trying to make this work is Freelancers Union, a decade-old Brooklyn-based nonprofit that calls itself a "federation of the unaffiliated" for the nearly one-third of the workforce that works independent of a steady employer. But it's not just graphic designers working from home in their pajamas: Founder Sara Horowitz was spurred to do something for freelancers when she took a law firm job and saw she was classified as an independent contractor, with no health insurance or retirement benefits. In 2008, she started the for-profit Freelancers Insurance Co., and in the fall opened the Freelancers Medical Center in Brooklyn. The group hopes to offer unemployment insurance as well. But some freelancers outside New York complain that they'd love to join the group, but wish it offered medical insurance west of the Hudson. (The group offers dental, 401K and disability nationally.)

Unions, though, typically require concentrated centers of population for some of their collective action to work, and in a creative class decentralized by a half century of suburbanization and several decades of the Internet, that's harder and harder to find.

Despite all the difficulties and challenges faced by unions, there's also one recent major success by a creative class union: The Hollywood strike of 2007 and 2008 led by the Writers Guild of America.

The strike was launched over writers' frustration at getting left behind by the shift to digital media. "We had been sucker-punched on a lot of previous technological advances," says screenwriter Howard Rodman, now a WGA vice president, who was active in the strike, offering a long list going back to videocassettes and cable. With the Internet developing as a way of distributing films and television, the union decided to plant its flag in cyberspace, rather than wish they had a decade later. "We knew if we didn't get it in that negotiation," he says, "we never would."

Despite the decline in union membership, workers still strike, and technological changes are sometimes the cause. Recently a number of symphony orchestras have fought with management, and found themselves on the losing end: The Minnesota Orchestra, asked to take a large pay cut by management, has been locked out, with no medical benefits, since October. These stories are depressingly familiar.

But here's what happened in Hollywood: The writers struck for 100 days ... and in the end got most of what they wanted. So, what happened?

Part of the writers' success came because the Hollywood unions—including the Screen Actors Guild, the Directors Guild of America, the Teamsters, and various unions of "below the line" workers—have deep roots in the movie business. (By contrast, the effects houses—one of which, Rhythm & Hues, filed for Chapter 11 right before winning an Oscar for *Life of Pi*—are not unionized.) But previous Hollywood strikes have fizzled, like the strike of 1988 over video royalties.

The 2007–2008 campaign was also better run than most. Support by high-profile stars—Steve Carell calling in sick to *The Office*—helped, as did enlisting the showrunners who head a television program and often come out of the writers' ranks. "These were people who made a lot of money for the studios, and who were used to working at the highest levels of the networks and studios," says Rodman. "It wasn't the suits versus the barbarians."

During a period that cut into many writers' savings, the union offered loans to some, which kept screenwriters' homes from being taken or their medical coverage from being cancelled. (No strike is an unalloyed victory: The studios, who employ the writers, lost hundreds of millions it could have earned. The Los Angeles area, including its florists, caterers, and other support workers, lost even more—something the messaging firm hired by studio management made clear as it worked to demonize the striking writers.)

Part of the reason Hollywood strikes can work is that the unions protect their position: Anyone who symbolically crossed the picket line can never be a member. "You can never come back—you are exiled," Rodman says. That doesn't mean that some writers (including some who penned soap-opera scripts) didn't keep working. But there were not enough scabs to undercut the union.

"At the end of the day, the studios would rather deal with a writer than want to be in the cesspool trying to determine credit," he says. "They don't want to give the unions everything they wanted, but to borrow a title, it's better than dealing with 10,000 maniacs."

Some say Hollywood's unusually liberal culture give unions power. But ask a striking graduate student at NYU or Yale, or the public radio staff whose unions have been broken or deflected, about how unsupportive liberal cultures can be.

Hollywood executives often support liberal social issues after hours, they don't typically let politics get in the way of their earnings or their dealings with talent. And Hollywood films have hardly been consistently pro-union. *On the Waterfront* is a great film, but it also takes a cartoonish view of union leadership. Similarly, for decades gangster films—including the *Godfather* movies—portrayed unions as handmaids to the mob. For every *Matewan*—made outside the Hollywood studio system, incidentally—there is enough material like *Blue Collar* for an anti-labor film festival. "Remember that movie, *The Replacements?*" Frank asks of a 2000 film starring Keanu Reeves. "It's about a scab football team and how awesome they are."

The recent film *Won't Back Down* shows Maggie Gyllenhaal and Viola Davis as plucky heroines who stand up to a reactionary school system—weighed down by an ingrown teachers union—to save a Benetton ad's array of kids. It was funded in part by plutocrat Philip Anschutz, who also supported the anti-teachers union documentary *Waiting for Superman.* It's only a matter of time before the Koch brothers make one of their own.

Rodman sees unions as more important than ever, and the only institution making the middle-class writer and the working actor possible at a time of historic income disparities. "As the conglomerates change, as entertainment becomes a smaller percentage of [multinational's] earnings, we'll see if that changes."

It may be that the crisis in capitalism—a system with which unions have a fraught but also symbiotic relationship—means unions can't operate the way they used to. Some union advocates see the twenty-first century economy as a return to the smoky early years of industrialism, before unions made themselves felt—the Information Age version of sweatshops and endless work weeks.

Technological shifts, in some ways, are making things harder. As the blue-collar employees who traditionally made newspaper production possible are replaced by automation, unions lose members and their strength dwindles further: The process is cumulative. "A union derives its power from organized action, with a strike as the big stick," Martelle says. "If you can limp along putting out a paper with managers, then you can't use that stick. They can always fill a paper with bullshit. But if you can't put it on a truck, you're in trouble."

That was the old model. "If you look at the stories from the last few days—corporate profits up, with no hiring coming—you see the problem," he says. "If people aren't working, there's nothing unions can do."

Still, newspapers with strong guilds—the *New York Times* and *Washington Post*—have seen fewer layoffs and less brutal severances, on the whole, than those without. And the business was ailing in 2007, as well, but the lack of union protection at the *Tribune's* two largest newsrooms, LA and Chicago, is part of what made Zell's dirty deal—build on employee pension plans—possible.

There is certainly no shortage of problems—new and old—that an artists' collective of some kind could address. In his insightful recent book, *How Music Works*, David Byrne talks about the difficulty of getting musicians paid for songs on Pandora, Spotify, and other services. "Spotify has reached agreements with the major labels, just as MTV did before them," he writes. "And just as before, the artist, who should be entitled to a share of that equity, is missing from the equation. Maybe this time around that will get fixed, and if it does then streaming will be an additional source of income for artists—especially if the artists hold on to the rights to their songwriting and recordings." Without a powerful musicians guild, it's hard to imagine this resolving any better today than it did in the MTV eighties.

"We know that a union would be a good thing," Frank says, "but it's very hard to start a union in a white-collar environment. When unions swept the country in the 1930s, very large workforces were concentrated in one place." Creative professionals simply don't have the numbers, and freelancers in the decentered age of the Internet are scattered geographically in a way that's very different than the way legions of workers would get together under one roof every morning at a Manchester cotton mill or Detroit auto plant. "It's harder for them to catch fire. You need unions, but you probably won't get one."

Gioia sees the current problem replaying the struggles of medieval guilds. "The biggest challenge to organizing creative labor is the large number of people willing to do the same work for free. This isn't a problem when you are a coal miner or factory worker. But if you are a photographer, painter, musician, poet, or some other creative talent, you soon figure out that the same gigs that you depend upon to pay your bills are someone else's hobby. That other person might even pay for the opportunity to do what you are doing to make a living. This makes collective bargaining extremely difficult, because you have very little leverage in the negotiation."

Some of the creative fields may figure a way out of the current mess; some won't. It may have less to do with ingenuity and more to do with how fast the respective pies are shrinking. Despite some disruptions, and an output heavy on fourteen-year-old-boys' testosterone fantasies, Hollywood studios continue to make enormous profits. Newspapers, magazines, book publishers, and record labels, by and large, don't.

Rich Yeselson, a DC-based writer who worked in the labor movement for two decades, considers unions the institutions that can best cut against income inequality and protect workers. "But a union can't compensate for an industry whose business model is in crisis," he says, "which is the real problem with the newspaper industry. If the business can't generate surplus profits that might go to unionized workers, rather than to shareholders (that's what the tug of war between management and labor is about), then the union is only bargaining, effectively, over severance and other closing costs (which is not nothing, but not wages and benefits going forward either).

"It often shocks conservatives to be reminded of this, but unions are capitalist institutions, they were founded in the early nineteenth century pretty much simultaneously with the development of modern capitalism. Managers and owners usually hate unions, but even the most militant unions look to cut a deal with management because the point is to use the union's power to extract more money and better working conditions for workers. But there have to be profits to extract—unions can't trump a dying industry."

Somebody may figure out a way to make this brave new world less inhumane. But it's going to take a while, and there will be plenty of pain along the way.

[*Salon*, March 18, 2013]

CHASING MUSICAL LEGENDS IN JOSHUA TREE NATIONAL PARK

TYPICALLY, WE GO TO THE DESERT at least once a year. We love the expansive space, several of the inns and restaurants and, of course, the otherworldly foliage of Joshua Tree National Park. We also enjoy the musical legacy of Gram Parsons, the former Byrd who overdosed in Joshua Tree in 1973, at age twenty-six, after virtually inventing the alt-country movement that would blossom two decades later. We feel these echoes and others—the twangy music, the land's natural contours, the local cuisine—when we're there.

But this year, my wife, Sara—a former music journalist—and I had one complication: our eager but mischievous son. Ian is no more difficult than the typical three-year-old boy, but he loves life so unambiguously that he can be hard to corral. Traveling with a toddler is a whole different ballgame: We figured some things would be better, some things worse, but we didn't know quite how it would all work out.

Well, we said, here we go.

Knock-knock

The drive to the high desert was already different: Ian demanded that we play Buddy Holly songs almost the entire way. But he got into the spirit of the excursion, singing harmony with Parsons on the Byrds' yearning "Hickory Wind," admiring the windmills off of Interstate 10 and laughing his head off at deliberately unfunny knock-knock jokes. ("Who's there?" "Ian." "Ian who?" "Ian yellow black!!" Laughter.)

We had booked at the 29 Palms Inn, known for its relaxing vibe and the privacy offered by its guest houses and adobe bungalows. Its restaurant—unlikely to dethrone Lucques or Mozza but offering fresh food and a full bar—is also convenient in an area where the wide-open spaces leave you miles from anything but a gas station and a stretch of asphalt. And as much as we love our son, we weren't quite willing to visit the high-desert equivalent of a Chuck E. Cheese's.

After checking in, we rushed out for a quick hike in the park. We were pleased to see that the winter's heavy rains had coaxed out the wildflowers and held back the infernal heat. As we drove in, the ranger handed us a junior ranger guide, full of things for Ian to look at and color. He has learned about the desert in kids' books on the Sahara, so he can tell you the difference between a Bactrian and a Dromedary camel, a skill not terribly useful in Southern California.

Hiking with Ian through the cacti and looming rocks turned out to be both challenging and a blast. He's still young enough to ride on my back, which is in some ways easier. But we wanted him to get some exercise.

While hiking happily near Barker Dam, we heard a blood-curdling scream. Ian was a few feet behind us, crying, cowering, and pointing at a long black snake that turned out to be . . . a tree root. The desert ended up being much more perilous and exciting through the eyes of a three-year-old.

By our next hike, near the aptly named Skull Rock, Ian had become more unshakeable. "Snakes, camels, and coyotes . . . we're keeping our eyes peeled for snakes, camels, and coyotes!" For a while he was making a strange sound—he called it his "honk-whistle"—to attract them. After we pointed out that animals are more likely to come out when it's quiet, he spent the rest of the hike shushing us.

We had dinner at the Crossroads Café in Joshua Tree, a casual, friendly hangout with healthy sandwiches and beer on tap. Ian was welcome here and offered milk with Ghirardelli chocolate. Afterward, I played a little guitar on the cabin's porch without, from what I could tell, waking the neighbors, and we went to sleep. So far, I thought, looking up at the startlingly bright desert stars, so good.

Plans unravel

The next day was carved out for Pioneertown, an Old West village built in the forties, in part with money from Roy Rogers, that became a set for Hollywood westerns and *The Gene Autry Show*. Some of the area burned in 2006 during the Sawtooth fire, but the village survived, and we looked forward to the old-school bowling alley and Pappy & Harriet's Pioneertown Palace, a country music-oriented restaurant with memorable baby back ribs. I'd also made a vague appointment to check out a musician-run ranch.

I did not schedule any of this very rigorously—perhaps I was trying for a laid-back, California-desert frame of mind—figuring the day would fall into place. That's the way a vacation is supposed to work, isn't it?

But the cool coffee shop—Water Canyon, which we think of as the gateway to Pioneertown—had recently closed. The bowling alley, it turned out, isn't open during the week. And Pappy & Harriet's is closed Tuesdays and Wednesdays.

The great old buildings, of course, were still there—Ian got a kick out of posing in front of the town jail in his cowboy hat and a villainous scowl—and I checked out the modest and affordable Pioneertown Inn, which just had reopened in late March. But aside from acres of parched sand and a few people sitting and gossiping in the hot sun outside the bowling alley, there wasn't much going on.

The wood-smoked ribs I'd been looking forward to at Pappy & Harriet's disappeared from my imagination. And I hadn't heard back from the manager at Rimrock Ranch, the funky complex of cabins I was hoping to check out. Flaky musicians! I said to myself. But I knew the bad planning was my own.

A second chance

I was pretty discouraged when we drove back to the inn. I had dragged my wife and son to a literal and figurative ghost town. As consolation, I told Sara we would pull over at the next stop promising lattes or cappuccinos (the only surefire way I know to talk my wife down from anger).

While she and Ian sat in a smart new shop called Ricochet Gourmet—espresso machine whirring—and I browsed through the cowboy hats and western shirts at Ricochet's vintage shop, my cell rang. It was Rimrock manager Jon Bertini apologizing for missing my call.

We were already in Joshua Tree, at least twenty minutes from the ranch, so I told him it looked as if we'd miss each other. But we started talking about music—he'd been in an early alt-country band, played mandolin, loved the Louvin Brothers—and before we knew it, we were turning around the car and heading back to Pioneertown.

Our tour of Rimrock ended up being one of the highlights of the trip. As you pass Pioneertown's center, the topography takes on new contours, mesas with blankets of yellow wildflowers come into view and the temperature drops a few degrees. With the sun going down the scene looked positively honeyed.

Jon and his wife met us at the ranch's entrance, which, at 4,500 feet above sea level, looks out over the whole region. The ranch—four mid-sized cabins, one large three-bedroom lodge that would suit two families, a pool, a central courtyard, and a refurbished Airstream trailer with a leopard-skin rug—was a thing of beauty. I especially liked the mix of old-school desert architecture and modern design, down to great poster art and what Sara called ironic taxidermy. Ian enjoyed all the open space, climbing up and down the stairs, and the various representations of animals. We left in much better moods than we'd arrived.

It was our last night. Tired from our adventures, we grabbed dinner at the inn. Its bar is a decent place to eat, and a rib-eye steak and glass of Pinot Noir improved my mood even more. I don't always love people playing music while I eat, but at the 29 Palms, which also hangs work by local painters, it's part of the high-desert atmosphere. We saw the guitar-fiddle duo Randy Godfrey and Bobby Furgo, who played fine traditional acoustic blues, closing with a spot-on "Key to the Highway," popularized by Mississippi bluesman Big Bill Broonzy.

We love the inn, but I'm curious to stay at Rimrock the next time. It puts us closer to Pappy & Harriet's—where I got a heavenly tri-tip sandwich on our way out of town—and I've already made plans to bring a friend who plays mandolin, our music-loving wives and our small sons, who are more than capable of pitching in on harmonica. That and a case of beer will make a great weekend in the desert as far as I'm concerned. And I'm sure Gram would understand.

[*Los Angeles Times*, May 30, 2013]

HOW THE *VILLAGE VOICE* AND OTHER ALT-WEEKLIES LOST THEIR VOICE

THERE WAS SOMETHING ELSE THERE, but you couldn't see it. There were notes coming from somewhere—maybe adding up to a melody—but you couldn't quite hear them. Growing up in and around this sprawling, elusive city in the 1970s and 1980s, Lynell George would see things, hear things, that never showed up in the daily press.

"I didn't always find my city in the newspapers," says George, who grew up black in racially mixed neighborhoods and was so inspired by the city and its contradictions that she decided to become a writer who'd decode LA's sense of place. She was tired of reading about the wealthy Westside, Hollywood deal-making, and society ladies in Beverly Hills. "Sometimes there were just little glimpses," she says, of something else.

Documenting the city—its racial and ethnic fault lines, the brilliant corners of its music scene, its overlooked literary life—was something, George realized, she could tackle more effectively as a journalist for alternative newsweeklies rather than a novelist. She'd spent years driving to Book Soup, a store on Sunset Boulevard, to pick up the *Village Voice* and read Greg Tate on black culture or Guy Trebay on the Bronx's crack epidemic, or to Venice's Rose Cafe or Tower Records to pick up *LA Weekly*.

"I wanted it on Thursday; I couldn't wait," she says. "If you didn't get it, it was gone. I wanted to be part of that conversation."

Talk to readers and writers about the heyday of the alternative press and you hear stories like this. For all the good memories, though, 2013 has been a rough year for alt-weeklies. The *Boston Phoenix*, among the oldest and most storied, collapsed in March, putting about fifty employees out of work, just six months after an optimistic move to glossy stock; the paper was losing roughly $1 million a year. Susan Orlean, a *New Yorker* writer who, like Joe Klein, Janet Maslin, and David Denby, worked for the *Phoenix* early on, compares it to the disappearance of her alma mater. "I am a child of the alt-weekly world," she says, "and I feel like it has played such an important role in journalism as we know it today." The *New Haven Advocate* was folded, along with two other weeklies, into the *Hartford Courant* this month after a year that saw heavy layoffs. In May, the two top editors of the *Village Voice* resigned rather than cut a quarter of the staff.

The troubles are not confined to the northeast: The *LA Weekly*, whose issues typically offer less than half the pages they did a decade ago, recently announced substantial cuts in its theater coverage, to which the paper had a three-decade commitment. Most places, page counts and staff sizes are way down.

Some of the causes of the alt-press meltdown are more complex than those of daily newspapers, which have been felled primarily by the Internet and corporate overreach. But the results are at least as tumultuous.

None of this sad trajectory was clear to Lynell George back when she became—in a chaotic office in Silverlake, a gritty gay neighborhood not yet declared cool—an *LA Weekly* intern in the late eighties and a staff writer in the early nineties. A tattooed performance artist manned the front desk, and pompadoured staffers in pegged jeans would arrive with guitars in preparation for after-work gigs. "You didn't know what you'd come into in the morning—I loved that. It reflected the music scene, the art scene." And "alternative," she realized, meant asking, "'What's really going on?' And to come at it in a different way."

Despite its association with the counterculture, the alternative press had its origins in the Eisenhower era—in the Red Scare, in fact. Though mainstream culture circa 1955 was sleepy and reactionary, Norman Mailer, who helped found the *Village Voice* that year out of a Greenwich Avenue apartment, wrote that the paper would "give a little speed to that moral and sexual revolution which is yet to come upon us." Dan Wolf, another founder, described the era as one in which "the vulgarities of McCarthyism had withered the possibilities of a true dialogue between people."

Mailer's column for the *Voice*, the novelist wrote a few years later, gave him the kind of opportunity that would have made Jack Kerouac swoon: "Drawing upon hash, lush, Harlem, Spanish wife, Marxist culture, three novels, victory, disaster, and draw, the General looked over his terrain and found it a fair one, the Village a seed-ground for the opinions of America, a crossroads between the small town and the mass media." Avant-garde filmmaker Jonas Mekas became the paper's film critic, urbanist Jane Jacobs wrote important pieces on the destruction of lower Manhattan neighborhoods, Nat Hentoff chronicled jazz and politics, Robert Christgau helped invent rock criticism.

The *Voice* surged from its initial print run of 2,500 copies (sold, originally, at five cents apiece) to 150,000 readers by 1970. By that point, the paper had company: What began as a music-heavy publication in 1966, *Boston After Dark* would become the more comprehensive *Boston Phoenix*, and in 1970, anti-war students at Arizona State founded the first *New Times* paper to protest the Kent State killings. The year after, the *Chicago Reader* was inaugurated by a group of college friends, and the following year, the first of the *Creative Loafing* papers, which would spread across the South, began in Atlanta.

These papers inherited varying degrees of the *Voice*'s political edge, emphasis on hipness and personal style, and pugnacity toward the mainstream. When *LA Weekly* rolled out its first issue in 1978, Jay Levin, one of its founders, wrote, "the smog in LA was so bad that much of the year you could barely see the hookers on the corner of Sunset Boulevard and Western Avenue."

Before long, the *Weekly* had dug into the cozy relationship between government regulators and polluters and turned out forty stories on smog and the people responsible for it. This was the paper's mission: "We would challenge all the official stories." (Today, now that LA's smog problem has improved, you can see the hookers clearly.)

Alt-weeklies thrived in conservative and conventional times. "The Reagan years were in some ways the alternative press's glory years," says Tom Carson, who wrote for the *Voice* and *LA Weekly* from 1977 to 1999. "We knew we were playing an adversary role. Peggy Noonan was right: It was a revolution, destroying what was left of the New Deal, making this into a very different country. And we were the only ones calling (Reagan) on it, besides a few scattered op-ed columnists."

At a time when corporate rock thrived and the blockbuster culture was gearing up—Steven Spielberg and George Lucas were no longer mavericks, Phil Collins and hair metal raced up the charts—and the president refused to utter the name of a plague killing thousands of gay men, the lines were clearly drawn. The alternative press knew which side it was on.

Though sometimes dismissed as hippie rags, alt-weeklies exerted an influence on mainstream, straight dailies. "The alternative press should get credit for pushing the daily press to cover culture and the arts," says Doug McLennan, a former *Seattle Weekly* staffer who now runs *ArtsJournal.com.*

But the influence went the other way, too: By the nineties, with the first popular Democratic president in three decades, corporate studios starting indie-film wings and "alternative rock" albums shooting up the charts, the lines became more blurred: Alternative weeklies and mainstream papers were harder to tell apart.

Manohla Dargis was writing for the *Village Voice* when she saw a *New York Times* story on the Nuyorican Poets Cafe and realized that things had changed. Cultural shifts, and an interest in youth and fringe culture by the mainstream press, meant that alt papers were losing their distinctiveness. And without a Republican White House, alt-weeklies were losing their political edge.

"When you take away the politics—if you don't have an editor with a very aggressive political agenda—all the other coverage is up for grabs," says Dargis. "Mainstream journalists started to cover that stuff. Mainstream papers started to poach, and some writers were comfortable in both worlds. Why shouldn't they be?

"People like Greg Tate and C. Carr were never going to work for the mainstream press." But Dargis says she realized that the terms had shifted, and by 2002, as film editor at *LA Weekly*, she was tired of toiling for alt-press wages. "I could stay there or make twice as much money in the mainstream. I couldn't say 'f---' anymore, but maybe I could make a living." She is now a movie critic for the *New York Times.*

In terms of circulation and revenues, the 1990s seemed like a good time for alternative weeklies. But the seeds of demise had been planted. It wasn't just what social critic Thomas Frank has called "the conquest of cool" or the pressures that pushed the *Voice*, for instance, to stop charging for its publication in 1996. It was a wily company from Arizona.

New Times began opening new alt-weeklies and aggressively acquiring existing ones in the nineties, and their model emphasized investigative reporting but not progressive politics. In 2005, New Times, led by founder Michael Lacey, bought the *Voice, LA Weekly*, and other papers and renamed itself Village Voice Media. At the original *Voice*, jazz critic Gary Giddins, photographer Sylvia Plachy, Pulitzer-winning cartoonist Jules Feiffer, and senior editor and gay-rights crusader Richard Goldstein were pushed out before New Times arrived; writers Hentoff, J. Hoberman, Christgau, Michael Musto, and James Ridgeway after. From 2005 to 2007, the *Voice* cycled through five top editors. *LA Weekly* was cannibalized, too. For those writers left, it was a culture shock.

"I got out in the nick of time," says Carson, the former *LA Weekly* and *Village Voice* employee, who now reviews movies for *GQ.* "I could not have survived the New Times era. They seemed motivated by hatred of everything the alternative press stood for—the left-wing politics, the countercultural sensibility, the value placed on intellectualism. These guys were just aggressively demolishing everything that weeklies were good for."

Of course, Craigslist and the Internet consumed much of the advertising that both alternative and mainstream papers depended on and altered the whole landscape. "These retail shifts have made it harder for publishers to distribute their weeklies," wrote press critic Jack Shafer, a onetime alt-weekly editor in San Francisco and Washington, DC. "Before Tower Records went under, a paper could drop thousands of copies a week at the store's many locations, and the stacks would disappear in a day or two. The video stores that once distributed them? Gone." Instead of opening an alt-weekly as you waited for your subway car or girlfriend, he says, young folks now pull out their cell phones.

"The alternative press comes at a very specific point in American history, and its demise does, too," says Dargis. "People are going to look at it as completely a technological issue, which is totally reductive. By the time the Internet arrives, the alternative press had already given it up. It had lost its mission."

A journalism career's start

As it happens, I am not a disinterested observer in these questions. I became a journalist largely because of the alternative press. As a left-leaning, college-radio-loving teenager in a moderately conservative Reagan-era suburb in Maryland, I found the *Voice* while working at a bookstore: From its political engagement to its underground music coverage to J. Hoberman's ability to make broader sense of mainstream films, this was a world I'd suspected existed but had never quite found before that.

By the latter nineties, when I was in my late twenties, I was editing a film section and writing about culture for New Times's LA paper, *New Times Los Angeles*, which the company formed after it bought two smaller weeklies and, in my boss's phrase, "machine-gunned the staff." I was told over and over again by my bosses about what a bunch of lazy, pontificating hippies sat across town at the *Weekly*, even as I blushed at the quality of their arts coverage. At *New Times* I met a very sharp bunch of journalists, but a business model clearly built on the promiscuous use of job termination. (I was fired once, then rehired.) They weren't quite right-wing—more macho libertarian, with a bullying streak—but when Sarah Palin broke out and began to run down coastal "elites," I felt like I was back in a Monday editorial meeting.

For all the emphasis on reporting—the implication being that columns, essays, or reviews were somehow unmanly—it was a film critic, Peter Rainer, who earned a Pulitzer finalist spot during my time there. Jonathan Gold, who worked for *LA Weekly* until last year, won his Pulitzer as a food critic.

But what seemed strange about the *New Times* crowd is that sometimes they were right. And sometimes they were right on important things, as when the paper helped break a scandal in which the *Los Angeles Times* secretly shared profits with an advertiser.

It was sad, then, when the company shut *New Times Los Angeles*, in 2002. I had decamped to the *Los Angeles Times* by then, and I watched with amazement as New Times swaggered back to town, took over the *Weekly* and started butchering. (Two longtime New Times editors told me the alt-press troubles come from the economy and the Internet and not anything the company did and declined to speak on the record. Similarly, the Association of American Newsmedia has said the *Boston Phoenix*'s closing and other turmoil is not a sign of a larger decline.)

New Times's owners killed my old paper's online archive, so most of what we wrote disappeared. They later dumped almost all of the *Weekly*'s archive of old papers, which contained what one scribe called "the secret history of LA." They moved the paper from a gritty, almost-hip location on Sunset Boulevard to a freeway-adjacent corporate box that former staffers liken to an Ikea set down in Siberia. Joe Donnelly, a gifted editor hired by one "Weekly" regime, fired by another, is not alone in thinking the owners ruined the paper. (Disclosure: I've worked with several people in this story, including Donnelly.)

In 2012, Lacey split to take control of Backpage, an online classified service heavy on escort services that has been linked to underage prostitution. (*New York Times* writer Nicholas Kristof has called it "Where Pimps Peddle Their Goods.") He has compared his departure to Backpage to his youthful protest over the Kent State dead and to Grove Press's Barney Rosset's fight to publish D. H. Lawrence.

What's the significance of all this for people who read weeklies rather than write for them? Los Angeles, which had three alt-weeklies in the eighties and nineties—including an *LA Weekly* with fact-checkers, researchers, and a large writing staff—now has just one, with a skeleton staff and fewer than 100 pages of copy. (Matt Groening's *Life in Hell* comic, a precursor to *The Simpsons*, ran in one of the papers New Times killed, the *Los Angeles Reader*.)

Over the years, alternative papers have paid attention to neglected issues and unjustly obscure rock bands. The members of the Pixies met through the classified pages in the *Boston Phoenix*. Giddins's jazz writing in the *Voice* remains as daring and clear as a Charlie Parker solo; Ridgeway's work on neo-Nazis and militias has no peer. *LA Weekly* helped document parts of its city that would literally explode in the 1992 riots, and then documented the carnage, in words and pictures, better than any other outlet. Even the New Times papers have published an enormous number of gutsy investigative stories on crony politicians, corrupt sheriffs, kids victimized in foster care and vile religious cults. "Yes, we're under tremendous pressure in the digital age, like everyone in the media," says Sarah Fenske, editor of *LA Weekly*, before naming stories that make her proud to be in the business. She cites a piece about lawyer Carmen Trutanich, whom she calls "one of the biggest bullies in LA politics"; one on accusations of exploitation of would-be filmmakers on YouTube; and a third arguing that an epidemic of hit-and-run accidents has been ignored by the police.

"What factory that we'd once hear about dumping toxic chemicals are we not hearing about anymore?" asks Ted Drozdowski, a onetime *Boston Phoenix* editor. "There are less watchdogs, which is why we hear less barking."

When those papers go down, or cut pages and staff, those stories disappear and those writers find another way to pay the rent. But it's not just what we don't see; it's the way seeing itself has changed. "When the *Voice* was in muckraking mode," says Carson, "and we'd go after some shitty landlord or some awful politico, that story was on the cover, and it was all over the place. Today, you can see that story online and you may be the only person reading it. A physical paper is a physical presence—and you'd see it all over the city."

[*Al Jazeera America*, December 28, 2013]

DOWN WE GO TOGETHER

After a while, I got accustomed to walking in circles. Most days I told myself things would be okay, but then I'd get news so unpleasant and disorienting—or have to pass something grim over to someone I cared about—that all I could do was slowly orbit, phone in hand, whatever room I was in, either trying to understand what was going on or working to make the person on the other end feel better. It's hard for me to do this while standing still.

This time, I was in Portland, Oregon, in the basement of the home of an old college friend, just waking up and getting ready for a day trip into the countryside. Then my cell phone rang, the face of my wife back home in Los Angeles showing up on its small screen. She didn't waste time. "The bank," she said, "is suing us." She'd woken up to a courier posting a note on our front door. "I'm sorry," was all he said before taking off. Pulling the photocopied forms off our door—in triplicate—she saw that one of the largest banks in the world had initiated legal action to take our little house from us. While offering various reassurances, trying to keep my wife from despair, I think I paced fast enough to wear a groove in my friend's stone floors.

The bank's action was not entirely unexpected. There had been bad news, dire warnings, and false alarms—as well as form letters sent to our address offering, in both English and Spanish, to "help"—for some time. In 2008, a risk-taking real estate mogul had bought the newspaper I wrote for. In the months immediately before and after he drove the company into bankruptcy, the paper laid off hundreds of us—more than a third of its staff. We should have seen it coming. Various owners and regimes had come and gone, but we mostly ignored them, telling ourselves we were laboring for "the reader"—someone we'd never met, but whose idealized interests and curiosities we hoped to engage. The reader was of little help, as a combination of market forces, new technologies, and clueless corporate overlords tore our business apart.

As my family limped through the next few years—I kept writing, but for less and less money—I found myself telling my five-year-old son over dinner one night that we'd be leaving the house he'd been raised in but we didn't know when, we didn't know where we would go, and we couldn't really explain to him why. "But then," he said, looking up from a Scandinavian high chair purchased in better times, "we'll come back, right?" Within a year or so, it was done, and I couldn't help but notice that the locksmith who arrived to lock me out of my first house drove a fancier and substantially newer car than my seventeen-year-old Honda.

Of course, I had plenty of company. The collapse of several of the best-known banks and trading firms on Wall Street in the same season as my layoff meant that not only journalists were suffering. I'd spent my two decades in the business writing about culture of various kinds—rock bands, graphic artists, piano tuners, classical composers, underground cartoonists—so I knew a lot of people who'd been hammered. Architects I knew watched their practices implode. Some of my favorite bookstores sold off their stock in a hurry as they closed their doors. A talented and energetic friend—a photographer who'd become a photo editor as a means to stability—lost his job, twice. A cousin in Oregon who'd started a small graphic design firm closed the company and moved into his brother's basement. A sweet, gifted couple, both of whom worked in art galleries, left for a midwestern family farm. For those who stayed, marriages and friendships often became collateral damage. An animator neighbor whose cheerful little daughter played with my son lost his job and, eventually, his health and his marriage. A close friend—a landscape painter who'd seen his income cut in half with the market crash—came over one night with a mandolin and we started an acoustic duo dedicated to slow, sad country songs, some of them from the Great Depression. (The band was intended more as fun than therapy, but the gallows humor may have been lost on our wives, who wondered how long we'd be able to keep our hold on the middle class.) Before long, my friend and his family sold their house and left the country. I worried that we too might have to go into exile.

My path into the creative class—as an observing reporter—was pretty typical. Growing up a middle-class kid, I had no illusion that I'd ever become wealthy, but I had a sense that I could get really good at something if I worked as hard as I could and surrounded myself with what someone once called—in a phrase that now sounds antique—the best that had been thought and said. Mine was a pragmatic, find-a-summer-job, get-Triple-A-and-change-your-oil-regularly kind of family. But there was also a respect for culture. Reading James Joyce's *Dubliners* showed me a new way to see: there was a world behind the world that you could discern if you squinted just right. People around me would often tell me they were not religious, they were *spiritual*, but I was neither: art and literature did all that religions were supposed to, without Crusades, or cults, or scented candles.

Whether it was endlessly spinning the Beatles' *Revolver* in elementary school—until I knew every detail of George Martin's production—or obsessively rereading Kurt Vonnegut in high school or sinking into the work of Thomas Pynchon and Billie Holiday in college, or Elizabeth Bishop's and Luis Buñuel's in the apprentice years that followed, I wanted to bathe in the work of great artists, even if I had no expectations of becoming a jazz singer or a surrealist filmmaker. I saw myself in the third generation of people who had worked in culture without either striking it rich or going broke. My grandfather had played piano on the vaudeville circuit and wrote songs for black-and-white cartoons, my grandmother was a dancer in Ziegfeld's shows, and my dad—their son—wrote about politics for a living. My mother and many of the women on her side of the family taught school; some were English teachers who passed on their love of literature. My aunt and uncle were RISD-trained graphic artists.

Stanford University Hospital had welcomed me into the world; my father studied in the school's journalism program while recovering from serious wounds he sustained in Vietnam, so going into that field made a kind of symbolic sense. Despite my teenage dream of becoming a "writer"—I'd had some minor success penning short stories in high school—working as a journalist seemed like the right compromise for a risk-averse child of the suburbs like me. So I did everything I could—writing for the college paper, working at a record shop and bookstores for something like minimum wage, moving six times over two years as I chased graduate journalism school and unpaid internships, running up enormous student loan debt—with the goal of devoting my adulthood to chronicling the makers and making of culture. I wrote for free often enough that I won the dubious honor of becoming a staff writer at a publication that did not pay. But for a while, it was going pretty well. In my first real job, I filed deadlined copy by day; by night, I got lost in smoky rock clubs, or chased Bach down what James Merrill called his "eternal boxwood mazes."

By my early thirties I was writing for one of the nation's Big Four newspapers, one emerging from complacency with a new energy, and a few years later I had what seemed like a dream job: working for the best editor I'd ever had, interviewing novelists and writing about authors and intellectual trends in the literary world. The work was around the clock, but that's the way fulfillment sometimes works. Like most new parents, my wife arid I were woken up at least once a night, and I was able to put myself to sleep by reading one of the numerous books I was responsible for knowing about. The abrupt end in the fall of 2008, a few weeks after a modest raise and some praise for how "productive" I'd been, came when a woman in Sarah Palin glasses and a clipboard told me I had until five o'clock to clean out my desk and exit the building. And in spite of a White House that spoke about the importance of protecting people who worked hard and played by the rules, no significant relief came for those who struggled to hold on to their houses after job losses. (Simultaneously, the enormous bank that owned our mortgage—a bank that had been saved from collapse by our tax dollars—refused to negotiate with us to save the place.) An entire political movement, inspired by the writings of Ayn Rand and a hatred of those who hoped the government could do something to help them during difficult times, would swing elections and become strong enough to shut down the nation's government five years later. They would denounce people like me as "losers" and sometimes worse.

But I'm telling this story not because of what happened to me, or what happened to my friends. As I took a broader look at where our culture was going, I saw that the predicament we found ourselves in was about more than the Great Recession. And while the Internet and other digital innovations had taken a huge bite out of some professions—disemboweling the music industry, for instance, through both piracy and entirely legal means—this was about more than just technology. Some of the causes were as new as file sharing; others were older than the nation. Some were cyclical, and would pass in a few years; others were structural and would get worse with time. There was a larger nexus at work—factors, in some cases unrelated ones, that had come together in the first decades of the twenty-first century to eviscerate the creative class.

These changes have undermined the way culture has been created for the past two centuries, crippling the economic prospects of not only artists but also the many people who supported and spread their work, and nothing yet has taken its place. The price we ultimately pay is in the decline of art itself, diminishing understanding of ourselves, one another, and the eternal human spirit.

Though highlighted and exacerbated by the Great Recession, these shifts started earlier and almost certainly will extend for years into the future, even as other elements of the economy recover. The arrival of the Internet and the iPhone, while crucial, are not the only forces at work here. And for all the current complaints about Miley Cyrus and YouTube videos of cats playing the piano, we appear to be at the beginning—not the middle and certainly not the end—of historic shifts that threaten the creative class.

While the fading fortunes of the creators of culture is alarming, it's equally disturbing that their often-mocked supporting casts—record store clerks, roadies, critics, publicists, and supposedly exploitative record label folk—are being forced out of the culture industry. This broader cultural middle class has long played an underappreciated role in connecting artists to their audiences. Without them, too much quality art becomes a tree falling in empty woods, and each artist, regardless of temperament, must become his or her own producer, promoter, and publicist.

Several important strands have tangled together and become hard to separate. They add up to a cheapening of the culture and to the fraying of the middle-class middle ground that allows the creative class to thrive. They reinforce existing notions that the only thing that matters is money and winning. In the long run, people who have to earn a living will find something else to do. "Do you really think people are going to keep putting time and effort into this," David Byrne asked, "if no one is making any money?" The only people who will be able to work in culture will be those who don't need to be compensated—celebrities, the very rich, and tenured academics.

How did we get here? Some of the roots are historical, others are economic, yet others are technological. Still others involve shifting social norms.

Since the Renaissance, we've associated the arts and culture with the wealthy and powerful. Michelangelo, Titian, and others like them became cultural gods; popes and emperors bowed to them. That was fun while it lasted, but the relationship created deep long-term problems. More recently, two centuries of Horatio Alger stories have built to a blockbuster culture that venerates celebrity above all else, overlooking the forces of history and ignoring material conditions. On the other side, artists' discomfort with the market economy, which dates at least back to the time of Charles Baudelaire, has led to a bohemian self-deception that has created another dead end. (Historical research on nineteenth-century Paris, for what it's worth, makes clear that the day's bohemians and bourgeoisie—classes that defined themselves in opposition to each other—had far more in common than either side let on.)

Simply put: Since the birth of the modern era, we've been kidding ourselves. We've become accustomed to seeing creative beings as either soaring deities or accursed gutter dwellers. Certainly, some were, and some are. But these two associations have obscured the fact that culture, as we understand the term, tends to originate in the middle class, depends on a middle-class audience for its dissemination and vitality, and leads most of its practitioners, if they are lucky, to a middle-class existence. There are plenty of exceptions. But Virginia Woolf and the rest of the upper-mid Bloomsbury circle were not anomalous; much of Anglo-American culture has roots among the burghers as well. The Beatles were essentially middle-class for their time and place, despite American associations of them with Liverpool's proletariat; it's even more true of the Rolling Stones, in spite of their self-mythologizing as raw, dangerous bohemians. Much of British rock music since the 1960s, including glam-rock and politically radical post-punk, sprang from the middle-class world of art schools. Most American jazz artists, black and white, square or hip, have begun middle class, and hoped to end up that way; many were able to establish themselves because of programs like the GI Bill. Most literary writers, and visual artists, and architects, and journalists, and curators, and publicists, start in the middle and end up there if they can. But these tales are rarely told, and the economic roots of the many thousands of the creative class who do not appear in magazine profiles are even more obscure.

There is, then, an invisible class of artists and artisans whose fortunes are worth taking seriously. We rarely hear about them, and we don't have a stable context in which to consider them, because of centuries of myths and misperceptions. We need to understand the situation, and its various layers, as clearly as possible if we're going to work to repair the current fracture.

Creativity fascinates people both inside and outside of the creative class. Malcolm Gladwell and his disciples write with verve and insight about the way product designers and computer engineers approach the creative process, discussing them alongside genuine, unimpeachable artists—W. H. Auden, Bob Dylan, the Beatles—in a way that emphasizes what these figures have in common. Pundits like David Brooks write about the way bourgeois bohemians have adopted the tastes of creative people—casual wardrobe, fancy coffee, laptops, an interest in aesthetics—no matter what they do for a living. These authors are right in a lot of ways. But it's important to note that the actual artists these corporate mavericks and hip lawyers are emulating are not, for the most part, doing quite as well. Nor has the fashionableness of the artistic lifestyle—late hours, black clothes—created more opportunities, or even a broader audience, for people who work in the arts or who pursue creative impulses outside a corporate structure.

What is this thing called the creative class? Richard Florida, the urban theorist who has done the most to describe it, defines this group as effectively anyone who works with their mind at a high level—so research scientists, medical professionals, and software designers are thrown in with jazz trumpeters and lyric poets. This may make sense in some contexts, but a more useful understanding of the creative class would include anyone who helps create or disseminate culture. So along with sculptors and architects, I mean deejays, bookstore clerks, theater set designers, people who edit books in publishing houses, and so on. At least since the Renaissance, a supporting class has been crucial. Our image of the lone creative genius is mostly a relic from the romantic age. Without these other figures, culture does not reach the audience. It's one hand clapping.

Any "class," by nature, includes a wide range. The middle class, for instance—a term we've been using, despite its ambiguity and elasticity, for many decades now—contains everything from auto workers to elementary school teachers to aerospace engineers, with many possible gradations along the way. (George Orwell once described himself as coming from the "upper lower middle class.") But the usefulness of any such sociological term does not depend on its contents being homogenous.

A novelist I admire has argued that people like him—independent artists, motivated by the irrational, romantic urge to write, paint, whatever, with an assumption that material rewards will never come—have little in common with those, however creative, who work in a guild or a profession, whether architects or journalists or publishers. I acknowledge these differences, but I think all of us in the creative arts, at whatever level, have a lot in common. The sciences divide themselves into "pure" and "applied" categories, and numerous subfields, but they're all, at their essence, up to the same thing. The late poet Donald Justice wrote about the compulsion to create, and I think it fits most of us in the creative class, regardless of what niche we occupy. My novelist friend is right in one major respect: This kind of life usually means giving up the comforts and certainties of a more conventional path.

"At a certain point in life, usually during adolescence, the artist dedicates himself or herself to art," Justice has observed. "The vows may not be codified and published, but they are secretly known and one does take them. I am perfectly serious about this. Years later the significance, the great emotion involved in this commitment, may prove difficult to recall, and especially hard to keep in mind during the excitations and fluctuations of a career, the temporary successes and, if one is lucky, the only temporary failures. . . . It may be that we become like the priests in the stories of J. F. Powers, so much taken up with affairs in the parish that the high moment of original dedication seems a contradiction. But for some of us it is always there, if only as a nagging whisper or the twinge and throb of guilt." Social critic Lee Siegel points to "the sense that something is missing, that doesn't satisfy you in everyday life—so you turn to these invisible things."

For all of Justice's romanticism about an aesthetic calling, he titled his essay "Oblivion: Variations on a Theme," because it's oblivion, not fame, where many of even the most talented figures typically end up. And all of us—once we've moved beyond school or our parents' couches—depend not just on that original inspiration, but on an infrastructure that moves creations into the larger culture and somehow provides material support for those who make, distribute, and assess them. Today, that indispensable infrastructure is at risk, imperiling an entire creative class.

Creativity, in the end, is not about self-fulfillment, but about work, focus, and rigor. The short-story master Tobias Wolff sees this all in pragmatic terms. "The literature that makes life possible for me and others is not a given," he writes. "It has to be made, day after day, by those who are willing to take on the solitude and uncertainty of work. Writing affords pleasure too, but mostly it's hard work."

Whether we work as a songwriter with a penthouse in what Leonard Cohen calls the Tower of Song—the place where the best lyrics and melodies live forever—or as a bookstore employee passing on a passion for Ursula Le Guin, we're all in this together.

The group I'm describing, then, is broad. But I'll concentrate on a few specific patches of the larger map. I'm not particularly interested in James Cameron, for instance, or Kanye West: Celebrity and corporate entertainment—good and bad—hardly needs defenders. And the luckiest and best financed figures within a structure like movie studios or major labels will, if they can keep from self-destructing, earn enormous riches and convince the rest of us that everything is fine. Although figures like these are undeniably creative, they're so far out on the edge of the reality of the creative class as to be anomalous. Similarly, when Apple or Facebook or Warner Bros. experience a big quarter, it doesn't mean that the creative class is thriving, any more than record profits for Big Oil translate into prosperity for the middle class. What's left, when you remove the wealthiest and most overexposed entertainers and their flacks and stylists, is an enormous group that encompasses film, novels and poems, music, journalism, theater, and much else.

In the end, the challenge to the creative class is broader than it may seem. My main concern with this set of issues is seeing not simply that creativity survives—that aspect of human experience will never entirely die—but that its exercise remains open to any talented, hard-working person. The stakes here are bigger than the employment prospects of video store clerks or architects. It comes down to something not merely aesthetic, but something that speaks to American identity and even our founding national myth and folklore: the idea of meritocracy. Is a life in the world of culture, whether producing it or distributing it or writing about it, something available to only the very lucky or well born? Furthermore, if working in culture becomes something only for the wealthy, or those supported by corporate patronage, we lose the independent perspective that artistry is necessarily built on. This goes double for the journalist.

If we're not careful, culture work will become a luxury, like a vacation home. Just as a democratic nation benefits from a large, secure, and informed middle class, so too we need a robust creative class. Painting a landscape or playing a jazz solo does not guarantee that an individual will become nobler or more virtuous. But a broad-based class making its living in culture ensures a better society. This book is about why they're worth saving.

Someday there will be a snappy moniker for the period we're living through, but right now—years after the crash of 2008—American life is still a blurry, scratched-out page that's hard to read. Some Americans have recovered, or at least stabilized, from the Great Recession. Corporate profits are at record levels, and it's not just oil companies that are flush. Technology corporations have become as big as nation-states: Apple's market cap is as big as the GDP of Taiwan or Saudi Arabia.

For many computer programmers, corporate executives who oversee social media, and some others who fit Florida's definition of the "creative class," things are good. The creativity of video games is subsidized by government research grants; high tech is booming. This creative class was supposed to be the new engine of the United States economy, post-industrial age, and as the educated, laptop-wielding cohort grew, America was going to grow with it.

But for those who deal with ideas, culture, and creativity at street level—the working or middle classes within the creative class—things are less cheery. Book editors, journalists, video store clerks, all kinds of musicians, novelists without tenure—they're among the many groups struggling through the dreary combination of economic slump and Internet reset. From their vantage point, the creative class is melting.

That implosion is happening at all levels, small and large. Record shops and independent bookstores close at a steady clip; newspapers and magazines announce repeated waves of layoffs. Tower Records crashed in 2006, costing 3,000 jobs. The bankruptcy of Borders Books in 2011—almost 700 stores closed, putting roughly 11,000 people out of work—is the most tangible and recent example. One of the last video rental shops in Los Angeles—Rocket Video—closed soon after. On a grand scale, some 260,000 jobs were lost in traditional publishing and journalism in the three years after 2007, according to U.S. News and World Report. In newspapers alone, the website Paper Cuts tracked more than 40,000 job cuts in the three years after 2008.

Some of these employees are young people killing time behind a desk or a counter; it's hard for them, but they will live to fight again. Having education, talent, and experience, however—criteria that help define Florida's creative class, making these supposedly valued workers the equivalent of testosterone injections for cities—does not guarantee that a "knowledge worker" can make a real living these days. "It's sort of like job growth in Texas," said Joe Donnelly, a former deputy editor at *LA Weekly*, who was laid off in 2008 and poured savings and the money he made from selling his house into a literary magazine. "Governor [Rick] Perry created thousands of jobs, but they're all at McDonald's. Now everyone has a chance to make fifteen cents. People are just pecking, hunting, scratching the dirt for freelance work. Living week to week, month to month." The British-born singer-songwriter Richard Thompson likens the current situation to the brutal Highland Clearances of the eighteenth and nineteenth centuries, in which the commons were enclosed, at the expense of peasant farmers, as aristocratic families seized the northern part of Scotland. Aristocrats "preferred the idea of sporting estates to having people actually working the land," he said. "So people were forced out to Canada and Australia."

In today's Britain, the situation has become dire even for accomplished novelists: forget about those toiling to break in. Hanif Kureishi, celebrated for the novels and screenplays *My Beautiful Laundrette* and *The Buddha of Suburbia*, is now struggling. The veteran award-winning novelist Rupert Thomson—perhaps appropriately for a writer influenced by Franz Kafka—has given up his office to construct an attic space in which he cannot entirely stand up. "All I want is enough money to carry on writing full time," Thomson said. "And it's not a huge amount of money." Writer and journalist Robert McCrum calls the changes since 2008 a revolution. "To writers of my generation, who grew up in the age of Penguin books, vinyl records, and the BBC, it's as if a cultural ecology has been wiped out." It wasn't just what the British call the post-2008 credit crunch, or the shredded safety net, or Amazon, "but the IT revolution was wrecking the livelihoods of those creative classes—filmmakers, musicians, and writers of all sorts—who had previously lived on their copyrights." He calls copyright "the bone-marrow of the Western intellectual tradition. Until the book world, like the music world, can reconcile the extraordinary opportunities provided by the Web with the need for a well-regulated copyright system, artists of all kinds will struggle."

Past groups punctured by economic and technological change have been woven into myth. Charles Dickens wrote sympathetically about Londoners struggling through the upheavals of nineteenth-century England; British folk songs valorized a rural village culture destroyed by the Industrial Revolution. John Steinbeck brought Dust Bowl refugees to life; Woody Guthrie wrote songs about these and others with no home in this world anymore. One of his inheritors, Bruce Springsteen, did the same for America's declining industrial economy.

But the human cost of this latest economic and technological shift on the prospects of our creative class has been largely ignored. Many of us, said Jaime O'Neill, a writer in northern California, are living in a depression. "It's hard to make the word stick, however, because we haven't developed the iconography yet," he wrote in an essay that asked, "Where's today's Dorothea Lange?"

Perhaps a fading creative class—experiencing real pain but less likely to end up in homeless shelters, at least so far, than the very poor—may not offer sufficient drama for novelists, songwriters, or photographers to document.

But journalists themselves also have downplayed the story. In fact, the media—businesses that have been decimated by the Internet and corporate consolidation, as surely as the music industry—have been mostly reluctant to tell the tale of this erosion. Some newspapers, of course, have offered responsible coverage of the mortgage meltdown and the political wars over taxes and the deficit. But it's harder to find in the pages of our daily newspapers stories about people who lose their livelihoods, their homes, their marriages, their children's schooling because of the hollowing-out of the creative class and the shredded social safety net. Meanwhile, coverage of luxury homes, fashions, watches, cigars, and sports cars continues to be a big part of magazines and newspaper feature sections.

Optimists like Florida may be right that America doesn't make industrial goods anymore and perhaps never will again, because what the United States produces now is culture and ideas. Unfortunately, making a living doing this has never been harder. It wasn't supposed to be this way. The Internet, it was widely thought, would democratize culture while boosting the prospects of those who make it. Allison Glock, a magazine journalist and writer, recently returned to her native South because she and her novelist husband could no longer afford to live in New York. "Wasn't the Internet supposed to bring this class into being?"

Much of the writing about the new economy of the twenty-first century, and the Internet in particular, has had a tone somewhere between cheerleading and utopian. One of the Net's consummate optimists is Chris Anderson, whose book *The Long Tail: Why the Future of Business Is Selling More*, championed the Internet's "unlimited and unfiltered access to culture and contents of all sort, from the main stream to the farthest fringe of the underground." With our cell phones, MP3s, and TiVos, we're not stuck watching *Gilligan's Island* over and over again, he suggested. Now we can groove to manga and "connect" through multiplayer video games.

In 2009, Anderson came out with a second book, the intelligently argued *Free: The Future of a Radical Price*, which suggested that new revenue streams and the low cost of computer bits meant that both businesses and consumers would benefit as the Internet drove down prices. It's nice to contemplate, but the human cost of "free" becomes clear every day a publisher lays off staff, a record store closes, or a documentarian finds her film uploaded to YouTube without her permission.

Of course, the meltdown of the creative class can't be blamed entirely on the Internet. David Brooks's influential *Bobos in Paradise: The New Upper Class and How They Got There* traced a multi-ethnic, meritocratic elite and a fantasia of latte shops, retro-hip consumers, and artisanal cheese stores. The cheese stores are, in some cases, still there, but much of what Brooks predicted has fallen through. He wrote—in 2000—that we were living "just after an age of transition," with the culture wars dead, a "peaceful middle ground" politically, and a nation improved by the efforts of a class that had reconciled the bourgeois ethos with bohemianism. This was easier to accept when things seemed to be humming along. But even after the 2008 crash—where unemployment hit 12 percent and above in California, which, thanks to Hollywood and Silicon Valley, is also the state most driven by the creative class—blind optimism persists.

Florida argued that the creative class would make cities rich in "technology, talent, and tolerance" and jolt them back to life. His 2010 book, *The Great Reset: How New Ways of Living and Working Drive Post-Crash Prosperity*, wrestled with the difficulty of the past few years. But he continued to put faith in knowledge workers to bounce back stronger than ever.

Others were more suspicious. The new economy "is good for whoever owns the computer server," said Jaron Lanier, a computer scientist who has done pioneering work with virtual reality. "So there's a new class of elites close to the master server. Sometimes they're social network sites, other times they're hedge funds, or insurance companies—other times they're a store like the Apple Store." Lanier debunked a lot of Internet hype in his first book, *You Are Not a Gadget*, and he goes even further in

Who Owns the Future? which argues that the Internet has destroyed the livelihoods of the creative class's middle tier-musicians, photographers, and journalists—but that it will move on to undercut other middle-class jobs. We're just getting started.

Andrew Keen is another Silicon Valley insider who's seen the dangers of the Net. "Certainly it's made a small group of technologists very wealthy," he said. "Especially people who've learned how to manipulate data. Google, YouTube, a few of the bloggers connected to big brands. And the social media aristocracy—LinkedIn, Facebook." In his first book, *The Cult of the Amateur*, Keen looked at the way the supposedly democratizing force of the Net and its unpaid enthusiasts has put actual professionals out of work. It's not just the Web, he said, or its open-content phase, but a larger cultural and economic shift. "We live in an age where more and more people think they have a book in them," he observed. "Or a film in them, or a song in them. But it's harder and harder to make a living at these things."

When Google is used as an excuse to fire the librarian, or "free" access to information causes circulation to drop and newspapers to lay off staff, the culture pays a very real price. Will the result be a neutron bomb culture? Lots of art and information left standing, but no people making it?

As cultural workers lose their jobs, where will they they go? Not only is the person who works in the book/record/video store a kind of low-paid curator, but these jobs have long served as an apprenticeship for artists, including Patti Smith, Quentin Tarantino, R.E.M.'s Peter Buck, and Jonathan Lethem.

Joe Donnelly, who co-edited the Los Angeles literary magazine *Slake*, has watched numerous friends leave writing, art, and acting. "I've seen a lot of people go into marketing—or help companies who want to be 'cool.'

What artists do now is help brands build an identity. They end up styling or set decorating. That's where we're at now."

The hard times and frustration are not confined to actors and writers. Eric Levin is a kind of entrepreneur of the creative class: he owns Aurora Coffee, two cafes in Atlanta that employ artists and musicians as baristas, and Criminal Records in the Little Five Points neighborhood, a record shop that thrived for twenty years and then was saved by a community effort after going on economic life support. One of his coffee shops closed in 2013. When asked if he knows anyone who's hurting, he replied, "Everybody I know." And he emphasized that independent businesspeople are in the same boat with writers and musicians. "Main Street U.S.A. is suffering. If you like big-box retailers—they're winning. Corporations are winning."

The arts—and indeed, narratives of all kinds—can capture a time, a place, and a culture, and reflect something of the inner and outer lives of its people. "But the tale of our times," Jaime O'Neill wrote in his piece on the silence of the new depression, "is mostly being told by our unwillingness to tell it."

[From *Culture Crash: The Killing of the Creative Class*, 2015]

LEAVING LOS ANGELES

REMEMBER THAT BITTERSWEET FEELING, halfway between queasy and liberating, when you've decided you're going to break up with someone but don't know when, where, or how you'll pull the trigger? Someone, that is, with whom you still share a connection but can no longer abide? I've lived with this weird ambiguity for almost a decade now. And I'm not talking about dumping my wife.

Each spring, sometime around when the magnolias on my street start to bloom and the elaborate flare of jacarandas, it happens: The Hollywood Bowl summer schedule comes out, the local soccer league announces sign-ups for the fall season, and universities look for commitments from teachers for the next term. Like my landlord's annual query about whether my wife, young son, and I will be staying in our rented cottage for another year, these all require us to figure out how much longer my family and I will be in Los Angeles.

We've been this way for years, existing here psychologically from month to month. As the world's economy shuddered in the fall of 2008, I lost my job as a writer-reporter covering books and authors at the *Los Angeles Times*. The relentlessness of the cutting was amazing: Not only were my two closest colleagues at the paper executed the same day, a favorite editor who took me for a consoling lunch at Musso & Frank was himself eviscerated a few months later. As my profession foundered and wages fell, even working full time as a freelancer earned me so little, I lost my house in 2011. The "recovery"—a period during which middle-class wealth actually declined—had sent rents up. Way up. By the time a sympathetic landlord took a chance, renting us a cottage in Burbank, the monthly tithe had nearly doubled since I'd last been in the game.

We're not unique. For many of us in Los Angeles—a metropolitan area that 57 percent of Angelenos can't afford to live in, according to a recent study—this is a city from which we are constantly on the brink of slipping away. Average rent in LA is $2,550 for a two-bedroom apartment. In fact, the disparity between wages and market prices here is the worst in the country, nastier than in New York City or the Bay Area, and it's become the toughest American city in which to buy a house. It's easy to forget now, as gaggles of tourists cross Hollywood Boulevard and Eastside neighborhoods carve themselves up into luxury condos and small-plates restaurants, but Los Angeles and California were hit especially hard by the Great Recession, and the damage lingered longer than almost anywhere else. LA County's unemployment rate was up around 12 and 13 percent for *years*, and along the way hundreds of thousands dropped out of the labor force entirely.

The economic contraction affected people at all levels, of course, from immigrant construction workers to board-certified doctors. Journalists like me were already reeling from the changes in reading habits wrought by the Internet. But the recession only made things worse, hastening my own layoff while rippling through the terrain of artists, novelists, and actors I'd made a living writing about for decades.

Over the last four years I've met an animator whose mental health deteriorated after a painful layoff, architects whose design firm (and marriage) became collateral damage, an accomplished musician and much-published poet who lived out of a van he parked under Silver Lake streetlights. My best friend in LA, a landscape painter who lived with his wife and son in a tiny Craftsman in Venice—a hub for artists in the sixties and still an affordable neighborhood when they arrived in 1998—saw his collector base, and income, collapse soon after Lehman Brothers tanked. There are scores of others with similar stories.

Some have remained, but many have left for jobs or reasonable rents they can't find in LA. For those of us who've stayed to continue the struggle, life here feels distinctly temporary. There are layers of significance in going to California and especially in moving to Los Angeles. But what's the meaning of leaving?

Los Angeles has been the site of fantasy, boosterism, and magical thinking for so long that it can be difficult to see the place clearly. People have come here from all directions: To the Japanese, this is the East. To Latin Americans, it's El Norte. And to multitudes within the country—whether impoverished Okies or blacks fleeing the South, or the beats, or British rock musicians, or artist Ed Ruscha in his old Ford on Route 66, or film people coming to break into Hollywood, or small-town suburban folks looking to "make it" in the big city—the movement west has had a special resonance.

The area's pull is as strong as ever. Sandal-wearing Silicon Valley types are buying up midcentury Westside homes from which to commute to Mountain View because it's cheaper here than South of Market. With so many art schools and galleries in Greater Los Angeles, the city is attracting striving artists who, willing to live on a shoestring, would have once considered New York the only place to be. For them, trading one high-rent city for another isn't that difficult. For prominent creatives like Moby,

Chloë Sevigny, and Lena Dunham, relocating (or at least buying property) here means more square footage and sunlight than in New York, which, conventional wisdom holds, has become blander as the middle class has been pushed out by exorbitant property values. And thousands of wealthy Chinese nationals are buying into the San Gabriel Valley, making a newly mansionized Arcadia "the Chinese Beverly Hills."

I have no doubt that it must be a blast to be young, rich, or famous in today's Los Angeles; I used to be one of those things, though it didn't last as long as I'd expected. Let me try to make this sound like a song: I arrived here one summer near the end of the century, at the tail end of my twenties, to work for a new weekly. ("Good riddance, dreary New England!" read a postcard an LA friend sent me; the burned-out mills on the reverse side vaguely resembled the Connecticut port city I was leaving.) It didn't take long for my life to ascend to the level of cliché: I found myself with a blond Midwestern girlfriend who loved to drive her Jeep to the Malibu beaches at all hours. The head-spinning LACMA show on video artist Bill Viola made me rethink what art could be, while *Boogie Nights*, out right before Christmas, had me wondering whether I was in some baffling mix of retro fantasy and urban Gomorrah. I could walk to Rhino Records on Westwood Boulevard and spend countless hours there. In older, more settled places, you've missed your chance to really belong if you weren't born there, but LA is different. You typically become a local a year or two after landing. Like others I spoke with, I felt I'd found a long-lost home, rushing to discover every film noir location or Beatles haunt or lingering bit of vernacular architecture.

The next year I met a different girl—an LA native—at an indie-rock show at the Troubadour, and we moved in together within sprinting distance of Canter's and the old Largo. We hiked in Joshua Tree, drove to remote, tree-shaded wineries in Santa Ynez. We were married in an old stone church in Pasadena, bought a small house in the Verdugo foothills, and brought our son home from Cedars—our room was next to Jack Black and Tanya Haden's—one spring day as the roses in our front yard burst forth.

Along the way I became not just an enthusiast but a partisan of California culture. I wrote stories about the fifties West Coast jazz scene and the sixties art explosion and sang the praises of modernists, forgotten painters, overlooked composers. I called the book I coedited about contemporary LA novelists and poets *The Misread City*, a title that practically screamed, "Take *this*, you blinkered, provincial Easterner."

As prosaic as it sounds, all this sunlit glory was accessible because of middle-class jobs and an economy that had made the city and state the envy of the world. The tens of thousands of careers that the aerospace industry provided in the postwar years helped make today's LA possible. There's been wealth here since the late 1800s, when industrial barons bought summer homes in the area. But the region offered room for millions of others to thrive on the money they made at jobs that didn't require a professional degree or investor funding. Firemen could afford to live in LA instead of thirty miles away from the city they were protecting.

Much of the manufacturing base was already gone by the time I met my wife. LA was pricey but not insanely so. She worked as a freelance writer and later as a teacher and school librarian while I labored as a scribe. We split $1,200 for our place near Fairfax, and although it took a lot of searching to find an affordable house, we made it happen. At a certain point, without quite sensing the change, I assumed we'd die here someday.

After my job went, my house, my credit, and any hope of eventual retirement followed. On groggy, unshaven mornings, as I run up narrow streets with my son to make the elementary school bell, the sun shining on the Griffith Park hills, I still feel like I could stay in the city forever. But even when things were going well, we gradually realized that to be middle class in twenty-first-century LA puts you on the sidelines. Now with my wife (despite two master's degrees) half a step from a layoff of her own, we know we'll always be downwardly mobile. Certainly we aren't homeless or poor, the way hundreds of thousands of Angelenos are. We can struggle to remain sideways. But as much as I like Los Angeles—which has been "home" longer than my Maryland hometown was—I'm no longer willing to be a third-class citizen here.

If LA began as a love affair with a beautiful and engaging (albeit neurotic) young woman, the city now seems like the girl who cheated on me and passed on a disease. During the first few months I was in town, I was both here—digging the sun and the bands and the beaches—and away, pining for places and people I'd left back east. Since my layoff, I've been partly here, partly in the next place. But where is that? I can tell you about the elementary schools in Portland, the coffee shops of Louisville, the guitar stores in Asheville, the yoga opportunities around Amherst—all areas we've considered moving to.

Though money, more than disenchantment, often drives a departure, one can lead to the other. Art critic Holly Meyers was elated when she came out here after graduating from Yale. But when she returned to the recession-raked landscape from three months in the silent Colorado mountains during an attempt to write a book, the city looked *different*. LA went from being "the city I was made for" to a place of so much auditory and social and professional noise that she knew she had to leave. Being broke helped the decision to head for Santa Fe.

David Shaw, who worked in sales for two indie-rock labels here, never quite got his groove back during the Great Recession; he ended up leaving town and now works for a label in Chapel Hill. He misses a lot of things about LA—the vegan restaurants, "the massive number of dreamers" who give the city its energy—but he noticed an anxiety settling over him like ash from a forest fire. The smog, crushing traffic, and creeping drought slowly made him fold up inside. He's happier now. For essayist Richard Rodriguez, LA was a city of wit and conversation—it made him think of the intellectual life of eighteenth-century London, only with sliding-glass doors and better-looking people. He retreated to San Francisco, where clouds and the dour Yankee ethic meant he could get work done.

One aspiring screenwriter pulled into town, after days on the road, with "Surfin' Safari" on the stereo and promptly ended up on I-405, going the wrong way. He compares his nine years in LA with the downward spiral of Naomi Watts's wide-eyed character in *Mulholland Drive*. He took an instant dislike to the place, but hiking, mountains, and a few teasing forays into Hollywood kept him from realizing it until he left for grad school in Michigan, coming back only to get his stuff out of storage.

It's no surprise that when you have kids, making the pieces fit is especially difficult, as novelist Katharine Noel puts it. She wrote in a corner of her Los Feliz living room while her husband, Eric Puchner, also a writer, toiled in a corner of the bedroom. They spent four to six hours a week commuting to their teaching jobs in Claremont, concluding that they would not ever be able to buy in a decent school district for their two kids. Johns Hopkins recruited them, and they now live comfortably in a leafy part of Baltimore. Noel misses strip-mall Asian restaurants, Eastside coffee shops, and the Silver Lake Reservoir, but they're getting ready to buy, and they walk to work. As my wife and I look at various neighborhoods—trying to sync up costs and decent schools with commutes and basic urban pleasures—I think of them.

In a sense you can never really leave Southern California: Put on the Byrds or Dr. Dre, or watch *Three's Company* or *M*A*S*H* or a John Ford movie, and you're back here, even when it's a location pretending to be somewhere else. Los Angeles has colonized our imaginations. Visit many other cities, Rodriguez points out—Houston, Atlanta, Vegas, Austin, Seattle—and you're in a place that's emulated LA's rambling horizontalism.

But there's another, deeper way we can never leave LA: The city transforms people. Even those who arrived here as adults and then left consider themselves Angelenos. A former film publicist who lived in Los Feliz (for $625 a month) listens to KCRW online from her house in Portland, Maine. Siobhan Spain, who resettled in the Midwest when the Chinatown gallery she directed shut down, remembers LA as a magical place: "Where else, on any certain day, could you witness Esa-Pekka Salonen conducting at Walt Disney Concert Hall, walk by a homeless person defecating on the sidewalk, swim near dolphins at Point Dume State Beach, help install artwork by Sanford Biggers, sit in traffic for over an hour, watch your friend act in an episode of *Nip/Tuck*, and go to sleep with ghetto birds circling your neighborhood?"

The musician Stew grew up here, founding the group the Negro Problem, but has come and gone several times. New York, Amsterdam, and Berlin gave him the sense that he was at the center of something rather than being eclipsed by the industry's heft. "Los Angeles," he says, "had a tendency to make you feel small." He left in 2004 for New York, partly because of a commission by the Public Theater for what became the musical *Passing Strange*. The east is full of philanthropists supporting culture. "In LA you're kind of on your own," Stew says. Today he lives in Brooklyn, in a brownstone near Prospect Park. But not completely. "You take LA with you wherever you go," he says. "I will never be a New York artist. I will always make music from the garage in the backyard." He's a Beach Boy, not a Ramone.

It's human nature to try to make meaning out of life, to build narrative shapes out of events and images. That may be, in the end, what creativity is about. But there may be no way to craft a life story around leaving LA, moving to Iowa or Chapel Hill or wherever. The energy is just so much stronger in the other direction. "To leave Los Angeles to go to Baltimore—that's not really a heroic journey," Noel says. "It didn't have to do with geography or any kind of larger narrative. It had to do with making a life as a writer."

That's the reality shaping my own story. As much as I'd like to think the city will mourn my family's departure, others will replace us. They may not be a small family trying to lead a middle-class existence, but I have no doubt that Los Angeles and its culture will go on whether or not we stay. My band of exiles, for all their disparate destinations, continue to see LA as mysterious, alluring, electric, just out of reach. Someday soon I will, too. The vagaries of employment and other economic issues mean I can't tell whether I will be gone by the time you read this or still plotting my escape. But in the restless spirit of a true Angeleno, I can't wait to get there.

[*Los Angeles Magazine*, July 6, 2015]

SEARCHING FOR A GREAT AMERICAN ROCK SHOW

TWO MUCH-AWAITED SERIES ABOUT ROCK 'N' ROLL made their debuts on prestigious cable networks this year. One has already been cancelled, after generating its share of hatred from the very people who should have loved it. Another has not quite lifted off, and may not last beyond its initial season, either. With a third series drawing mostly bad reviews, it's enough to make you wonder: Is it even possible to make a decent television show about rock music?

One of these shows, Denis Leary's *Sex&Drugs&Rock&Roll*, didn't arrive with enormous expectations, so it hasn't been met with the severe disappointment of the others. But *Vinyl* was set in a period that currently generates immense fascination—New York in the pre-punk seventies—helmed by Martin Scorsese, Mick Jagger, and Terence Winter of *Boardwalk Empire*. And *Roadies* was created by Cameron Crowe, the former music writer who directed *Almost Famous*, with executive production by Winnie Holzman, creator of *My So-Called Life*.

Two veterans of rock journalism tried to puzzle out with me why these shows didn't work. All three of us wanted to like these series, but somehow the shows didn't quite arrive. We disagreed, though, over whether the genre of the rock-show could be saved.

Part of the problem with *Vinyl*, which was cancelled after a single season that cost about $100 million, is that it was aimed at exactly the kind of serious rock fan that would be annoyed by how many of its details it got wrong. (Critic Caryn Rose recapped the show for *Salon*, focusing on the authenticity of its portrayal of the time period and the artists, and found it often came up lacking.) "My sense of *Vinyl* was that it was a kind of glorious failure," says Ira Robbins, a music critic best known as the editor of the *Trouser Press* guides to alternative rock music. "They made a costly, painstaking effort to recreate an era. And then having reproduced it, they laid on these sloppy anachronisms, coincidences, and fictionalized history." And the show's creators offered brief appearances by actors playing actual musicians, to almost no effect.

"It was like wax figures—Madame Tussaud's. The story didn't need any of the real people." The real parallels—Gram Parsons showing up in a visit to LA—were like a series of non sequiturs.

One of the biggest problems was the Nasty Bitz, a band led by Jagger's son, which bore almost no resemblance to any band in New York at the time, Robbins says. (The other rock critics I spoke to disliked the show almost as intensely.)

Mitchell Cohen wrote about rock music in New York in the years *Vinyl* was set, and took a job in A & R a few years later. He found it "ridiculous on every level," with a "smug, in-the-know name-dropping" even while failing to create anything like the real atmosphere of those years.

Part of rock music's appeal is exclusivity, the sense of being inside a dangerous subculture and getting all the jokes. *Vinyl* seems to have failed to resonate with people who like music for that reason, and it somehow failed to reach the people who aspire to be part of its dark, urban demimonde.

Another side of rock is more democratic and mainstream, driven by passion for the music but in a more sincere, open-hearted way: This is what Cameron Crowe offers, in movies like *Say Anything* and *Almost Famous.* So when his *Roadies* went on air this spring on Showtime, it seemed like his warmer approach to rock music might fit our tense times better than the too-cool-for-school coke-fest of *Vinyl.*

But while there have been no announcements of the show's cancellation, and it's simply impossible to hate, *Roadies* has failed to generate excitement. "*Roadies* is a completely nebulous show that exists in its own universe," says Robbins. "And then they sprinkle in some musical references. It's simple and obvious and predictable."

There is some good acting in the show—Imogen Poots plays a bruised young idealist very convincingly—but also a lot of missed connections, as in what's supposed to be romantic tension between Luke Wilson and Carla Gugino's characters. I've watched all five episodes made available to the press, and keep wanting each one to be better. At some point, I fear, I'll have to give up.

"I think it would be better if it was either smarter or dumber," Robbins says. "They're not telling enough about the reality, and they're hiding behind the culture. This is so glossed-up it's like *Happy Days.*"

Cohen likes *Roadies* a bit better, but his descriptions are the definition of faint praise. "It was nice to see a show where there wasn't a lot at stake," he says. "It's mostly people doing their jobs. The big tension is whether someone can get to the computer in time to put in the new set list. I kind of like that. While *Vinyl* was trying to make these grandiose statements about the power of rock."

Part of the problem, though, is that after a few episodes of small stakes, it's hard to keep wanting to tune in again. "This is a band on the road, and not a lot happens," Cohen says. "*Almost Famous* was two hours—what is this, ten hours?" The tension isn't exactly building. "Are they gonna change the set list again?"

So between these two shows and Leary's—"a lame rerun of Leary's better hits," the *Atlantic*'s David Sims judged—I'm wondering: Can anyone do this right?

Robbins thinks not. The audience for rock music ranges so widely in generation, favorite style, and level of commitment that it's hard to get everyone on the same page, he says. There's just not enough consensus. "How would you take that enormously fragmented audience and make something both insightful and entertaining?" he asks. "You can't narrowcast a TV show. It's hard for someone like Cameron Crowe to make a show that would interest a twenty-year-old. You could make a show that nobody understood—with sophisticated references and in-jokes—or a show that's not really about anything but sort of set in that world. And neither of them would be entirely satisfying to anybody."

But Cohen disagrees. "I don't think it's impossible. I keep coming back to *Mad Men*. It's just about advertising." The show's premise doesn't sound like a natural hit. "'Really? Are they gonna do TV commercials and layouts for *Esquire* magazine?'" The show worked, though, because it was smartly written, acted, and constructed.

But there's something else that *Mad Men* and Aaron Sorkin shows like *The Newsroom* and *Sports Night* have in common that these rock shows don't. *Mad Men* creator Matt Weiner didn't love advertising, but he wanted to get something across about the role the industry played in sixties culture. Sorkin felt for the plight of TV journalists, but he was after character and story. Few people turned to *Mad Men* because of their passion for Madison Avenue.

Similarly, the best movies about rock music—*This Is Spinal Tap, School of Rock*—were made by directors who cared about rock music, but there's a sense of ironic distance alongside the love of its characters.

Loving rock music and the people who make it is, as far as I'm concerned, a virtuous stance. But it may not lead to good TV. If someone can balance their ardor with their art, may he or she please stand up now. In this dreary year, we could sure use it.

[*Salon*, July 23, 2016]

THE REVENGE OF MONOCULTURE

Is IT GONE? DO WE MISS IT? Do we want it back? Are we glad it's history? I'm talking about the so-called monoculture, and I'm not sure whether we were supposed to be nostalgic or gleeful about its so-called passing.

The fight over the monoculture is a funny, ambiguous one: Some have argued that having a shared Anglo-American culture gives us a communal sense of belonging together, sharing concerns and values at a time when politics, ethnicity, and religion often divide us. Being able to share in the wonder of a groundbreaking new Beatles album, to exalt over the release of Purple Rain, to welcome a big summer movie, was a sign of a culture that worked, where people listen to each other and connect through their tastes. Figures as different as Robert Christgau—the Silent Generation journalist who helped invent rock criticism—and Touré—the Gen Xer who writes on a wide range of topics, especially black music—have lamented the loss of this kind of shared experience. Touré wrote about what he calls Massive Musical Moments this way:

> In these Moments, an album becomes so ubiquitous it seems to blast through the windows, to chase you down until it's impossible to ignore it. But you don't want to ignore it, because the songs

are holding up a mirror and telling you who we are at that moment in history.

These sorts of Moments can't be denied. They leave an indelible imprint on the collective memory; when we look back at the year or the decade or the generation, there's no arguing that the album had a huge impact on us. It's pop music not just as private joy, but as a unifier, giving us something to share and bond over.

But cyber-utopians looked at the downside of this kind of cultural unity and offered something else: Instead of the lockstep world of three networks, a handful of radio stations and a limited number of news sources, the Internet would offer a wild range of options. Chris Anderson's book *The Long Tail* was only one of the celebratory works that made it sound like an eclectic digital paradise was inevitable and imminent: Every bit of niche culture would find its audience, and the idea of the mainstream—all that obligatory stuff everyone was expected to like—would wither away. Why listen to tired AOR playlists and watch the same old sitcoms when manga, K-pop, Nordic metal, comedy offerings on YouTube, and infinite indie everything would be available around the clock, to anyone with an Internet connection? As Anderson wrote:

An analysis of the sales data and trends from these services and others like them shows that the emerging digital entertainment economy is going to be radically different from today's mass market. If the twentieth-century entertainment industry was about hits, the twenty-first will be equally about misses.

With "diversity" a rallying cry for most on the liberal left, this fit what about half the audience wanted. Since many conservatives were urging a breakdown of the "mainstream media," there seemed to be something in here for almost everyone. (Silicon Valley's Peter Thiel talked in his speech at the Republican National Convention about the "ossified monoculture" that his hero Donald Trump would help to defeat.) And if you are a Pop-timist—the strain of music critic who exalts popular taste over stuffy old critical biases—the disappearance of the monoculture is a good thing, too: It sets taste free. Who can object to freedom?

Looking at the summer of 2016, it's still hard to determine whether a monoculture is something we want or we don't. (In agriculture, the issue is similarly vexing.) But one thing that's becoming clear: While there is plenty of diversity—of opinion, of musical style, of offerings in television and movies—the monoculture is as strong as ever. Whether it's better or worse is a whole other question, but the mainstream, rather than fragment-ing, has reinforced itself in a big way.

So while it's possible, as it's always been, to retreat from pop culture and rely entirely, say, on a diet of eighteenth century Baroque piano music, Japanese anime, and *Twilight Zone* reruns, the gravitational pull of the mainstream is strong. Log onto Twitter, and be drawn into sports culture whether you want to or not: Not just from notifications, but from the NFL games that will stream there.

How about movies? Of the ten highest earning films of 2016, the top nine are either kids movies or comic book properties. The last one—*Central Intelligence*—is a comedy-action movie with blockbuster actor Dwayne Johnson. These are also the movies that get talked about online, in all but the artsiest magazines, in the ads that probably take up more space in your newspaper than the reviews do.

Meanwhile, even the most serious actors—Ben Affleck, Scarlett Johansson, Robert Downey, Jr.—are devoting a lot of their time to superhero films and action movies. We've barely had time to recover from Affleck's appearance in *Batman v. Superman* before we get the chance to see his cameo in *Suicide Squad*, to catch his starring role wielding a gun in *The Accountant*, and to see the new trailer for *Justice League*. Whether or not you like Affleck's sometimes drowsy and wooden style, this is a guy who made his name with indies by Richard Linklater and Kevin Smith.

What else happened this week? The pop culture news that has broken through the onslaught of the political conventions has mostly involved Comic-Con, which attracted 130,000 people to San Diego this year and which movie studios ignore at their peril.

To be clear, there are all kinds of "culture" coming right now, including a wide variety of music. But the media coverage of music this week—the way most people hear about what's being released and what matters—was mostly about MTV's Video Music Awards. The VMAs have nominated, over the years, Herbie Hancock for "Rockit," Cindi Lauper for "Girls Just Want to Have Fun," Paul Simon, Talking Heads, the Verve, Beck, D'Angelo . . . Stylistically, that's all over the place.

This year, it's Adele, Beyoncé, Drake, Justin Bieber, and Kanye West: Kiddie pop, and superstar R & B. Some of these videos are of high quality—Beyoncé's "Formation" is the centerpiece of the aesthetically and politically daring *Lemonade* and would be nominated in any year. But the only surprise here is that Taylor Swift didn't get nominated. And Swift is so huge—and celebrity so dominating a force in both culture and the way we talk about it—that we don't have to look far to find her. There she is, in the video for Kanye West's "Famous" . . . and in the articles about Taylor Swift being snubbed by the VMAs this year. She's here even when she's not here.

"Many people have categorized the 2016 presidential election as a referendum on the very soul of America," Amy Zimmerman wrote in a Daily Beast story about the awards, topped with a picture of Swift. "But I would argue that nothing has illustrated the eternal, nationwide battle between good and evil quite like Taylor Swift and Kanye West's seven-year beef." She's kidding, in part, but plenty of people who aren't kidding see things this way.

So are we better off than we used to be? That's hard to say. But if the mainstream used to mean AOR acts like Fleetwood Mac and The Eagles, "uplifting" Oscar movies alongside Spielberg-style action films, and bland network programming, only one medium has broadened drastically in the Internet age. Television is not only more "diverse"—both racially and in terms of style—and smarter, it's got a discourse around it that debates *Breaking Bad* and *Game of Thrones* and *Empire* and everything else. At the Emmys, *Transparent* and *Master of None* and *The Americans* will all be in the mix.

But when it comes to the movies and films that make money and draw attention, the list gets pretty thin. It's songs by corporate-branded celebrities (at various degrees of quality) and comic-book movies.

So why did this happen, when it was supposed to go the other way? Like any cultural change, it likely comes from a swirl of economic, technological, and sociological factors that we'll only understand fully in retrospect. History shows that capitalism tends towards monopoly unless some counterforce pushes back, and the Internet has not yet found its Teddy Roosevelt. The biggest musicians and actors bombard us with tweets, puffy magazine stories, and online marketing until their "brands" are ubiquitous. But part of it may be the Paradox of Choice: If everything is available, all the time, we're likely to get overwhelmed and just fall back on what we know already (or what's been the most aggressively marketed to us.) If you've ever stared at an enormous, multi-page menu and decided to get the burger or the steak, you know how this works.

The Internet's near-infinite offerings are not the only cause, but it's worth looking at what's happened since it arrived. We've always had popular and fringe, overexposed and undersung, but the proportion has changed. In 1986, thirty-one songs hit number one, and came from twenty-nine different bands or artists. By the period from January 2008 to September 2012—we're into the first years of digital dominance—half the number one songs are turned out by just six artists. (That's Katy Perry, Rihanna, Flo Rida, The Black Eyed Peas, Adele, and Lady Gaga.) *New York* magazine calls it "the monopoly at the top."

And the changes in online media have followed similar contours. "The top ten web sites accounted for 31 percent of US page views in 2001, 40 percent in 2006, and about 75 percent in 2010," Michael Wolff wrote in *Wired*. Now with Facebook increasingly the way most Americans get their news, the faux-consensus will be even tighter.

So we might not all buy the same album anymore. But the whole country was talking about the latest *Star Wars* last winter, and that seems likely to repeat for at least the next few years. Just as television news—whether on the left or the right—has picked up the hectoring tone of Fox News broadcasts, most online media has borrowed the snark of Gawker. It's pretty clear that Taylor, Kanye, Bieber, the Kardashians, and numerous superheroes—most of which present themselves as misunderstood underdogs—will continue to be impossible to escape. We can pretty much bet what kinds of movies will dominate media coverage and the box office next year, and it won't be hard to guess who will produce the most celebrated videos and best-selling songs of 2017.

It may be an improvement over the Eagles. But if this isn't monoculture, I don't know what is.

[*Salon*, July 30, 2016]

HOW MUSIC HAS RESPONDED TO A DECADE OF ECONOMIC INEQUALITY

CULTURE, ESPECIALLY POPULAR CULTURE, always has some relation to the conditions that surround it, and these days, there is no shortage of music that reflects our economic reality.

But that reflection isn't always quite what you'd expect. During the Great Depression, which saw widespread homelessness and US unemployment reaching 25 percent, popular films showed the very rich drinking cocktails in formal dress; cheery songs like "Pennies From Heaven" charted. And in the post-2008 decade of recession, instability, and income inequality, blockbuster acts spent a lot of time telling us the incredible time they were having.

The real story of the past decade has been harder to hear. A decade ago, as some Americans remember all too well, the US economy began to crumble, and took the rest of the world's markets along with it. First housing prices started to slide, revealing a nation caught in a deflating real estate bubble. Bear Stearns and Lehman Brothers came next.

The cascade of damage was worldwide, but it took on an especially fierce pitch in the world's largest economy: Beginning in late 2008, the US was losing more than half a million jobs a month. By 2009, the Great Recession's first full year, national unemployment reached fifteen million people, or 10 percent—the first double-digit rate since the early 1980s. Trillions of dollars of wealth disappeared from the economy, and four million Americans lost their homes in just two years.

Meanwhile, the nation's biggest songs in the year after the crash were numbers by Flo Rida, Chris Brown, and Coldplay that had little to do with economic strain. It takes any cultural form—movies, books, visual art, whatever—months, sometimes years, to respond to social, political, or economic change. But pop music has less lag time than most other genres.

(In previous centuries, folk songs about hangings or train crashes could appear almost instantly. And it wasn't for nothing that Public Enemy's Chuck D once called hip-hop black America's CNN.)

By the end of 2009, though, the biggest-selling singles were songs like Jay-Z's "Empire State of Mind," Lady Gaga's "Bad Romance," and various party-hearty numbers by the Black Eyed Peas. And so it went, into the teeth of the recession.

Popular music, of course, becomes popular partly because it takes people away from their lives. Be it the blandness of affluence or the pain of personal difficulty, there has always been an element of aspiration and fantasy to popular culture.

But from Woody Guthrie singing about the Dust Bowl and the Great Depression's devastations in the 1930s to rock and soul bands of the sixties and seventiess writing about war and civil rights to British punks shouting about unemployment and the working class to rappers spitting about injustice and racism, popular music has always also delivered social critique—much of the time including economic issues.

What we see in the decade following the 2008 stock market crash, though, is a relatively tame popular music world in which best-selling artists and left-of-the-dial "alternative" musicians share an apparent lack of interest in the nation's economic state.

"Most people in the mainstream music world—whether it's pop, indie, or country—don't want to offend any of their fans," says Margo Price, a country singer-songwriter who has been outspoken about economic structures. "Their big labels don't want them to, either."

After the pain of the 2008 crash, the nation experienced an economic recovery that shifted a massive amount of income from the poor and middle class to the very rich. The big banks got bigger; huge bonuses returned. Just two years after the crash, the nation's Gini coefficient, the standard measure of wealth distribution, was at forty-six and nine tenths, making the US among the most unequal of modern democracies.

We can call the past ten years the decade of inequality. So what, then, does the music of inequality sound like?

The tropes of mainstream pop music are far removed from audiences' economic realities

Part of the paradox here is simply that monetary wealth gives musicians— at least, the tiny minority experiencing material bounty—something to sing about.

Musicians are not unique here: In the years since the Reagan administration, a reveling in what used to be called heartless materialism has become de rigueur. (The shift in personal style from an old-school rich man like Warren Buffett, who made his early fortune in the 1950s, to Donald Trump, a product of the gilded 1980s, is hard to miss.)

Artists singing about how much wealth they had accrued fit cleanly into a *Lifestyles of the Rich and Famous* culture. The Beatles, the Rolling Stones, and Marvin Gaye were filthy rich, but it's hard to imagine them crooning about their money and mansions. Nor can we imagine Joni Mitchell, Patti Smith, or Liz Phair posing in a bath of diamonds, as Taylor Swift does in the 2017 video for "Look What You Made Me Do."

Many of the songs about luxurious possessions and lavish lifestyles—the sonic equivalent of *Keeping Up With the Kardashians*—are the descendants of "Mo Money Mo Problems," the 1997 Notorious B.I.G. song. But in many cases, there seem to be no serious problems besides having too many women or possessions to choose from.

"When inequality is high, it's driven by the superrich, because [the poor] can't go lower than zero," says Keith Payne, a University of North Carolina psychology professor and author of *The Broken Ladder*, a recent book on wealth disparity. "People feel poorer but aspire to higher standards. This leads to a risk-taking kind of life: People are more likely to gamble, play the odds, use drugs or drink, commit crimes. It also orients people to the very wealthy as opposed to the poor."

These are the classic tropes of hip-hop, a musical style that, Payne points out, surged in ubiquity in the same years as the rise in inequality. A mixtape of conspicuous consumption and runaway consumerism could be assembled from songs like Post Malone and Ty Dolla Sign's "Psycho" ("got diamonds by the boatload!"), Lil Uzi Vert's "Money Longer" ("money got longer, speaker got louder, car got faster"), and Lil Pump's "Gucci Gang" ("Spend ten racks on a new chain / My bitch love do cocaine.")

The style became so ubiquitous that the satirical trio the Lonely Island parodied the genre of gold-plated gloat with "I'm on a Boat," a 2009 rap song featuring T-Pain that makes "yacht rock" numbers like Christopher Cross's 1980 hit "Sailing" look modest and egalitarian.

More cutting is Lorde's 2013 song "Royals," which seems to be aware of how mismatched the music is to the times: "But every song's like gold teeth, Grey Goose, trippin' in the bathroom / Bloodstains, ball gowns, trashin' the hotel room / We don't care, we're driving Cadillacs in our dreams . . . "

Part of what looking across the genres shows you is that the big-selling, celebrity-driven mainstream of just about every style of music offers very little social or economic critique. If that's what you're looking for, look to the edges.

Music engaging with inequality tends to be on the fringes of popular genres

Mainstream country music, a genre rooted in the rural red-state South, is no stranger to poverty or songs about risk-taking. But it very rarely deals with inequality, says Payne, a native of Kentucky. "The only economic theme is, 'We grew up poor, but we didn't know it at the time, and now we've got everything we need.' That's the theme of countless country songs," he says.

The country songwriters interested in exploring economics more assertively don't find a receptive industry, whether radio, country labels, or other gatekeepers. "They are so scared of coming out on an issue that offends Trump America," says R. J. Smith, a music journalist and author of a recent biography of photographer Robert Frank. What you get, instead, is "good short story-ish songwriting about how people are living, but with little sense of why poverty happened."

To the extent that there's been a consistent protest, it comes, curiously, from the fringes of country. Despite its recent political and cultural conservatism, country has been the music of the poor and working class since the days of Jimmie Rodgers and the Carter Family. And the alt-country movement, which has co-opted the folk tradition, continued the grit and social criticism of the old days after the big-hatted mainstream moved into formula and political reaction.

This has led to what we could call empathy songs and plutocrat songs: The empathy song looks at the plight of someone crushed under the economic wheel, sometimes speaking in his or her voice; the plutocrat song is typically more overtly political, targeting the damage done by the very rich.

Honorary Americana artist Billy Bragg (who is British but has made several albums of Woody Guthrie's music with alt-country pioneers Wilco) began performing Guthrie's "I Ain't Got No Home" after the 2008 crash. (The song is explicitly class-based, describing a "rich man [who] took my home and drove me from my door.")

And Margo Price's songs are among the strongest economic critiques post-Great Recession: Numbers like "Pay Gap," "About to Find Out," and "All American Made" ("And I wonder if the president gets much sleep at night / And if the folks on welfare are making it all right") sometimes combine feminism with scenes from the class struggle.

Veteran singer-songwriter Loudon Wainwright III worked in a vaguely country-folk tradition with his 2010 album, *10 Songs For the New Depression*. The songs alternated from despairing to lighthearted (the number "House" is both), and name-check Alan Greenspan and John Maynard Keynes. (One cheeky number is called "The Krugman Blues.") Peter Himmelman's "Rich Men Rule the World" is a brutal song in the same vein.

Two classics from the edges of country actually predate the Great Recession, perhaps because the rural South never quite caught the postwar boom like the rest of the nation did. James McMurtry's "We Can't Make It Here," from 2005, tells of a struggling, wounded Vietnam veteran, empty storefronts, a failing bar, and the pinch of a stagnant minimum wage. (The novelistic vision is appropriate for the son of *Lonesome Dove* author Larry McMurtry.) And while their most recent album is more about race and politics in general, Drive-By Truckers' 2005 album, *The Dirty South*, is a forceful look at American poverty and inequality, highlighted by the song "Puttin' People on the Moon."

"In our hometown," Drive-By Truckers leader Patterson Hood says of Florence, Alabama, "the economy collapsed in the early 1980s: During the so-called Reagan boom years, we were like Flint, Michigan. They closed the Ford plant, and there was a domino effect."

Along with the songs of the late Merle Haggard, Bruce Springsteen's work serves as a template for bands like the Truckers. The Boss has written some of the best work about the way economics shapes and limits lives— songs like "My Hometown" and the Dust Bowl-inspired *Ghost of Tom Joad* LP. He has not quite matched these since; his energies have largely been elsewhere. But the 2012 *Wrecking Ball* LP, with songs like "We Take Care of Our Own" and the Wall Street-dissing "Death to My Hometown," is a solid stab at addressing what much of the country has been through.

And while the late, great soul musician Charles Bradley largely sang about racism and his personal travails, his "Why Is It So Hard," from 2011, may be the single most emotionally powerful recent song about poverty and income inequality.

Hip-hop, too, gets more political and anti-capitalist around the edges. The Coup, the Oakland hip-hop group led by Boots Riley, released a 2012 album called *Sorry to Bother You*, which would eventually lend its name to the new breakout movie. The album takes a far-left stance on issues of economics and inequality, heavily informed by Riley's communist beliefs, with songs like "Strange Arithmetic" ("Economics is the symphony of hunger and theft / Mortar shells often echo out the cashing of checks / In geography class, it's borders, mountains, and rivers / But they will never show the line between the takers and givers") and "WAVIP" ("I am with the people on the bottom, fella / We gonna riot, loot, rob till we rich as Rockefeller").

Meanwhile, much of mainstream hip-hop went from fierce anti-racist politics, decades ago, to celebrations of hedonism. Music historian Robert Fink of UCLA points out that in the years after the stock market crash, the nation experienced its first black president, who was widely popular, especially with black people. When Obama was replaced with a man with a reputation for antagonizing black people, alongside a rash of police killings of young African-American men, politically minded hip-hop and R & B artists increasingly focused their attention on Black Lives Matter and related movements, rather than economics.

"I can't think of a single hip-hop song about people getting subprime mortgages or that kind of thing," Fink says.

Inequality is not a natural driver for slick, commercial pop songwriting

"There is very little in the mainstream music business about economic hardship," says music historian Ted Gioia. "Are Katy Perry, Justin Bieber, Lady Gaga, Taylor Swift trying to shake things up?" Some artists sing about race and gender, he says, but economics has largely been overlooked in the slick and commercial pop mainstream.

Gioia characterizes the lip service the music industry pays to social issues as a decades-old problem: MTV and the rest of the business largely slept through the AIDS crisis in the 1980s; this time, Gioia says, economic inequality has become the forgotten issue.

But some artists have made an end run around these forces.

One of the most realized looks at the Great Recession and its discontents may not be a political piece of hip-hop or an angry piece of outlaw country, but rather a musical. *Hadestown* was an off-Broadway "folk opera" in 2016, relocating the story of Orpheus and Eurydice in a post-apocalyptic Great Depression with a wink toward the present. It's based on an album by folk singer Anais Mitchell that includes contributions from Ani DiFranco, the Haden Triplets, and Bon Iver's Justin Vernon.

Finally, there was a four-disc compilation in 2012 called *Occupy This Album: 99 Songs for the 99 Percent.* The styles and quality range quite widely, from Michael Moore singing Dylan's "The Times They Are A-Changin'" to songs by Yoko Ono, Toots and the Maytals, and Nancy Griffith. (The video for "United Tribes," a song by Thievery Corporation with rapper Mr. Lif, captures the energy of the movement it emerged from.) Still, it's hard to miss that many of the songs are old, or only obliquely related to Occupy itself.

One reason songs about the recession and inequality are hard to find may be psychological. The Brooklyn musician Pauline Pisano lost her job as a web designer when the recession hit, and has struggled financially since. But it wasn't until an NYU course and an exposure to the books of David Graeber that she focused on economic matters and the corrosive effects of debt. ("I feel like the people who cheated won," she says now. "And for the people who played by the rules, the rules changed.") She's since led a musical tour of the South talking to people across the political spectrum about the subject, and her work has been politically energized.

"I was hit by the recession very heavily—why didn't I put that in my art?" Pisano asks. "Maybe I thought, 'This is just the way things are.'"

As crucial an issue and as destructive a force as inequality is, it's not a natural driver for songwriting. "Inequality is the ultimate abstraction," says Keith Payne. "Art is not typically about abstractions—it tends to be about concrete images. Inequality is neither wealth nor poverty, but the distribution of resources. And who wants to sing about that?"

What does it mean when popular music does not really express most Americans' lived experience?

One glaring irony here is that the past decade has also seen the vast majority of musicians struggling even more than they did previously: The collapse of the sale of recordings has made most of them all too aware of income inequality, especially when they compare themselves to one-percenters of the past (the Eagles) or present (Lady Gaga).

Alan Krueger, President Barack Obama's chief economist, gave an important speech about the way the winner-take-all economy devastated many rock musicians in 2012, and there are few signs that the musical middle class has been restored.

The larger issue here—the lack of genuinely popular songs about the biggest economic event since 1929—is pop culture's claims of being a democratic art. What if popular music does not really express and describe what the mass of Americans is experiencing? And in an era when the phrase "check your privilege" has become commonplace, does it matter if the biggest hits are being made, in many cases, by fantastically privileged people?

Taylor Swift, for instance, comes from a long line of bank presidents; her father relocated to Merrill Lynch's Nashville office and later bought a share of a record label to help her career. (See also "Uptown Funk" producer Mark Ronson, from one of Britain's wealthiest families.)

"If it becomes clear that our popular culture is a rich kids' project, it loses its legitimacy," UCLA's Fink says. "Even more than in Britain, we have Horatio Alger pretensions here." Once we get a sense that our popular culture is the preserve of the very rich, it's not quite "popular" in the democratic way we typically use the term.

But it also may be that the unpopularity of a president who himself comes from the plutocrat class will finally focus musicians and their handlers on inequality and other pressing issues. "I think that we are living in a very dangerous time," says Price. "People as a whole are distracted by social media, celebrities, unattainable wealth."

But things can change, and Price believes they might: "We're in a turning point right now, and musicians and visual artists have a chance to move mountains with their words. If they would only use them."

[*Vox*, July 30, 2018]

AFTER A DECADE, WILL GUSTAVO DUDAMEL STAY AT THE LA PHIL OR LEAVE ON A HIGH NOTE?

THE FIRST TIME GUSTAVO DUDAMEL CAME TO LOS ANGELES, his reputation soaring after winning a prestigious conducting contest in Germany, the twenty four year-old walked into the Hollywood Bowl's rooftop restaurant and was greeted by artistic administrators who had flown in from across the land expressly to meet the emerging legend. Chad Smith was one of them.

"He spent like five minutes at the dinner," recalls Smith, today the LA Philharmonic's chief operating officer, "and was like, 'Naaah . . . ' He went to that hot dog place on La Brea."

These days Dudamel prefers sushi and Nancy Silverton's restaurants, but that night fourteen years ago it wasn't Pink's celebrated chili dog he was after. He just wasn't ready.

"I think you have to protect yourself," Dudamel says today, sipping sparkling water at Bar Marmont as a Bill Evans Trio record plays in the background. Dressed in casual black with artfully weathered brown boots—a goth preparing for a strenuous hike—he adds: "You have to respect others, but you have to respect yourself." He makes clear that he shook everyone's hand that night at the Bowl and later caught up with Smith over a burger in West Hollywood.

In the year or so following his unexpected triumph in Bamberg, Germany—and the bombardment of offers and accolades that followed—Dudamel thought often of his mentor, the late Venezuelan conductor Jose Antonio Abreu, who had always urged: "reflection, thinking, time to breathe." Abreu had routinely counseled that a mind is like a bottle of wine, and that half an inch of air between the cork and the juice is what makes it all possible—you need space to let your soul exhale. Dudamel loves metaphors and uses them liberally when trying to get a musical idea across to the orchestra: *Play your instrument like you are swimming naked; you are flipping through a book and see a picture you cannot touch. . . .*

Despite his initial hesitation, Dudamel ended up, of course, accepting the music director position with the Phil after being pursued by orchestras from around the world; he just guided it through the recently concluded 100th season, which may have been the most ambitious and extravagant season by any orchestra on the planet. In September he will mark ten years with the Phil, having hired nearly a third of its 106 musicians and, arguably, transformed its sound. As the most famous classical musician in America and the public face of an orchestra considered the world's most daring, Dudamel inevitably informs the next century of the Phil—and fuels speculation about whether a man so ferociously restless will remain at its helm a second decade.

To appreciate the Dudamel phenomenon, it's necessary to consider the recent state of classical music in the English-speaking world. Simply put, LA was a ravaged—or at least dispirited—land craving a savior. A bit like diminished Democrats eternally pining for JFK, classical music folk have been yearning for a figure who could galvanize the general public the way Leonard Bernstein did in the mid-twentieth century. "Everybody's looking to us as a symbol," Dudamel says. (Dudamel uses "we" or "us" more often than "I," wearing his humility and love of what he calls his family on his sleeve.)

By now the story of Dudamel's arrival has nearly passed into myth. Some have compared it to the grooming of a Hollywood star; others see biblical parallels, with Abreu—founder of the Venezuelan-based music program El Sistema that's rolling out across much of the world—as God and Dudamel as his earnest prophet and charming son. There are parallels to the arrival of Elvis, the British Invasion; Dudamel's public appearances, especially overseas, are sometimes likened to Beatlemania, with the young conductor-as-rock-star mobbed by even younger admirers.

The reality is far more prosaic. The son of two musicians—a salsa trombonist and a voice teacher—Gustavo Adolfo Dudamel Ramírez was born and raised in Barquisimeto, Venezuela's fourth-largest city and a place known for its universities and musical tradition. Despite the temptation to see his ascent as a rags-to-riches tale, Dudamel grew up middle class; as a boy in the eighties, he was into soccer, movies, and violin. He began music lessons at age five, waking at 3:00 a.m. to journey 225 miles to Caracas—like driving to LA from Morro Bay—once a week with his grandmother. One detail of the Dudamel legend is the eight-year-old musician "conducting" Fisher-Price toys after seeing an especially moving performance. He learned a love of serendipity from a grandfather who took him on long, aimless drives.

At age eleven, as a violinist in a youth orchestra, Dudamel grabbed a baton when the adult conductor who led the group was a few minutes late—as Dudamel began waving it, the other kids started playing behind him: "It started as fun; a few minutes later it was serious." Holding a baton for the first time, Dudamel has said, felt "like the most natural thing in the world." That day he became the conductor's assistant; a few years later he was summoned to Caracas to study with Abreu. Two years after that, at eighteen, Dudamel became music director of the Simon Bolivar Youth Orchestra, El Sistema's showcase band and a group he still leads, free of charge, out of his commitment to musical education.

It may now seem inevitable that the world's most glamorous conductor ended up leading what may be the world's most admired orchestra, that a young Latin American hero would settle in a Latino-majority city that likes to tell itself it will never grow old. But it could have just as easily not happened at all.

That star-making Mahler competition in Germany? Dudamel almost didn't show. He'd just been in Berlin, apprenticing with the celebrated conductor Simon Rattle, and was worn out. "I was trying to find any excuse not to go," he says, remembering unease about his unsteady English. "My maestro said, 'It's only two weeks—go.'"

His performance launched numerous calls from scouts and observers to rave about the young Venezuelan—most essentially, LA Phil's then-conductor, Esa-Pekka Salonen, a serious musician not known for empty praise. But the Phil was just one of many suitors, and Dudamel took his time committing. "He thought I was a stalker," jokes Deborah Borda, then the Phil's president and CEO, who received Salonen's call and has remained a Dudamel booster since decamping for the New York Philharmonic, "chasing him all over the world to get him to sign the contract."

Another thing that's rarely mentioned, in part because Dudamel has become a symbol of Los Angeles and speaks about his love for the place and his enthusiasm for seeing shows at the Bowl, eating at In-N-Out Burger, and other regular-guy signifiers: He really didn't much like it here or know what to make of the place the first few times he visited, even though LA superficially resembles the rambling, palm-tree-lined Caracas. "It was difficult for me to see the city," he says, describing a vague, cryptic place he could not interpret. "It was very abstract: Do I like or not like the city?"

A few years later he was leading a free five-hour concert at the Hollywood Bowl complete with fireworks spelling out his name, thunderous ovations, and Spanish-language subtitles. A star was born.

None of the rest of this would matter—the fireworks, presumably, would have spelled out someone else's name—if not for Dudamel's musicianship. Alongside the popular excitement about his arrival, there was some grumbling among critics suspicious of this barely known twenty-something following Salonen, a first-rate conductor and composer who modernized and streamlined the Phil over seventeen years. Age was part of the bias, though Europeans have a tradition of young composers: Gustav Mahler took conducting jobs in his twenties and led Vienna's main opera company in his thirties; a century later, Rattle took over an important English orchestra at twenty-five. The LA Phil, atypically for a US orchestra, likes young talent: Salonen came in at a boyish thirty-four; Zubin Mehta when he was twenty-six.

Some credible critics have seen limits to Dudamel's musicianship, and there's been a dull murmur since his arrival that the *Los Angeles Times* is too smitten to give a realistic assessment. Anne Midgette of the *Washington Post* in 2010 described his conducting as "uneven, superficial, moment to moment"; the *Wall Street Journal's* David Mermelstein lamented that after a decade Dudamel "hasn't quite put his stamp on this orchestra in the way that Messrs. Mehta and Salonen did in their day." Every artist has a personality, built on aversions and preferences, strengths, and weaknesses. The standard critical take on Dudamel is that he's better on the warhorses—the familiar Mozart to Mahler fare—than with the modern and contemporary music that has become central to the Phil's identity. These criticisms aside, Dudamel is widely respected by orchestral music insiders and beloved by the musicians he conducts. Some overseas players have been known to beg friends in LA to get a message through about their eagerness to work with him.

Yuja Wang, the young piano soloist who has toured with Dudamel and performed with him at the Bowl on July 25, likens him to the late Italian titan Claudio Abbado. "Both are so intuitive and sensitive with their gestures and expressions," she says, "they don't have to speak." When Dudamel does, she adds, "he jokes in his funny English to put the musicians at ease."

Pianist Herbie Hancock, who heads the Phil's jazz wing, says it's not always easy to perform with orchestras or classical conductors, but Dudamel gets it. "He just has this warm feeling—it's just like playing with a jazz musician. He's courageous, interested in trying new things—he's not stilted. He can feel that jazz rhythm and interpret it for the orchestra." A piece of music, Dudamel says, is like a work of philosophy that he must first interpret for himself and then translate to the musicians, who bring it to the audience. He makes the process sound nearly sacred.

People tend to talk about Dudamel's "intuition" with music and musicians. Chad Smith is one of them: He credits Salonen, an avant-leaning Finn, with developing a "clear, crystalline sound" and Dudamel with making the orchestra "more flexible, richer," finding new depths. Smith, who takes over as artistic director of the Ojai Music Festival next year, points out that over the decade of Dudamel, the Phil has commissioned more new music than the orchestra did during its previous ninety years.

But when people compare Dudamel to other conductors, it's generally to Leonard Bernstein, a childhood hero—he once conducted using "Lenny's" old baton and accidentally broke it—and the last American classical figure to really capture a mass audience. (Jamie Bernstein, who thinks her father would have adored Dudamel, is one of many to have drawn the parallel.) "He doesn't look like Bernstein when he conducts," says Alex Ross, the *New Yorker's* music critic, who allows that the warmth and emotion may be similar but Dudamel's style is more precise, less emphatic.

But when people speak about the similarities between Dudamel and Bernstein, they're not really talking about musicianship. They're talking about fame.

Within the world of orchestral music, and even in the jaded precincts of the press, Dudamel is sometimes characterized a bit like that line from *The Manchurian Candidate*: the kindest, bravest, warmest, most wonderful human being I've ever known in my life.

Dudamel is in fact not only massively talented but a genuinely likable guy. He clearly enjoys people and doesn't waft desperation or neediness the way some celebrities do. Like Tom Cruise and other famous men, he's shorter than you'd think, but no Napoleon temperamentally. When he took the stage at a party at the Hollywood Bowl on a cloudy May evening around sunset, after the audience had chatted through every previous speaker, the place went silent. Dudamel never raised his voice above a murmur and did not say anything particularly memorable, but the crowd was as quiet and attentive as if Young Elvis had risen to address them. Like many who have spent a lot of time outside their native tongue, he communicates with gestures and eye contact as much as with words but never seems to play to the gallery. He's focused. He's there. He's listening.

Simon Woods, an understated Englishman who took over the Phil from Borda, calls this, "the indefinable charisma of star power—you can't describe it; you can't bottle it. But you know it when you see it." The Phil, he says, was smart to follow Salonen—who had his own style of charisma but could never be described as exuberant—with someone entirely different.

To most Angelenos, Dudamel is a guy who stands onstage in front of 100 musicians and thousands of audience members, waving a baton and then taking bows an hour or two later. But he spends the vast majority of his time offstage working, too—planning the season, meeting the donors, urging some musicians on and others to retire. He guards his privacy, an "introverted extrovert," as a colleague describes him. Dudamel and his first wife, journalist and dancer Eloísa Maturén, divorced in 2015 and have an eight-year-old son. Two years ago he married the Spanish actress María Valverde in a secret Las Vegas wedding.

When Dudamel travels, which is often, he lugs not one but two suitcases full of books. He is unsurprisingly fond of Latin American writers— Carlos Fuentes, Octavio Paz, Pablo Neruda. His favorite seems to be the philosophically minded Argentine Jorge Luis Borges, especially "The Aleph"—a short story about paradox and infinity. "The best time I have is when I read," he says. "Engaging my imagination. I'm very simple—I'm happy with simple things."

Has success changed The Dude? "What's amazing is that Gustavo is exactly the same guy," says Alberto Arvelo, a filmmaker who met Dudamel when both lived in Caracas; they now regard each other as long-lost brothers. "Becoming a celebrity is something that has not affected his soul. The rest of what happens—the comedy of celebrity—is not what he is looking for. He wants more and more and more—to explore the boundaries of music, classical music, contemporary music, folk music, other art forms."

***

Sometime around 2002 Dudamel's mentor, Abreu, took his protégé to a charmless, empty parking garage in Caracas. Can you hear the acoustics? he asked. Can you see the walls, the seats, the musicians on the stage? Dudamel smiles recalling it. The concert hall Abreu envisioned ended up being built on the site of the garage; it's since hosted thousands of Venezuelan kids and their instruments and audiences.

"Maestro Abreu had an incredible idea," Dudamel says. "We are spreading the idea around the world. It's about identity, about access to beauty, about using harmony to create. To be poor is to be no one. But culture is an identity. And culture is universal."

Music education, El Sistema, maestro Abreu, and YOLA (formerly Youth Orchestra Los Angeles, inspired by Abreu's program) are the things Dudamel is most likely to talk about, and talk about most earnestly, when the questions stop. "He is present every day," Dudamel says, gazing heavenward as he mentions the late maestro as his most important influence. (Abreu died last year [2018] at seventy-eight after a long illness.)

Dudamel is not El Sistema's only admirer. It's been hailed as both a way to create an audience for an aging art form as well as to help break kids out of cycles of poverty. YOLA currently has four sites here, with more than 1,200 students. In fall 2020, its reach will expand significantly when a new concert hall, designed by Frank Gehry and acoustician Yasuhisa Toyota— the team behind Walt Disney Concert Hall—opens in Inglewood. (In May Dudamel conducted a free neighborhood concert with YOLA and Phil musicians at a church near Lafayette Park in Westlake.)

But not everyone who's looked at Abreu and El Sistema has been persuaded. To skeptics, the maestro was a skilled but cynical petrol-state power broker—the kind you might find in Saudi Arabia—who is good at charming politicians. Despite the fact that classical music includes many eras and styles, Abreu's repertoire centered on overplayed, overhyped showpieces—a mainstream monoculture that has nearly wiped out everything else around it.

For all the claims made for the power of the program to lead a youth revolution, "we now see that El Sistema has been grinding people into dust," says Robert Fink, a UCLA musicologist who heads the university's music industry program. Fink calls it "a fantasy version of what people in the West believe about classical music. It's a worldview where classical music is an unqualified social good, is inclusive, solves social problems, and keeps the canon intact."

The most damning assessment comes from the book *El Sistema: Orchestrating Venezuela's Youth*, which includes a chapter on Dudamel. Geoffrey Baker, a music professor at the University of London, visited Caracas out of his enthusiasm for music education only to find a cult of personality of nearly North Korean proportions. Baker's book argues that Abreu, whose training was primarily in economics, just wanted money and power, and sold the idea of art-as-uplift to persuade politicians to give them to him. Baker also wonders why nonwhite people in former European colonies have to play orchestral music. Why not jazz, which values individualism and spontaneity? Why not music native to their own region? The fact that El Sistema unfolded during the reign of Hugo Chavez—who came to office a populist and died more resembling a dictator presiding over a broken nation—makes things even stickier. (Dudamel conducted at Chavez's funeral.)

As Venezuela has subsequently collapsed, economically and otherwise, Dudamel's silence about the government that supported the program drew substantial criticism. Dudamel eventually denounced Chavez's successor, Nicolas Maduro, and now finds himself effectively barred from his native land, the country where his family lives and where he still, on paper, leads an orchestra. "I urgently call on the President of the Republic and the national government to rectify and listen to the voice of the Venezuelan people," Dudamel posted on social media after anti-Maduro demonstrations and crackdowns two years ago. Maduro responded by canceling a tour the conductor had scheduled with Venezuela's National Youth Orchestra. Dudamel has been both emphatic and careful. "I'm with you!" he told the Venezuelan people in January while getting a star on Hollywood Boulevard; he later said he wasn't taking sides.

Dudamel is clearly pained by the situation back home and has heard the criticisms before. It's the one subject where his enthusiasm takes on a defensive, slightly emphatic edge. Politics, he says, is "very complex—you see what's happening onstage, but what really happens, happens backstage."

He gives a long defense of Abreu and El Sistema when pushed. "Since 1975 El Sistema has been a program of the Venezuelan state," he emphasizes, "not the government. Governments change—states don't." The program and the youth orchestra have survived eight regimes. Dudamel gets flustered as he talks about the beauty of the country, the pain of its devolution, but his message is clear: Hundreds of thousands of kids—including once upon a time, one named Gustavo Dudamel—have learned and grown because of El Sistema.

Two or three decades ago, there were few phrases more discouraging than the announcement that a classical program would include a piece of new or "contemporary" music—buzzkill for both progressives and old-timers who want the same Beethoven and Tchaikovsky pieces over and over. But in the intervening years, academic avant-gardism was flushed out of the system; West Coast minimalism opened up ways to approach traditional tonal music; young, post-Bjork composers from Scandinavia and earnest mystics from Eastern Europe showed up along with the emergence of such composers as John Adams, Nico Muhly, and young Pulitzer winner Caroline Shaw.

Orchestras used to have to choose whether they wanted to be "progressive"—new pieces, edgy composers—or populist, offering flashy fare for a broad audience and summer seasons involving Kenny Rogers or George Benson. The combination of Dudamel—who has preserved the edginess of the Salonen years and aimed to democratize simultaneously—and Woods—who seeks to extend Borda's triumphs—means that the LA Phil can do both at once: It doesn't have to decide which one is more important. That the Phil has more money than any US orchestra certainly helps. You can have a Thomas Ades commission and lessons for kids in the hood. But Dudamel's star power also means that the Phil can do just about anything, and audiences, donors, and the press will take it seriously.

There remains concern—some of it justified—about the "graying of the audience" for classical music in the US and UK, but the Phil has seen the median age of its attendees fall from sixty-one to fifty-six during the Dudamel years. So the second century of the Phil and the second decade of Dudamel's term are beginning in a sunnier state than most American arts groups find themselves. Still, he and the Phil have a sense of unfinished business.

Three of LA's major classical music organizations are now helmed by men with Spanish surnames. Besides Dudamel, Placido Domingo stands as the longtime general director of the LA Opera, and Jaime Martin recently made his debut as the LA Chamber Orchestra's music director. Despite earnest efforts to diversify audiences, Latinos are still underrepresented at concert halls. But under Dudamel the Phil's proportion has nearly doubled. (Woods calls continuing this trend one of his top priorities as Phil CEO.)

As for Dudamel's artistry, even some of his admirers think he needs to step back a bit to grow as a musician and thinker. "I've seen his schedule," Rattle said a few years ago, "and I do not see how he has time to breathe."

But the most pressing question about Dudamel is how long he'll stay. It may be difficult for the Phil to keep him past the end of his contract, which ends with the 2021–2022 season. He was hard to land and could likely prove harder to hold.

Some speculate he will not rest until he arrives at the taproot of the tradition. For a young Mozart- and Mahler-loving man from the edge of the classical music world, the center is not California. It's the German-speaking heart of Old Europe. Dudamel clearly adores much about Los Angeles and digs living in the Hollywood Hills, but he may still feel out of place here. Despite massive emigration out of Venezuela since Chavez's election, the Latin American population in LA is mostly Mexican and Salvadoran. And being close to Caracas is no longer much help when you are an enemy of the state.

In addition to the question of whether the Phil can keep Dudamel, there is the issue of whether it should—for the sake of the orchestra, the conductor, and the audience. There's a notion in the arts that holding the same leadership post for more than ten years is dangerous, for both the boss and the organization, leading to complacency or defensiveness. The days of three- and four-decade grand-old-man tenures seem to be over.

"The players themselves are the arbiters as much as anyone else," says Thor Steingraber, a veteran of LA performing arts life who runs the Soraya center in Northridge. "They've been in the middle of a great love affair; that's what makes for a great orchestra. How long does that last? Nobody knows." Still, Steingraber, says, even if he splits in 2022, "Dudamel will probably be woven into the fabric of Los Angeles for the rest of his life: This was his first big gig, and he rolled out El Sistema here."

The Phil's philosophy of permanent revolution also syncs up with Dudamel's own sensibility. The Phil—and the city itself—is about what Dudamel calls "a vision of the new," a commitment to risk-taking and boundary breaking and genre blending.

For Dudamel the possibilities continue to seem endless. The ideal tenure for a conductor, he says, is not about a magic number but a healthy relationship. "If the relation is good—if you have the space to breathe, to build things, to create things—I don't see an end."

[*Los Angeles Magazine*, August 12, 2019]

ACKNOWLEDGMENTS

WHEN HEYDAY'S PUBLISHER, STEVE WASSERMAN, first brought up the idea for this book, it was in the greeting line at Scott's memorial service, just a week after my husband's death by suicide. What a blessing. For the next couple of days, it gave my shocked, disbelieving brain something to do—come up with a list of articles by Scott that could be considered his very best and most essential. This was something hopeful to hang on to when my soul was shattered and everything seemed incomprehensible, so my first of many thank-yous goes to Steve, one of Scott's favorite and most infuriating cocktail party and newsroom sparring partners.

The generosity of Dana Gioia, Roberta Ahmanson, and Katrina vanden Heuvel made this book possible. Much gratitude goes out to Ted Gioia for writing his perfect introduction, and to the editors and designers at Heyday, especially Emmerich Anklam.

Journalists work in a delicate and complex ecosystem and there are so many to thank. To the editors and writers at the *New London Day*, especially Milton Moore, who helped Scott become a cultural critic. To Rick Barrs, Jack Cheevers, and Joe Donnelly, editors at the now-defunct *New Times Los Angeles*, who helped shape some of his first Los Angeles writing. To Bret Israel, who smartly poached Scott from *New Times* and brought him to the *Los Angeles Times*, and to Maria Russo, for being Scott's dream editor. To the many *LA Times* writers who allowed Scott to bounce ideas off them (sometimes—often, I'll bet—when they were on deadline), including Reed Johnson, Christopher Reynolds, and Lynell George, all of whom helped find and select articles for this book.

To former *Los Angeles Magazine* editor Matt Segal, who took a chance on Scott's bittersweet kiss-off to LA, a rare thing for a city magazine. To Scott's friends who shored up our family before and after his death, including Tim Page, Boris Dralyuk, and Steve Mirkin. And words can't express my gratitude for Susan Carpenter, David Daley, and Jeffrey Boxer, three of Scott's treasured friends, for being my friends, too, giving solace and professional advice when it was most needed.

More thanks go to Scott's family, my family: siblings Amanda, Sam, and Craig, as well as Kelley, Ruey, Lee, Pat, Rosemarie, and Todd, and especially to Scott's mother, Jane, who has been hit with more than her share of tragedy but who consistently rises to every occasion with remarkable grace and optimism. To my mother, Laura Scribner, who made Scott's daily life easier so that he could write so well.

Finally, and especially, to Ian, Scott and my only child, and the real reason why this collection exists. I hope this book makes you proud of your dad. He would be so very proud of you.

—Sara Scribner

ABOUT THE AUTHOR

Scott Timberg, a former arts reporter for the *LA Weekly* and the *Los Angeles Times*, wrote on music and culture and was a contributor to *Salon*, the *New York Times*, and *Vox*. He was an award-winning journalist, a blogger on West Coast culture, and an adjunct writing professor. His previous book, *Culture Crash: The Killing of the Creative Class*, was published in 2015 by Yale University Press. Richard Brody of the *New Yorker* called *Culture Crash* "a quietly radical rethinking of the very nature of art in modern life," and Ben Downing, writing in the *Wall Street Journal*, said, "Mr. Timberg succeeds in assembling a large, coherent, and troubling mosaic . . . weaving all manner of information and opinion into a fluent narrative of cultural decline." Timberg died by his own hand on December 10, 2019, in Los Angeles. He was fifty years old.

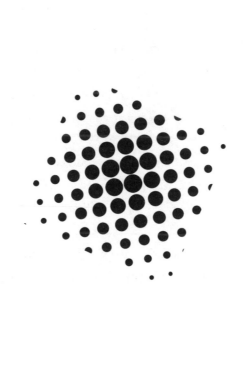